Message from the Himalayan Sages:
Timely & Timeless

Guru Sakalamaa

(Smt. Jyothi Pattabhiram)

notionpress.com

INDIA · SINGAPORE · MALAYSIA

Copyright © Sakalamaa Smt. Jyothi Pattabhiram 2024
All Rights Reserved.

ISBN 979-8-89446-046-8

This book has been published with all efforts taken to make the material error-free after the consent of the author. However, the author and the publisher do not assume and hereby disclaim any liability to any party for any loss, damage, or disruption caused by errors or omissions, whether such errors or omissions result from negligence, accident, or any other cause.

While every effort has been made to avoid any mistake or omission, this publication is being sold on the condition and understanding that neither the author nor the publishers or printers would be liable in any manner to any person by reason of any mistake or omission in this publication or for any action taken or omitted to be taken or advice rendered or accepted on the basis of this work. For any defect in printing or binding the publishers will be liable only to replace the defective copy by another copy of this work then available.

CONTENTS

This book is a loving and devotional offering to   vii

Mission made possible – A chronicle   ix

Section 1

1. Submission – a Yearning to Utter!   2
2. Saga of Radiant Serpent   6
3. The Fulcrum of Polarities, Bridging the North and South Divide!   13
4. Early Chapters of My Life!   20
5. A Journey Towards Elevation Beyond the Karmic Cycle   35
6. The Dance Steps and the Jingle Bells: Tha-ka-dhi-na-tha   45
7. My Guru Paramparā   54
8. My 'Master,' Bhole Baba Swami Rama   59
9. Venerable Bengali Babaji   61
10. Mukti Baba – My Great Grand Master   64
11. Sri Vidyaranya Bhārathi Tradition   68
12. The proximity of Three Gurus   70

Contents

Section 2

13. Ten Steps Towards Bhole Baba — 75
14. If Swami Rama Wills, there Can Be a Shower of Dollars!! — 77
15. Shield of Pirouetting Shri Chakra — 82
16. Accept me as your Guru only when you are Convinced of my Power and Siddhis!! — 87
17. Baba visits Bengaluru – 1992 — 93
18. Guru's Disembodied Love — 100
19. Beyond the Veil: Two Supernatural Experiences with Swami Rama — 105
20. A Guru's Promise - A Serpent Headed Rudrākshi — 110
21. Yogananda Paramahamsa in the Train! — 114

Section 3

22. A Journey To Satyaloka- The Real World — 122
23. Part 1: Chinnamastā Means a Severed Head — 130
24. Part 2: Chinnamastā Means Rebirth — 135

Section 4

25. Sage Agasthya's Messages — 148
26. Temple Cat and the Nurturing Mother — 150
27. Animā Siddhi Agastya Entered my Throat — 152
28. Mere Gaze Granted Mystic Moon Knowledge — 158
29. Chandra Vidya and Tithinitya Practice — 162

Section 5

30. Sage Durvasa: Ocean of Snow Inside a Volcano — 167
31. I Shalt Slit Thee, this Very Moment — 169

32. The Secret of the Wombed Face, Unveiled!	177
33. Unveiling Chandrakala Namaskar in the Presence of Rishi Durvasa!	185
34. What is Chandrakala Namaskara?	189
35. The Benevolent Son of Sage Atri	192

Section 6

36. Bengali Baba, the Illuminator of the Path	201
37. Have You Come For A Picnic?	202
38. A caged, Enlightened Soul	208
39. When Guru Visits as a Friend!	212

Section 7

40. Mother Renuka	225
41. Can't the Mother Inside not Come Out?!	227

Section 8

42. Bhole Baba's Instructions and Bholenath's Presence	237
43. Kalabhairava on a Varanasi Twilight	239
44. Darshan of Lord Kashi Vishwanath	249
45. Saptharshi Pooja – A Divine Experience	256

Section 9

46. Divine Experience in the City of Palaces – Dr. Rā. Sathyanarayana	262
47. The Grace of Samadhi by a Mere Gaze	264
48. A Plane that does not Fly, and Satyavan Savitri's Story	268
49. Guru's Dentures in my Hands!	277

Contents

50. Srividya – Universe in a Capsule	283
51. Tantric Practice System and Srividya	289
52. Guru Lineage is There!	293
53. The Journey from Savithri to Sakalamaa	295
54. Guru Lineage Continues!	298

THIS BOOK IS A LOVING AND DEVOTIONAL OFFERING TO:

My beloved Gurus and my guiding lights – Gurudēva Swami Rama, the luminous messenger of the magnanimous and sublime Rishi Parampara of the Himalayas. The one who 'Introduces the Guru in You to You'; And Dr R. Sathyanarayana or my Mysuru Gurugalu, as I fondly call him, an internationally acclaimed Danceologist, Musicologist and a venerated guru in Srividya Tantra belonging to Srividyaranya tradition.

AND

To the Himalayan Rishi Parampara and Sri Vidyaranya Bhārathi Tradition; the eternally alive, awakened and timeless traditions which are inter-connected, and find their roots in the Vedic era, continuing through an unbroken lineage of Sages to this day. The traditions that go beyond the bounds of all religions, nationalities, geographies, races, millennia, and ages; the beacons of the 'Ultimate Truth'. Their only mandate – constantly educating about the importance of meditation and guiding in the path of spiritual liberation - is to all of humanity.

Gurudeva Swami Rama   Rā Sā Gurugalu (Mysuru)

Parameshti Guru
MUKTHI BABA

Parama Guru
BENGALI BABA

Swaguru
SWAMI RAMA

Himalayan Rishi Parampara – Guru Lineage

Sri.CHANDRASHEKARABHARATI SWAMY

Sri.BRAHMAVIDYANANDANATHA

Sri.PUNDARIKAKSHANANDANATHA

Sri.SATHYANANDANATHA

Sri Vidyaranya Bhārathi Tradition – Guru Lineage

MISSION MADE POSSIBLE – A CHRONICLE

About 300 pages of this spiritual literature are in your hands today. A spiritual journey encompassing over 3 decades has culminated as a memoir.

It is a highly daunting task to consolidate the scattered experiences over the decades into a holistic picture. If that effort has borne results, it is only through the divine blessings of my Gurus and the guidance of the guru lineages of the Himalayan Bhārathi tradition and Sri Vidyaranya Tradition. At this juncture, I offer my deepest respect and gratitude to the sages of my Guru Paramparā.

I desired to write a book about my spiritual journey and my experiences for almost 25 years, through which I wanted to share about the Rishi Paramparā, which could serve as a guiding light for spiritual seekers in the generations to come.

'You will author a book, and it will make history,' the assurance given by my Gurudēva Swami Rama; and 'You shall write, but be grounded in reality,' the guidance I received from Rā Sā Gurugalu (Dr. Rā. Sathyanarayana); have served as my inspiration behind this attempt.

While attempting to record these divine experiences - from being tacit memories to a literary form, many scholars and disciples have lent their support, and I wish to remember them here.

My respect to Pandit Rajmani Tigunait.

I thank respected scholar Mr. Jagadish Sharma Sampa for thoroughly assessing the contents of the book and for all the suggestions for improvements.

I fondly mention Mrs Rajwinder Bajwa (Deputy Commissioner, State Taxes - Govt of Punjab), Retd. Col. Parminder Singh Bajwa (former Deputy Director - Defence Services, Govt of Punjab), and Dr Ashok Bhat and his family, for all their direct and indirect support.

I wish to remember the support received from my daughter Sadhana, my son-in-law Sanketh, my little granddaughter Mahathi, and the rest of the family.

I thank Karan Bajwa for designing the book cover and the various illustrations so beautifully. I appreciate the firm support I received from Gauravpreet Bajwa and Rajakumar. I love the help I received from Harish during the book review and editing.

My blessings and love to Pradeep and Roma for their initiatives in publishing and marketing the English edition of this book.

I deeply appreciate Vimarsha Jain, Shashank, Bhama Suresh, and my dance disciple Bhaskari for beautifully translating this book into English.

Lots of love to Shreelakshmi Rajakumar, Radhika Vitla, and Priya Kervashe for efficiently transcribing my experiences.

I thank Notion Press for their support and professionalism in publishing this book in English. Finally, I hope that the contents of this book will serve as a shining light to illuminate your path in your spiritual journey.

With a deep reverence for all my gurus – **Sakalamaa**

***

2025 year happens to be,
Gurudev Swami Rama's Birth Centenary.
I offer this book at His 'Lotus feet' as a
'PRELUDE' to the prominent celebrations in
in 2024 year itself!
Jai Gurudev- Sri Gurudev!
in devotion!

— Lakalamaa
21, July 2024.
Guru Purnima

ವರ್ಷ ೨೦೨೫, ಗುರುದೇವ ಸ್ವಾಮಿ ರಾಮರ ಜನ್ಮ ಶತಾಬ್ದಿ ವರ್ಷ!
ಈ ಪುಸ್ತಕವನ್ನು, ಮುಂದಿನ ವರ್ಷದ ಈ ಸಂಭ್ರಮಾಚರಣೆಯ
'ಮುನ್ನುಡಿ'ಯಾಗಿ ವರ್ಷ ೨೦೨೪ ರಲ್ಲೇ, ಅವರ ಪಾದ ಕಮಲಗಳಲ್ಲಿ
ಅರ್ಪಿಸುತ್ತಿದ್ದೇನೆ!

ಜೈ ಗುರುದೇವ - ಶ್ರೀ ಗುರುದೇವ!
ಭಕ್ತಿಪೂರ್ವಕವಾಗಿ!

— Lakalamaa.
21, ಜುಲೈ 2024.
ಗುರು ಪೂರ್ಣಿಮಾ.
(ಪುಸ್ತಕ ಬಿಡುಗಡೆ- ೨೨, ಸೆಪ್ಟೆಂಬರ್, ೨೦೨೪)

Section 1

- Submission – a yearning to utter!
- Saga of Radiant Serpent
- The fulcrum of polarities, bridging the north and south divide!
- Early chapters of my life!
- A journey towards elevation beyond the karmic cycle
- The dance steps and the jingle bells: Tha-ka-dhi-na-tha
- My Guru Paramparā
- My 'Master,' Bhole Baba Swami Rama
- Venerable Bengali Babaji
- Mukti Baba – My Great Grand Master
- Sri Vidyaranya Bhārathi Tradition
- The proximity of Three Gurus

1

SUBMISSION – A YEARNING TO UTTER!

One evening in 2018, I was visiting the residence of my Srividya Guru, Sri Sathyanandanatha (adoringly referred to as Rā Sā Gurugalu), in Mysuru. His house was nothing less than a temple to me, and I was lucky to see my Guru at the entrance itself, visibly delighted to see me. He welcomed me with his warm affection. During the conversation, I mentioned, 'Gurugale, for a long time, I have been longing to meet Sage Vasishtha' Though I was hesitant to ask this question, his voice boomed, ' Yes! You Shall!' with all the assurance that it is sure to happen.

Though mesmerised, I continued the conversation by asking, 'Gurugale, I have an ardent desire to write about You and Swami Rama, about our Rishi Paramparā, and share my direct experiences.' Gurugalu smiled, pleased upon hearing my request, and responded, 'Yes, why not! With no exaggeration, let your narrative be relatable and well received,' he blessed. As someone who firmly believed that the mercy of the Divine Mother and Guru's blessings are one and the same, I instantly felt confident that I was bound to fulfil this endeavour, and I started looking forward to the opportune time.

Though I had been in contact with Rā Sā Gurugalu since 1983, he arrived in my life as my Srividya guru almost 20 years later in 2000-01, And I was graced by Swami Rama, who guided me and helped me closely observe my own life's metamorphosis, layer-by-layer, since 1992; It is beautiful to see how both of these great Gurus helped me in my spiritual quest, by guiding me through Srividya, by mentoring me through multiple facets of life, by unveiling the reality of the external material world or Maya, and by preparing me to experience the deep compassion of the Divine Mother, Sridevi Srilalitha. They have literally handheld me through my journey and continue to do so even now.

My deep desire to help those who are interested in treading this path through sharing my own personal experiences has been blessed by my Gurus and my Rishi lineage. There is only one emotional driving force behind all of these efforts: sharing the magnanimity of this divine Guru-Shishya (Master–Disciple) Paramparā – its sweetness, solidarity, maturity, discipline, and unparalleled unconditional love.

Very recently, I was looking for an annotation of mine in the pile of my old books. During this Kadatha Yajna (Book re-reading & discarding process), I came across an old diary of mine. In one of the pages, the sentence 'at Swami Rama's ashram in Rishikesh' caught my attention. This entry was from the timespan between 1992-96. I had taken the blessings of Gurudēva and was about to leave when he announced, 'Whatever you write will become a historical document.' After reading those lines, I was even more compelled to write and share this book. I also had full confidence that at the right moment, this would surely happen, as I had blessings from both of these great Gurus.

In 2017, I took a group of spiritual seekers on a Yoga and Srividya retreat to the Tadakeshwar in the Himalayas to hold a few discourses on Srividya Tantra practice. We were staying at the Swami Rama Ashram, located within the perimeters of the Tadakeshwar Mahadev temple. This ashram is very close to Swami Rama and Bengali Baba's hearts. As such, as long as we were staying there, all of us kept experiencing their presence within us. During my discourse on Tantra, the title my hands inadvertently wrote on the blackboard read 'Messages of The Sages.' It flashed to my mind immediately that this should be the name of the book. Because the wisdom of the Rishi

Paramparā is eternally awake and highly potent and within the reach of any honest practitioner, I took it as a direct message.

Whenever I sat to discuss about this book with my team, I felt the strong presence of Gurudēva and Rā Sā Gurugalu. 'Change your core values' came a message during one of the meetings. It was very common to receive subtle signals, such as a flickering light or the lizard twitching as affirmations, whenever I had 'found' the answers to some of the complex questions. When I think of some of the experiences that filled me with unbound energy and positivity, I find myself searching for words to express my gratitude. In one of such focus team meetings, the team was left with goosebumps when a bee suddenly appeared, out-of-nowhere, inside a closed room and did the pradakshina (circumambulate) over my head. I remember nights when I was a bit preoccupied and was struggling to sleep; a single noisy mosquito delivered an inexplicable experience of deep serenity, and I was left teary-eyed, all through the simple vibrations it generated. When I was thinking about the challenges ahead of me to meet the expenses of publishing this book being a pensioner, answers in the form of symbolic messages started reaching me through random YouTube channels, leaving me with goosebumps many times.

What is new in this book?

Spiritual studies have been customary in our culture since ancient times, as the Supreme vidya - both in practical and theoretical aspects, as part of the Spiritual Science - to think of saying or writing anything new will be laughable. 'What is new in this book then?' should be a natural question, therefore. The aspects of the truth unfolded by the Spiritual Science remain relevant and prevalent even today in this era of science and technology, and one can learn this Vidya even today. The truth is that there is the whole Guru Paramparā, which has been perennially committed to this cause for centuries. That's not it! The Rishi Lineage, the giants of the divine echelons, have maintained this vidya in an eternally awakened state as a direct link to bestow upon the honest seekers, and they even guide each one along the way.

Another reason why it may win the hearts of the readers perhaps is this. Because most of the spiritual biographies tend to be by seekers with a desire to be a monk who go to the Himalayas in search of a Guru and eventually receive unparalleled experiences. But what you will perceive here is a complete contradiction. It is the story of a woman who was born in a small town to a very ordinary family, with a simple living between the 4 walls of the house, and the unfolding of her spiritual journey. As someone who had never been to the Himalayas and who firmly believed that the Rishis were legends from the past with no significance in today's world, I was overwhelmed to be blessed with a series of interactions and direct experiences. It is said that when the disciple is ready, the Guru will appear. Was this a display of that divine mercy? How can they all be so empathetic and so loving! I am humbled beyond words to express my gratitude for the compassionate nurturing process that they took me through.

Is this another addition?

We do come across many examples of spiritual seekers successfully capturing their spiritual journey in some or the other form of literature, such as autobiographies or documentaries, which are setting newer records in reaching their audience. In that long list of 9,999 books, is this another addition?

I submit each page of this book, as the petals of the holy lotus at the feet of the Himalayan Rishi Lineage - with deep devotion, a lot of excitement, tears of joy, and gratitude!!

***

2

SAGA OF RADIANT SERPENT

Its sharp tongue moved in and out like a small red flamelet!!! The sun appeared dull compared to its yellow-coloured body, emanating radiance akin to pure gold!! I found myself tilting my head upward to behold its towering presence. The giant serpent had a looming stature commanding all my attention. Despite a slight apprehension, I was enticed by its spellbinding allure. It held me in a mesmerised trance, captivating all my senses; that serpent was a breathtaking epitome of serenity.

***

During my college's summer break of 15 days, I decided to engage in some form of intense Sādhana. While pondering what Sādhana to undertake, I recalled my Gurudēva Swami Rama's words during my initiation, "In Srividya Samayāchārā tradition, other than Patanjali's Yogasutras, Soudharya Lahari is considered to be a significant text." Baba had given me the first 5 shlōkas of this sacred text in the form of mantras, and I was instructed that these are very potent mantras and were to be practised daily. Hence, I had read the text and several commentaries on it. I decided to undertake a 12 day japa anuṣṭāna on one of the Shlōkas from Soundharya Lahari during these 15 days.

Due to the text's assured potency to bestow siddhis with desired results, the Sādhana of any form of Soudharya Lahiri is highly recommended in our tradition. The text lists the benefits and fruits that sadhaka is bestowed upon practising each Shlōka. Suppose the practice doesn't yield the assured outcomes mentioned in Soudharya Lahari, then it is due to the shortcomings in the practitioner's Sādhana and not of mantra. These shortcomings might be due to a lack of diligence, low concentration, partially purified mind, wavering discipline, irresponsibility, or anything that hinders spiritual practice. In case of such lapses, the practitioner has to repeat the whole observation of rituals, i.e. anuṣṭāna, with full diligence and discipline until one achieves the results prescribed in the text. Considering this aspect of the result, I started looking for Shlōkas. My eyes effortlessly landed on the one which assured attainment of moksha, 'Japo jalpaḥ śilpaṁ sakalamapi mudrā virācanā ....' (Shlōkas 27, Soundharya Lahari), and I decided to undertake my anuṣṭāna on this mantra.

To engage in uninterrupted Sādhana, I started looking for a place with minimal distractions. While searching for a conducive location, I learned of a friend's farmhouse on Magadi Road near Bangalore. It was a 10-acre farmland with a small house with minimal connectivity to the outside world. There was a huge water-tank and vegetables, fruits and flowers were being grown over there. A family was taking care of the farm's day-to-day maintenance. I decided to undertake my 12 days anuṣṭāna in this place.

While scouting for a place to meditate, I chose the place under the water tank because it was 100 metres from my room, well-shaded, levelled with cement, and comparatively cooler throughout the day. I started day one of my anuṣṭāna by spreading the mat under the shade of the water tank. It was a four-line long mantra I had to practice at least 1000 times daily. I was observing the whole process as laid down in the scriptures. Due to its length, it wasn't an easy task to memorise the mantra. After practising 3 times daily, I could mentally recall it effortlessly on the fourth day.

At times, my mind threw tantrums. I used to get mentally tired. My mind would drift in the middle of Japa, and every time it did, I had to refocus and get back to chanting. In the midst of all these challenges, my practice continued. As days passed, I began suspecting whether I was on the right path and whether I was engaging in practice properly. And so on. Another hurdle was food. It seemed like the lady was new to cooking. Every day, either the food was too spicy or too salty, and I couldn't have it after a few days. Health is vital during spiritual practices, mainly when undertaking such anuṣṭāna because missing one day means restarting from day one. I couldn't afford to miss a single day, so I resorted to buttermilk and rice 3 times a day to stay healthy until I completed the practice.

In a day, I spent 6-8 hours performing japanuṣṭāna, and the rest I spent in my own company. At times, I burst into tears remembering my three-year-old adorable daughter, who was under my mother-in-law's and husband's care at home. Since I had resolved to 'no contact until I complete my anuṣṭāna,' I didn't venture out of the farm. I wanted to dive deep into myself and understand what I am. Only under such circumstances does one connect to the deepest fibres of our existence, or else we humans never ponder over questions like, Who am I?

As I was blissfully floating in the gentle waves of Soudharya Lahari, the tenth day suddenly started to feel heavy; I involuntarily started praying to Baba, and a realisation dawned on me that I was so preoccupied with the text that Baba hadn't crossed my mind. The very thought that 'I started this anuṣṭāna without seeking his permission' sent a wave of fear down my spine. This whirl consumed me. 'What would happen if I didn't complete what I started? Will Bhagavathi ever forgive me?' I immediately sought refuge in Baba. I prayed to him, 'Baba, Please forgive me for undertaking this anuṣṭāna without your permission.' I was experiencing all kinds of anxious moments and vacillations that a sadhaka undergoes. My mind oscillated between '2 more days to go, let me finish this' to 'no, come what may, I can't continue this anymore.' What should I say? The mind is such a trickster!!!

In spite of such confusion, inner conflicts, and anxious moments, after the completion of 10th day, I sensed a significant shift in my energy. It seemed like my prayers reached where it should. I felt an unbound joy springing within me.

On the eleventh day, I got ready early and walked towards the water tank to perform my morning anuṣṭāna. As I took a few steps outside my room, I suddenly felt light in my walk as if I was floating; my entire existence was brimming with bliss. I found myself alone on that track; farm workers weren't anywhere to be seen. In this state, I finished my early morning rituals and returned to my room for breakfast. After resting, around 10:30 a.m. with a book in my hand, I started walking towards the water tank spot, thinking I would sit until 1 p.m., the next break.

Humming a classical tune of a song to which I had choreographed dance in classical Bharatanatya, beating the counts of the rhythm of a Jati with my fingers on the notebook, oblivious to this worldly happening, I was threading through a narrow path towards my meditation spot. Despite the seething sun, the atmosphere was pleasant due to the gentle cool breeze. Both sides of the path were covered with 6-7 ft long overgrown grass. Suddenly, I noticed something move in the grass and stopped abruptly. I stared at what looked like a 6 and a half feet long, immaculate serpent!! It was standing erect on its curled tail with an open hood. There must have been hardly a three-foot distance between the serpent and me. Enchanted by the whole sight, I didn't notice the water bottle and notebook slipping away from my hand!! I stood there frozen with my mouth half open as if witnessing death!! I could hear my heart racing!! My quickened breath!! My body just refused to move!! My eyes were stuck on its piercing diamond-like eyes. I just couldn't move. Surprisingly, I was not thinking of running away or ways to safeguard myself from the serpent, not even for a moment. Rather, I was completely disconnected from worldly sense and that moment, totally mesmerised by the sight of a broad, hooded, radiating golden-bodied serpent.

Its sharp tongue moved in and out like a small red flamelet!!! The sun appeared dull compared to its yellow-coloured body, emanating radiance akin to pure gold!! That bright light from its body. The serpent stood motionless; its flickering tongue was the only sign of life. It possessed such a serene stillness that one could have mistaken it for a masterfully crafted sculpture. I found myself tilting my head upward to behold its towering presence. The giant serpent had a looming stature commanding all my attention. Despite a slight apprehension, I was enticed by its spellbinding allure. It held me in a mesmerised trance, captivating all my senses; that serpent was a breathtaking epitome of serenity. Time ceased to exist, and I'm not sure how long I had been in that state. The serpent slithered away from me and vanished into the shadow without a trace.

When I returned to my senses, my legs trembled, and my whole body pulsated with newfound energy. It took some time to regain my energy; I was stupefied, and not even my Guru crossed my mind. Though I was brimming with joy, my body was exhausted. It was as if somebody pulled my whole nervous system upward. I was in a fix. Should I proceed and complete my anuṣṭāna or just go back and rest? After a few minutes, I decided to complete that day's ritual as per my Sankalpa. So, with great difficulty, I reached the water tank and sat down to do my japa. I returned to my room after finishing my japa, had my lunch, and laid down to rest. I must have been half asleep; a thought dawned on me like a lightning bolt: 'That serpent is none other than Bhagavathi herself!!!' Simultaneously, a loud proclamation echoed from within: 'Your anuṣṭāna is complete!!' I leapt from my slumber and sat down. A profound sense of contentment washed over me. Even though I made a Sankalpa for 12 days, I felt fulfilled on the 11th day.

Evening I called Pattabhiji from a telephone booth near the highway and informed him, 'Tomorrow, I shall return home, and rest will talk in person.'

About less than a year after that momentous incident, we were graced with the presence of a venerable individual. He came to meet Pattabhiji; he asserted that he had the power to summon any divine energy! Since the location of our spiritual centre had been graced with the divine energy of Hanuman, Pattabhiji requested him to invoke that energy. That individual's facial expression and gestures were transformed drastically, and a lot of people there indeed felt the presence of Lord Hanuman. After Pattabhiji, many others came forward to ask questions and received satisfactory answers from him. After some time, this individual turned towards me and inquired, 'Whom shall I summon for you?' I said, 'More than any God, I love my Gurudēva Swami Rama a lot. Can you please invite him for me?' He asked for more details, like who he was and where he was from. I have to mention that by then, Swami Rama had departed from this world. After I answered all his queries, his facial expression and body language changed. Both Pattabhiji and I could sense the presence of Swami Rama on that day.

For a few minutes, I found myself doubting whether Baba would truly visit us through this individual's body. It didn't take long for my doubts to dissipate, as his body language, manner of speaking, and gestures perfectly matched Baba's. My body trembled. I was overcome with deep remorse, both for doubting this person and summoning Baba. I could feel it in my very being that Baba was displeased with me!

As I pondered upon these thoughts, I suddenly heard Baba's voice emanating from his body. "There was no need for you to go to a farm and do Sādhana!!" Why do you think Bhagavathi comes only when you suffer like this? I am already with you. You can do your Sādhana wherever you are! Itna kasht lene ki kya zaroorath thi? (What was the necessity of going through all this trouble?) Pattabhiji was particularly pleased to hear this, as he did not approve of my tendency to take risks by venturing into forests or isolated places to do Sādhana. He was concerned about my safety. He was relieved because after receiving such admonitions from Baba, he believed that I wouldn't embark on such risky adventures again. Being concerned for my well-being was his expression of love. In the end, Baba lovingly said, 'Beti, Kabibi yaisa math karna, ye sab karne ki tumhe zaroorat nahi hai, (Child, never engage in such things, you don't have to undertake such activities), I am always with you! In this manner, Baba bestowed upon me a blank cheque for life!!

***

Messages from the Himalayan Sages: Timely & Timeless

3

THE FULCRUM OF POLARITIES, BRIDGING THE NORTH AND SOUTH DIVIDE!

Himalayan ranges hold a special place of significance as the epicenters of spirituality in the hearts of Indians. The breathtaking valleys, the unending mountain ranges, the serene flow of the holy Ganga river, and the forests made of sky-high trees have all found their own place in the inner faculties of a spiritual individual. India is the birthplace of Yoga, and Yogis are directly associated with the Himalayas in our belief system. These associations come naturally to us as they are deeply imprinted on our minds. It is not just the Indians but also people the world over associate Yoga directly with India. Spiritual seekers across the globe agree with this reality.

This is not far from the truth. Himalayan ranges have served as the womb to the unveiling of all the eternal truths known to us. As such, a Yogi's seeking process is naturally bound to draw him towards these sacred mountains. The capstone is that Lord Shiva's abode is in the Kailash Parvath, in the Himalayas. It is supremely sacred for the seekers in their spiritual journey.

The roots of the belief in Himalayas are so strong in our spiritual ecosystem, that many would consider 'without Himalayas, a Yogi's life is incomplete.' In this backdrop, if we observe the lives of many yogis through their autobiographies, one can easily notice the inseparable connection between them and the Himalayas.

But in my adolescent years, I did not have any such magical experiences or any divine signals. Until I met my Guru, my thoughts and actions were that of any normal person. I was engrossed in a simple worldly life.

Normal living and mischief-making

My entire life - be it my birth, studies, job, marriage, or family – has been spent in the state of Karnataka, located in the southern hemisphere of India. When I completed my post-graduation in English Literature, I firmly believed in the superiority of the logical mind. I was someone who would often be demeaning towards the culture of this land, ways of life, and our belief system; I was a judgemental girl, to say the least.

For me, the western literature that I was teaching meant everything! So much so that I would quote Albert Camus, excerpts from British literature, romanticism, and even modern literature seamlessly in my arguments.

I would take pleasure in annoying my mother. I would keep asking nagging questions like 'Why do you do the pooja in this manner?' or 'Why do we need to light the lamp? What is the meaning behind it? I will not light the lamp if you don't answer my questions. But my mother did not have any answers! Most of the mothers in normal households were probably going through the same situation at home back then. Due to the unending invasions of the outsiders, our ancient disciplines to attain a meaningful life, which was part of our culture, had almost disappeared from people's lives.

It was a time when the entire nation was culturally struggling to find its roots. As a newly independent nation, the mindset of people - shaped by centuries of slavery - could barely be altered in a few decades of freedom. There was massive friction, and common people were in a confused state.

Course correction after meeting Swami Rama

My thought process and my outlook towards life changed forever once I met my Guru Swami Rama. I had a very normal meeting with him. I did not have any instant spiritual realisations or any internal voice screaming 'He is my Guru.' It may sound weird, but it is true. One can understand that meeting a guru does not always come with a spiritual upheaval, and need not be as dramatic as we envisage.

Now, coming to my experience with the Himalayas, once I had found my Gurudēva, the connection with the Himalayas automatically started building, though little by little. However, for someone who was accustomed to the South Indian weather, the extremely cold atmosphere and the food culture of the Himalayas were tough to adjust to. It was not too exhausting to reach Rishikesh, at the foothills of the Himalayas, and therefore I would settle for Rishikesh to meet my Guru.

But I attribute my own spiritual awakening to the Tadkeshwar Holy shrine located in the Garhwal region of the Himalayas in Uttarakhand. It is also the place where Swami Rama did his Sādhana in the cave, and it was a place frequented by Bengali Baba. Visiting places like Tungnath also had a highly positive influence on my spiritual awareness and my appreciation for the Himalayas went up further. But my roots firmly remained in south India.

After the fortune of meeting Swami Rama, I got initiated into Srividya through a Mantra in Sādhana Mandir, Rishikesh. I was in contact with Swami Rama for 4 years when he was still in his physical body. However, 'time' is not the appropriate measure to ascertain a Guru's proximity to his disciple.

A disciple might have spent 25 years in the service of the guru and may not have received the wisdom or spiritual advancement while another may get it within a few months. These are influenced by the preparations and the deeds from our past life, called Karma. But under a Guru's protection, one will see time and space operate differently.

Major transformations may occur to some people the instant they see their Guru, but to some nothing happens at all. But it is true that those 4 years of association with Swami Rama turned my life into a beautiful spiritual voyage. Even after leaving his physical body, Swami Rama used to visit us, whenever we needed his guidance.

Shastri ji, who illuminated my life, as foretold by Swami Rama!

Upon leaving his body, Baba appeared in the dream of Pattabhi Ji and sent us a message, 'I am sending both of you to a Shastri, an adept in Srividya, in South India. I want you to learn Srividya in the south Indian tradition from him.' But no other details were revealed, such as who this person is or how to find him. But Baba had willed, so the connections got established on their own. I got to continue my practice under the tutelage of Sri R. Sathya Narayana - or, as I reverently call him, my Mysuru Gurugalu or Rā Sā Gurugalu.

There is also one more topic I need to mention here. Swami Rama used to say that the north Indian Bhārathi tradition is the same as the Himalayan Paramparā. It is the same Rishi lineage. For this Rishi lineage, the bond with the Himalayas is inseparable. The exact opposite of the Himalayas happens to be southern India. Commonly, we see the Yogis who start their spiritual journey in the south of India, eventually culminating in the Himalayas. This is a very common thread we notice in most cases. But in my case, it was the exact opposite.

Though my roots are here in South India, it was my first Guru Swami Rama of the Himalayas, who then directed me to learn the Srividya in the South Indian tradition and sent me down south again in my spiritual pursuit. I believe that there is a strong reason behind this.

In his book, Living with the Himalayan Masters, Swami Rama mentions his visits to the south of India, witnessing the grandeur of Madhurai Meenakshi temple in Tamilnadu, and his meetings with many Srividya adepts. While explaining the importance of Dakshinachara Srividya (or the southern practice of Srividya),

Swami Rama proudly observes - the southern practices and schools of Srividya have retained their purest form, and the essence of this vidya is kept undiluted by the southern Srividya guru lineage.

Swami Rama willed for me to learn from the south Indian branch of Srividya under a specific Guru lineage. Eventually, when I ended up meeting Rā Sā Gurugalu of Mysuru, he never let down Swami Rama's trust in him. As long as I was learning Srividya under his tutelage, he showered immense love and affection and bestowed the entire Guru lineage's grace upon me without holding anything back. Those proved to be the golden days for my journey in Srividya. Through Rā Sā Gurugalu, I was initiated into the Sri Vidyaranya tradition of south Indian Srividya.

A spiritual journey in reverse flow, from north to south

My spiritual journey concentrated more around South India. Only when we look back at the Rishi lineage do we realise that the Rishi lineage has no limitations of these geographical boundaries. Our Rishi lineage is beyond all nationalities, languages, religions, or customs. Rishis belong to the whole world, and the whole universe is under their connectivity. They live by the rules of the universe and are not bound by the realms of this planet. Upon understanding this, I also realised that while north India, south India, the Deccan plateaus, and the grasslands - all have geographic or topological differences, in the path of spirituality, they are all One, singularly united.

Another reason I say this is because I also had the opportunity to witness the harmonious links between the Srividya Dakshinachara tradition and the Himalayan Srividya Tradition.

A major milestone in my autobiography!

In my spiritual practices, one of the Gurus I had the fortune to learn from is the legendary Sage Agasthya. Since that fortunate encounter, I have gained deeper learning in many topics, such as spiritual wisdom, Vidyas, and Thithi Nitya Upasana, an esoteric practice in Srividya. In South India, everyone knows about Sage Agasthya. He is originally a Himalayan Yogi and performed most of his spiritual Sādhana in the Himalayan ranges itself. Upon being instructed to widely spread the wisdom of the Yogic science, he travelled down south, crossing the Vindya mountain ranges and settling down in south India. Due to the vastness and treacherous topography, the Vindhya mountain ranges had a reputation for being impenetrable and were unconquered by any human – therefore, north India and south India stood divided by this majestic mountain range. Sage Agasthya conquered this challenge and continued his journey to the south, making it his mission to spread the benefits of yoga and yogic wisdom to humanity from here. Hence, the Rishi Lineage is meant for all. Small and big traditions, your tradition and My tradition - these distinctions don't exist at the higher realms. It is only a wisdom-system.

When it comes to spiritual seeking, we have all kinds of distorted imaginations. For example, all yogis must be from the Himalayas, It is essential to meditate in the caves for spiritual progress, one must go through the hard penance, only when you hunt for a Guru in the Himalayas you would find one – there are so many stories, myths, imaginations that influence our thinking in this regard.

I did not have to go through any of those. I was a very ordinary individual, living my normal married life. But the future held something else, my Guru visited me where I lived; and such a facility graced upon me by the lineage has eventually led me to pursue my spiritual practices.

Besides, my Srividya Guru, Rā Sā Gurugalu was also a married man, living a normal family life. He used to research a lot in the fields of his interest, such as Dance and Music. And he held a full-time job as a Chemistry professor in a college. Such was his greatness that he had attained the epitome of spirituality, the ultimate truth, being so surrounded by the mundane world.

I recollect the words of Gurugalu's son. The college where Gurugalu taught was very near to their house. So, Gurugalu would return home for lunch on a cycle or by walking, and of those 30 minutes which he had at his disposal, he would dedicate

15 minutes to his Sādhana and the rest to finishing his lunch and rushing back to work. Your job can never hinder your spiritual advancement, which is a big lesson I drew from my Gurugalu. He was a living demonstration of this concept for us.

***

4

EARLY CHAPTERS OF MY LIFE!

Every individual's life is a journey from ignorance towards wisdom. 'Thamasoma Jyothirgamaya' or 'Lead me from the darkness to the light;' these prayers to divinity refer to the same thing. Making this prayer the foreword, I am sharing some of the incidents from my life.

The carefree childhood

I was born in 1957. The birthplace is Sagara, in the Shivamogga district of Karnataka state. Grew up in Shivamogga and I had a very ordinary childhood. Nothing extraordinary happened around me, and neither can I say 'my life was different than others' in any way.

Those were the days of extreme poverty at home. Our joint family had 22 members. We were 8 siblings to our parents. There are unforgettable memories in my life, from as early as when I was 6 or 7 years old. One of them is lining up and waiting for hours to get the grocery supplies from the ration shop, and all the kids in the house would queue up. It could be early morning or late evening; we would be in the line. Every person would be given a small portion of rice, and we all had to eat. We would carry bottles to get Kerosene.

Early chapters of my life!

The distributed rice would usually be of the lowest quality. Even after washing the rice 4 to 5 times, it wouldn't lose its bad odour; the cooked rice naturally carried the same odour as well. We all had to share whatever was available, so we all would get a hand-made lump of rice in rotation until it was over. My mother (Amma) would take a large vessel, add the cooked rice, and mix it well with some basic accompaniments like Rasam (watery soup) or Sambar (thick soup with lentils and vegetables). She would also keep a bowl of water next to her. Every time, before forming the rice lump, she would dip her hands in the water. Since the hand would be watery and hence slippery, the rice would always be proportionate and equal. This was her trick to ensure everyone got a fair share. Amma would feed us kids directly, but for adults, she would serve those lumps on their plates. We would circle around her to be hand-fed and would race to play outside with other children as soon as the food was finished. We never observed when Amma or Ajji (grandmother) ate or how much they got to eat!

The war declared between India and China was in full swing during 1967. We had to snuff the kerosene lamps as soon as we heard the siren sound of the police from the night patrol. It was supposedly to avoid being tracked by the enemy camps and possible aerial attacks. We had to stop all our activities when the siren went off and go to sleep. Many times, the siren would be heard all night. As school-going kids, we struggled to complete our studies, homework, etc. It was a daily routine in our lives.

We siblings had a 2 to 3 years gap between our birth. Those days, government-controlled ration stores distributed clothes as well, not just food. Clothes, Sugar etc were not available for the public to buy. We would use jaggery to sweeten the coffee at home, as sugar was considered a luxury reserved for the rich.

Shopping for our clothes used to be an amazing experience as well. Once a year, our Appa (father) would take all the kids of the household to the tailor. As we headed out, Amma's instructions would follow: 'Tell the tailor to stitch the clothes a size bigger.' One had to buy the fabric for the dresses at the same tailor shop those days, by the metre's length. The boxy tailor shop would be dimly lit. All of us kids would try peeping inside to make a connection with the tailor. Being in his good books would be very important during that time!

Appa would ask us to queue up in front of the tailor and ask him to take our measurements. As soon as we heard those words, all of us would line up like obedient soldiers. One fabric material would be selected, and the same colour and print pattern would be used to make the clothes in an identical design. No design changes were allowed. An entire roll of that fabric would be bought, and we would receive our family 'uniforms' in one go!

It would be only during a special festival that we got to buy clothes, that too only once in a year!

Sharing of clothes used to be very common back then. I would always get to wear my elder sisters' clothes. My elder sister would wear it for some time, and when she outgrew it in a couple of years, the dress would come to me. This way, our wardrobes got filled up. The dresses used to be a bit baggy, like the oversized or plus-size fashion that is trending with the youth today. It was a logical choice, as the clothes had to fit the growing kids for a little longer. The quality of the fabric materials, back then, was undoubtedly superior. Even well-used dresses that had been worn for 2 or 3 years seemed pretty new when they reached me. If a dress wouldn't fit us, we had to pass it on to someone else. Our life was such, but it never bothered us from being joyful.

Amma and Ajji had to balance a lot of things for the family. Appa's financial contributions would be significant as well. But, for a family of that size, it seemed like a drop in the ocean. Appa had his tendencies for a few luxuries as well. Due to those expenses, there was a shortfall of funds for the household expenses.

In a way, my Appa had a very colourful personality. He had his own style with a strong personality. He used to be very style-conscious and would always wear costly attire. Two expensive pens had found their permanent places in his pocket. I think they were

'Parker' pens; one used to have blue ink, and the other was red ink. Writing with colour pens, as a hobby, is something I picked up from my Appa. And that hobby continues to this day.

My eldest sister also was like a second mother to us. If I bothered Amma with too many questions, she would say 'go and ask your sister.' And she was also mother-like to all of us. This emotional bonding was so deeply instilled in her that even after she got married and shifted to her in-laws' house, she would still behave like she was my Amma, whenever I visited her.

The guava tree in front of our house turned into our playground during holidays. We would climb the tree and sit on different branches. The telephone was a new invention at that point of time and naturally drew our interest. A few tins or boxes and some thread were all we needed, and a telephone was born for us to play. My brothers also would partake in this game. Playtime started early in the morning and went on even in the afternoons under the scorching heat of the sun. The play would go on until Amma shouted at the top of her voice to get back in. It is saddening to see how excessive homework is destroying kids' childhoods these days. At home, my sister used to review our homework. Even when we did not complete our homework, teachers were not really bothered. Not completing one's homework wasn't a punishable offence then, like it is today. There was joy in going to school.

Ours being a Brahmin family, my grandmother used to properly follow all the religious rituals. We children were an obedient lot, to it.

My Appa: the multifaceted Radio Narayana Rao

Appa used to be quite a popular person in Sagara, our hometown. His exceptional sharpness in his personality was one of the reasons for his popularity. His mechanical skills were unparalleled.

He was nick-named Radio Narayana Rao. He had a radio repair shop near Maarigudi Circle, in Sagara, called 'Radio House.' Appa's popularity was growing each day. People from distant villages would travel all the way to get their radios fixed. The transistor was the latest invention in those days, and the radio was the main source of entertainment and mass communication. Appa could repair any nonfunctional radio device. He hadn't studied the subject and had not studied beyond 10th in school. But he was a superhero who fixed any mechanical issues, and it came to him naturally. The way he would be engrossed in solving the mechanical issues mesmerised his customers. Sometimes, people waited for hours, and even days, to get their radios repaired by him.

Sometimes we also overheard people say, 'We don't give our radio for repair to anyone but Radio Narayana Rao.'

Another speciality of Appa's personality was his solid grasp of languages. He was smart and multilingual. If any stranger heard him speak in Urdu, his perfection and fluency could make them believe he was a Muslim from birth. We would amusedly watch him fluently converse in 6 to 7 languages. One more fascinating topic about Appa was his relationship with the banks. Our family had relocated to Shivamogga. In those days, there were not too many banks, and very few cooperative banks were in existence. Any bank manager transferred to Shivamogga would become his friend in no time whatsoever. His street smartness came very handy here. He would first find out the mother tongue of the bank manager and then speak in that language as one of their own, which helped him build strong relationships. Also, due to this, his loans got sanctioned quite quickly.

Appa used to have a car those days, quite a fancy one, the kind which British elites used. He knew about all its spare parts and could repair it himself. He would drive vintage cars of all types. He also knew how to repair these in no time, whenever they broke down. He used to be a good driver as well. I used to watch him drive, proudly, as he skillfully drove through the twisty ghat regions.

Appa was active in politics as well. The Congress Party was in power back then. Appa had identified himself as a leader of that party. He held some prominent posts also in the Municipality for a while.

He was a big fan of Dramas. Those days, stage shows by organised troops, called drama companies, were at the peak of their popularity. Whenever these drama companies visited our town for a performance, he would invite some of them to our house. Many would even stay at our home as guests. The dramas lasted the whole night. One of the most popular drama companies of that era was 'Gubbi Veeranna Drama Company.' The main actors of this troop, and even the owners, used to stay at our place. It is quite possible that Gubbi Veeranna himself had visited us, too, but I was too young to remember.

Life in Shivamogga was challenging. When we were in Sagara, we owned the house where my nephew continues to live even today. Even after many alterations and repairs, the house has retained its original form even now. When compared to Sagara, life in Shivamogga was expensive. We had taken a small house on rent, and it was overcrowded. Appa got us admitted into private schools. It was a time of limited means, and I did not understand why he sent us to private schools by paying high fees instead of the free education available in a government school. But meeting the school expenses was always a challenge.

Company drama, a visual spectacle!

My interest in classical dance and my teachings both started in Shivamogga itself. Had we continued to live in Sagara, learning the dance would have become a distant dream. In the entire town of Shivamogga, there was only one dance teacher. My Ajji (grandmother) probably would have looked for this teacher. Ajji was very interested in these matters, whereas Amma was busy with cooking, apart from overseeing the fundamental needs of our family. She was a total devotee! She would get emotional and start crying every day as she read 'Mookam karoti vaachalam, pangum langhayate girim' from the Bhagavad Gita, which roughly translates to 'A dumb person will start speaking, and the one without legs can climb mountains – when the divine blessing is with you.' She was emotionally linked to her divinity, and she used to sing very well. I remember hearing her singing the spiritual compositions of Purandara Dasa and many other devotional songs. Company dramas had a major influence on people's lives in those days. Dramas were usually musicals back then, and the majority of the dramas were stories from the ancient scriptures - called Purānās.

The songs performed in these dramas were inspired by Indian classical music. Back in Sagara, the place where the drama companies usually erected the performance stage was right across the road from our house within a short distance. While we couldn't get to see the performance, as we had to buy the tickets, the songs and the dialogue travelled to us clearly. We would watch the dramas through the door gaps of those temporary tents whenever possible. We got to see and hear the same drama for 10, 15, or sometimes even 90 days. We would mug up the dialogues and even know the next lines as well. Even when the performer on the stage fumbled, we would get it right. While we were busy imitating the dialogues, Amma would be blissfully rendering her voice to the spiritual compositions from the play. Those songs had such a profound impact on me that after completing my formal training in Bharata Natya, I eventually ended up choreographing them. I had embedded Amma's Purandaradasa songs into my dance choreographies as well.

Colourful medicines

My dance classes started when I was in the second standard, in Shivamogga. When we moved to Shivamogga, the responsibility of our family, too, fell on the shoulders of my Ajji. She was very dear to me. A lot of people thought we resembled a lot, too. More than the physical similarities, we also matched in our interests and traits. But Amma was the opposite of both of us. Soft-spoken and polite, she had never raised her voice at anyone out of anger. She also barely scolded us, even when we were being highly mischievous. Her home and her family were her world. Unless it was necessitated, she rarely stepped outside.

I remember going to a doctor's clinic with her. Those days, the doctors also acted as compounders. The doctor would examine the patient and make a prescription first. Then, the doctor would walk over to the medicine dispensary area to perform the duty of compounder. Very few could read, so the medicines had to be recognised by their colours. Even the doctors would explain the medicine dosage, timing, etc., by referring to the colour only. For example, the rose-coloured tablet was for fever; if the fever was accompanied by a cold, there would be another colour, and cough medicine would be of a different colour again. We would remember the dosage based on the colours and follow the instructions. In the follow-up visits to the doctor, we would explain things like 'Last time you gave red medicine,' and the doctor would understand. I sincerely wonder about the predicament of people with colour blindness back then! It wasn't a recognised condition, so it didn't exist! And they had to select and swallow the pill! Metaphorically fitting today's modern science.

Now, when asked what his fee was, the doctor always responded with 'whatever you want to pay me.' Those days, the calculations used to happen in annas (25 paise would be 4 annas, 50 paise would be 8 annas, and 100 Paise would make one rupee). If someone paid the doctor 4 annas, it was newsworthy. And he never asked for any specific amount from anyone. Due to our solid physical immunity, we were less prone to diseases. Rarely, due to the weather pattern changes or when we had some outside food, we would fall sick, but we also recovered quite fast with these basic medications themselves or home remedies like various concoctions made of spices and herbs, in Amma's kitchen.

In the company of 'Jaganmohini'

If we need to know about the outside food, then you need to know about box shops. Those days, most of the stores used to be 'box shops,' which were made with a curtain in the front and a metal sheet for a roof, and they resembled little boxes. If the curtain was closed, the shop was closed. If it was open, it was business time. The sweetmeats decorated the front of those stores as merchandise of attraction. The peppermint used to be a major attraction. There were no chocolates those days. There were candies of different sizes, colours, and shapes. I used to love the tangy peppermint. It was an unparalleled blend of sweet and sour! From our home, we had to turn right and turn left again a short distance later, and we were at a box shop. It had surrounded my childhood so much that I can clearly picture it in my mind even now. I used to irritate my mother by pressurising her, saying, 'Amma! Amma! Five paise for peppermint pls.. pls.. pls!' The pleading would go on until she paid!

Though we would ask for money from our mother, the finances of the house were under the control of our Appa. He was the head of the family, and he used to make all the key decisions in the household. He would also allocate clear budgets for different expense items, but Amma was a crafty accountant, to say the least. She would give accounts for every single paise, but she was smarter than Appa in financial matters. She knew how to confuse him in this matter and would save 10, 25 paise coins safely in a jar filled with black mustard to avoid detection. And if Appa ever doubted and asked if she was keeping money aside, she would shut him up by saying, "Look around. Where is the money? Do you see any? Why do I need your money!" But, usually, Amma would pick pocket Appa's money during his shower. She would sneak into the room and pick out a few coins every day for a rainy-day fund for the family. She definitely respected him and feared him to an extent as well. But that fear was overcome with her responsibilities towards her family.

Our pocket money used to come from the money pick-pocketed from Appa. But Amma was very disciplined in distributing that as well. If I received 5 paise today, I could expect my next pocket money only after another 2 weeks. But, as kids, we had our own internal understanding. With the money I got, I would buy 5 peppermints and share it with a few others. And when their turn came, they would also share it with me. Many times, when we didn't have any money, we begged the shopkeeper for a few peppermints on loan, promising to pay him the next day. He would just brush us off and send us back home, and sometimes, he would give us loans.

We would go and report it back at home, crying, to Amma. That was our world. A short while later that box shop got upgraded, and he introduced a chocolate-like sweetmeat. Possibly made of jaggery and milk powder; but it created magic. He would serve that sweet on a small stick, like today's lollipop. But, we had nick-named it 'Jaganmohini,' or 'the mesmeriser of the universe.'

Mad love for studies and the strict Jnanakshi teacher

I think I was in the 6th or 7th standard, and I remember going to my father and asking, 'Appa, exams tomorrow. I need to study. Can you wake me up by 3.00 am?' Appa made sure to set the alarm, eventually staying awake to ensure I didn't fall asleep. In reality, there was no need to wake up at 3.00 am. The syllabus used to be much simpler, unlike today and did not require such an effort. But this helped me instil discipline at a very young age. English was my favourite subject by then. It was one of the toughest too. In those days, Kannada (a language originating in Karnataka, India) used to be our medium of teaching for the first 5 years of education, and English language classes started only after 5th standard.

An English teacher would be treated like a celebrity. There was an English teacher, a Christian lady called Jnanakshi. Those days, the teachers who studied in 'convent schools' were considered the gold standard for teaching English. They would be hired for higher salaries and perks. Teacher Jnanakshi was known to be very strict. Being talkative and mischievous, I had seen the ire of quite a few teachers. My day wouldn't be complete without getting scolded by at least one teacher. After all the scolding, the Kannada teacher would say, 'Jyothi, you keep talking so much. If your mouth was made of wood, it would have cracked by now. But since I was good at my studies, they also liked me a lot. Though I was a chatterbox, I would absorb what was taught with full concentration.

English exams were like nightmares for us. We would lose sleep being anxious. Our biggest challenge used to be our spelling mistakes. During the dictation, we would get only one minute to spell the word given, and the teacher would move on to the next word, and she would not repeat the previous word even upon asking. Dictation classes were held every day. Once the teacher was giving the dictation a bit faster, and I was distracted. The teacher had given the words - 'Father' and 'Mother' - but for us, it was tricky at that age. Instead of 'Mother,' I ended up writing 'Mather.' Apart from losing a mark, I got a decent amount of scolding, and I had to stretch my palm and take some beatings in front of all my classmates. More than the beatings on my palms, the insult was hurting me more. I was doing my best to hold back from crying in public, but the tears were on a free flow. This upset the teacher even more, and she beat me a few more times. From then on, whenever the word 'spelling' comes up, I am reminded of that day. However, the early foundations for my passionate pursuit of English literature were laid by Jnanakshi teacher.

***

How to make coffee?

Our headmistress was a charming middle-aged lady with a fair complexion. As the headmistress, she commanded respect from all the other teachers. We used to have board exams in the seventh standard, and as such, there would be a lot of pressure to study. Even the teachers were committed to taking the classes. Another interesting aspect was that she took English classes for the seventh standard. Her classes used to be very unique. Nobody was allowed to be absent on the days of her classes. But, unfortunately, her English was average. In reality, she did not have much of a background in English either. But as headmistress, it was her decision to take the class.

Once she explained to us 'How to make coffee?' and I remember it even today. We had to write an essay in English on the above topic; but we were yet to start forming our own sentences. We were used to memorising the answers beforehand, and our teachers also expected the same from us. So, memorising was the only way we knew to face the test.

She always started her dialogues with 'Children, you remember..?' She wouldn't know how to complete that sentence in English alone. So, she used to have 6 to 7 templated responses. We used to wonder if she borrowed them from different textbooks. But they were excruciating for us to memorise, which she would make us do. We had to repeat those 6 lines throughout the 30 to 40 minutes of her class. And this wasn't for one class; rather, it would go on for weeks at a stretch. The topic was 'How to make coffee?' and the kids would have preferred to learn the process of making coffee in real life than go through the torture of memorising those lines.

The farce of a perfect score!

My Amma did not have much understanding about the subjects in the seventh standard, and she was not able to help us in our studies. She only knew that her daughter was considered good in her studies, and regularly got good marks.

She had studied only until her second or third standard. But she knew basic maths, calculations and how to sign. I remember her signing the documents as 'Radha' in her mother tongue Kannada.

As the board exams neared, I had made up my mind to aim for a perfect score of 100. Parents were less stressed about the exam results back then. So, we had the space to decide. But, I had aimed to get 100 out of 100 marks in every subject.

As the exams began, I would rise early to study and go to the exam hall well-prepared. And I had done well, too, until that one day. I remember coming home and entering the verandah, and there was a curtain separating the verandah from the living room, beyond which was a small room, followed by the kitchen; it was a tiny home.

It was noon when I had returned from my exams. During exams, the school used to function only for half a day. Since Amma knew about this, she did not bother coming out and continued her chores in the kitchen. I stayed in the verandah but could not draw the curtains and enter the living room. I was trying to disappear behind the curtains with a grim face and shouted from there, 'Amma!' She was busy cooking and said why don't you come inside and talk. 'No, come here,' I insisted, and this drama went on for a while!

Finally, Amma relented and came to the living room. 'Oh, you are here!' she said as she pulled me out of my hiding space behind the curtains. By the time she asked why I was hiding my face, I started weeping.

'What happened?' Amma was anxious.

I stammered, 'I.. I.. made a mistake in the exam today!' I was crying out loud by then. Amma was left confused as she was anticipating some major tragedy looking at the way I was crying and wasn't anticipating this response. It took some time for her to understand the entire situation.

She didn't know whether to laugh or to cry! She consoled me saying 'So what? You have made one mistake, and instead of 100 you will get 99. That's all! Come and eat now.'

'How could that mistake happen? 'I was still naggy. It was like my world had collapsed in front of me. I didn't eat well and kept sobbing through the day.

Those days, the mistakes were corrected by writing the correct answers a hundred or even a thousand times. I knew about the mistake I had made as soon as I submitted my papers. So, I started writing the correct answer a hundred times in preparation. I didn't want to wait for the teacher to point out the mistake. There was a high expectation about the board results, and the results day arrived. The score I got in English made me emotional again; it was 99 out of 100. In all other subjects, I received a perfect score of 100.

Those days the rankings were declared at a district level. Since there were one or 2 who had scored all the marks, I ranked third in the district that year. I was teary-eyed and grim again, as I had come in third place. The report card from the seventh board exams served me as a reminder of this whole episode and was with me until very recently.

Initial days of dance tuition

The Bharatanatyam (Indian classical dance form) classes used to be twice, weekly, and cost Ten or Fifteen rupees a month. It used to be a lot of money in those days.

Appa was never amenable to the idea of my dance classes. It is an interesting episode of how I asked him to let me join the dance classes. Appa was very temperamental, and we had to assess before asking such things. Approaching him when he returned home tired from work was to be avoided at all costs, as he would definitely decline to our demands. Once he said 'No,' it was impossible to revert him to a 'Yes.' When angry, Appa was just like sage Durvaasa. Amma would call him 'Hitler' at times.

That night, after Appa had finished dinner, Amma sent me to him. I was probably half past 6 or 7 years old by then. As he was resting, I went and sat on his lap. I shared all the stories from the school of that day, and once I was sure he was in a joyous mood, I carefully approached the topic.

'Appa, I heard there is a dance teacher who teaches really well. My friends have all joined that class. Can I also join?' I approached with all the cuteness and innocence.

He was amused but clear in his rejection of the idea, saying, 'What do you mean to dance? I don't like all this…!' and simply walked away without allowing for any responses. It was a clear deadlock. We didn't relent, either. Amma pitched in the next morning during breakfast, 'She is a child; wants to learn dance. Why can't we allow her to go and dance?' asked Appa softly.

'So, she has your support too! What are you people thinking? Being from a traditional family like ours, does she want to dance? Can't you see it? Can you even think?' he thundered and left.

It was an improbable quest to find answers before Appa returned home at night. How to convince him? There was no other way.

My Ajji (grandmother) really wanted to get me enrolled in the dance classes. But, how without Appa's permission? I approached the topic again with Appa after giving it a week's break. 'Again the same nuisance! Have you forgotten my decision?' he scolded me and sent me off. We all came to terms with the fact that he would never agree with this plan.

Finally, it was my Ajji and Amma who sat together to make a master plan. My Ajji declared her firm decision, 'Anyhow, her Appa comes home late at night after work. Before he returns home, I will take her to the dance class and bring her back as well. But she must learn Bharatanatyam,' with full conviction. What she suggested was practically possible. But how to pay the massive fees? Here, Ajji also took up the burden on herself.

***

5

A JOURNEY TOWARDS ELEVATION BEYOND THE KARMIC CYCLE

In this chapter, I am trying to chronicle the bittersweet memories of my birthplace, the time spent there, the surroundings, etc. My birthplace is Sagara, and my childhood was spent in the surroundings of Sagara and Shivamogga in Karnataka, India.

When we retrospect on the journey of life through the prism of spirituality, we find a broader context to life.

In the cycle of life and death, there is 'rebirth;' mention all our Shāstras.

When we believe we are born only once, there is no scope left to complete the unfulfilled tasks, desires, or any evolution in the journey of life. Hence, justice for the soul becomes non-existent in this thesis. The concept of rebirth, therefore, is more appropriate. It provides a great opportunity for the Atman to elevate itself. One needs such chances of advancement to be able to go beyond the cycle of life and death, to fulfil the purpose of one's life, and to break free from the karmic bondages.

In this backdrop, when we assess our birth, the environment around us, our parents, friends, relatives, and life as a whole - we can see they are all predetermined. These are detailed in the Shāstras.

Hence, my viewpoints are inspired by these aspects when I try to share about my birth and the environment. When we try to narrate based on the foundations laid by the events in our lives, as perceived by the mind in this material reality of the world, it tends to bring its own limitations as well. It will then just be recording someone's life without any spiritual perspective. As such, I am being extra conscious as I share my life perspectives with you.

It is true that I was born in Sagara. According to the Shāstras, it is highly probable I chose the place myself. It is possible my childhood and place of birth were decided in my previous lives, and so were my familial bonds. To fulfil the purpose of life or any unfulfilled desires, the Atman chooses the right atmosphere and people, and when we see life through this prism, it is quite likely that I chose Sagara and Shivamogga to spend my early life in this birth.

Sagara and Shivamogga were very conducive to building my life around literature and beautiful sensibilities towards life. Sagara is located in the Malnad region of Karnataka, right adjacent to the Shivamogga district, and is known for its rich plantations of betel nuts and coconut. The serene atmosphere, peaceful lifestyle, and family rooted in its culture were instrumental in developing my awareness of the world. Hence, the Atman bound with this body may have chosen that environment.

This freedom of choice is earned by us from our previous life. This freedom of choice is referred to as 'Buddhihi karmaanusaarini' in the Upanishads. It means our intellect works according to our past karmas. The Atman selects the environment that will be supportive to fulfil all the desires that are left unfulfilled in our previous births. It can be said that, the environment I was born into had a huge influence in the making of my individual personality. However, this wisdom or awareness happens to be a link to the present life, its forgetfulness can turn it into a bondage.

Literary and cultural abundance, called Shivamogga

While I was born in Sagara, Shivamogga is where I grew up. But Shivamogga that I know and grew up in is not the same as it is now. I am explaining the town it was 45 or 50 years ago. In a small town like Sagara, my Appa felt the opportunities were limited and restrictive. I keep wondering if Appa had not moved to Shivamogga, would my life have taken this turn, and would the spiritual path be in my life to pursue?

Every being will be trying to fulfil its unfulfilled desires relentlessly. It will keep building an appropriate atmosphere to achieve what it needs to achieve. That is called 'Karma.'

Shivamogga and Sagara were almost identical in most aspects. As I was growing up, I was also able to see the city grow swiftly. It was a city close to the heart of many celebrated writers, and the good samaritans of Shivamogga had nurtured the rich cultural heritage as well.

Many intellectual personalities come to my mind when I hear of Sagara, Shivamogga, Theertahalli etc. Some of the foremost novelists and writers in Kannada such as Kuvempu, Dr. U. R. Ananthamoorthy and many such legends of the literary world lived in Theertahalli and the surrounding towns, making me feel proud about my birthplace.

Shivamogga is known to be a cultural hub. The DVS College, where I studied; National College of Commerce, where I served as a lecturer; Kasturba College - all of them had built an atmosphere that nurtured cultural, literary, and performance arts. As such, I was drawn towards the theatre arts, too.

When I was studying in the DVS College, there was an intellectual group of professors and lecturers who wrote and published many thought provoking, progressive plays and also creatively directed those performances on the stage. As a student, and also as a lecturer, I had the opportunity to participate in a few theatre shows.

Such sensibilities towards art and culture laid the foundations for my inner growth. Along with this, I also got to learn and practice classical dance as well. These opportunities helped me to bring out the talent hidden within and express myself better. Even after my spiritual journey across the country and overseas, these fond memories of my childhood and adolescent years are etched in my mind forever. Whenever I see any new place, even while traveling abroad, the images of my hometown come rushing back into my mind. Endless stretches of betel nut, coconut, cardamom, pepper, and banana plantations; mountains, hillocks, and rivers adorn the rich canvass of Malnad. They remain as fresh in my memory.

Chance to be the lead actress in a movie

Cultural activities were abundant even during my student life. At this juncture, I need to share an important episode that changed the direction of my life, related to the Kannada Film Industry. Was it by luck or was it the direct display of the line 'Buddhihi Karmaanusaarini?'

I was at the tender age of 16 then, yet to start making my own decisions. It was an unexpected opportunity to act in the movies, and I was still confused. I was doing very well on the academic front. I wanted to achieve more in academia, and I was shocked when this opportunity knocked on the door.

Since there was pressure from Appa, I also accepted the opportunity.

A withered mind amidst the acting and the photoshoots

Shivamogga used to be a small town with its own limitations back then. On the one hand, there was the new generation that grew up with me, and on the other, there was the older one, with those who had seen me growing up. Both of these groups were not willing to accept my entry into the movie field and would exclude me from their groups. This hostility was making me want to back out. The lack of empathy from the groups and their mindset was difficult for me to fathom.

Another reason for this was the shooting itself. Bengaluru did not have the studio facilities, or the technology needed for movie-making back then. Hence, we had to go to Chennai (which was called Madras in those days) for almost everything. As such, the first screen test, make-up test, costume test, photoshoot, everything happened in Chennai itself. This necessitated frequent travels to Chennai, and that, too, was just for initial preparation work. I started missing my college classes, and my attendance also went down significantly. I was facing a lot of criticism and mockery at college, my friends started abandoning me for no reason, lecturers started acting weirdly distancing themselves, and all of this left me in a very fragile state. I was feeling lonely and orphaned in the crowd.

At the sensitive and tender age of 18, these were the mental blows I was dealing with, and I started getting into depression. But the pressure from my Appa was not easing. He was adamant that I had to act in the movies.

Bidding adieu to Cinema; shockwaves for Appa

I was the reason behind many quarrels at home. My elder brothers mustered their courage and started questioning Appa: 'If she is not interested, why are you insisting on her acting career? Why waste money on something she doesn't enjoy?' Since Appa had to take me to the shooting, his business was suffering as well. Every visit to Chennai meant massive expenditures. Differences of opinion started emerging among the family members.

Appa's ego got hurt by this, and he started taking it as a personal challenge. He wanted to see his daughter become a star, come what may! Our finances worsened at home. The smile had vanished from Amma's face. I started developing an inferiority complex. 'So much is going wrong because of me; what if I die, and when I am only not there, would they all be back to normal?' the suicidal thoughts were getting stronger.

This can be taken as an example of what happens when a normal girl, rooted in her culture, enters the film industry as an outsider. With all of these challenges, we completed shooting the first part of the movie.

By then, I had reached a mindset of complete dejection and didn't want to continue acting in the movie. My lack of motivation made me back out of the project. It was an unexpected blow to Appa's dreams. Since he had invested in the movie alongside others, the financial losses were also heavy. His hopes of seeing the movie hit the big screen and seeing some returns on the investment, as well as his dreams of seeing my talent recognised on a larger platform, were both dashed.

Reality was not syncing in for him. As a result of all of this, he stopped talking to me altogether. Feeling disgraced, he exited the movie makers group. Whatever he spent until then went into losses. A few shooting schedules and visits to Chennai had all cost Appa a lot. As such his business also closed down for some time.

I took up English literature, History, and Economics as my opted subjects and continued my studies. Slowly my mind started healing.

But, as a result of this entire episode, my relationship with Appa had really soured.

Post Graduation for a mere 5 rupees!

As the time passed, Appa's anger towards me also diluted. He himself supported me and sent me to pursue my postgraduate degree at Mysuru (Mysore then).

Those days, the university offering postgraduate studies was Mysuru University. Shivamogga's Kuvempu University was non-existent then. One had to go to either Mysuru University or Karnataka University, which is located in Dharwad. It was very difficult to get the seat on merit, especially in the general category. The fee was also very high. I did not have any hopes of getting a merit seat. However, due to my good marks, I not only got the merit seat in the general category but also a freeship. You may find it difficult to believe, but all I paid for the 2 years of my postgraduate studies was only 5 rupees! That, too, was paid to the Karnataka government to get my marks card, and the rest of the expenses were all waived.

Since I had to stay in a hostel for my studies, paying the canteen bill was proving to be a bit of a burden.

Manasa Gangotri, or the Mysuru University, had made its name for being one of the best universities. The Kannada research centre had just started and a lot of laureates of Kannada literature worked there. I completed my higher education in the campus with many fond memories from those days; the student life, the friends group etc made me joyful.

Dance or profession?

After post-graduation, my professional journey commenced. I was disappointed for not being able to focus on my dance. While at the Mysuru University campus of Manasa Gangotri, I practised dance, yoga, and music. I got to learn under the tutelage of Sri Muralidhar Rao, a sought-after Acharya in dance, and his student, Dr. Vasundhara Doraiswamy, who went on to become popular globally. I had learned under them with keen interest, and I did not want my journey with dance to remain only a hobby. I wanted to actively engage in dance and contribute back.

Given this, the path ahead was unclear and remained so for some time. I was at a crossroads when choosing my career path. The financial duress at home deterred me from quitting my job as a lecturer to pursue dance. I liked my job as a lecturer, too. So, after consulting my Amma, I decided to go ahead with the job as a lecturer. In those days, it was rare for people to attain post-graduation degrees in English literature. The number of people managing to do this could be counted by hand. Hence, these jobs naturally commanded respect. When the results were announced, and I was still awaiting my certificates, I already had the job offer in my hand. The first job in my professional life was that of a lecturer at the National College of Commerce in Shivamogga.

Appa's anxiousness!

My Appa became anxious as soon as he heard I was shortlisted for the interview. He was against going to the interview. 'Would you be able to stand in front of grown-up boys and teach? It will be tough. Why do you have to take so much trouble and teach?' he tried his best to dissuade me.

But I was adamant about going ahead. Since he could not stop me, he came to the college with me on the first day. The typical mindset of the parents back then used to be as such. Appa not only spoke to the Principal, but also with the Head of the Department in the English section and requested them to look after me well. My career started off in such a situation.

Those days were beautiful. Since I was new, I was very eager to teach exceptionally well. I was keen to learn a lot, so I could teach a lot. But my excitement was watered down by the lack of interest from the students.

Majority of the students did not enjoy studies at all and came to college out of compulsion. They valued the certificate more than the knowledge they could attain. It was a stark contrast to how I remembered studying. It was difficult to find passion for knowledge, as the rich students came just to pass time and the poor came hoping the certificate would enable them to find a job.

My belief that 'teaching is a noble profession' was being tested in this environment. My ballooning excitement to teach was getting needle-pricked, metaphorically speaking. I was getting disillusioned. But I would not relent, so I tried to muster all the energy and continue.

By then, another thing that was bothering me was the lack of opportunities to dance; there were no opportunities to learn, teach, or perform anywhere.

The feeling was deepening that I was wasting my life in that place. Due to that I also started to feel suffocated at work. During that time, a public notification came out from Karnataka Public Service Commission (KPSC), from the Government, stating there were roles open for English lecturer posts in the state-run colleges. Appa was keen on that, as it was a government job.

I saw it as an opportunity to go to Bengaluru and continue my dance pursuit. Therefore, we decided to apply for it after consulting with a few senior professors to seek their guidance.

I received the interview call. There were no written exams in the interviews those days. It would be a direct interview, and one had to conduct live classes to prove their capabilities. People like me, from the general merit category, had minimal chances of getting selected for the job. The competition was stiff, but I got selected for the job. I was adamant about working in Bengaluru.

I was finally posted at 'Maharani College' in Bengaluru. At last, I was in Bengaluru. I managed to find the hostel, canteen etc.

First task I took up when I moved to Bengaluru was to join dance classes again. There was a very popular artist by the name of Usha Daatar in Bengaluru those days. She was an expert in Kathakali and Mohiniattam, and Bharatanatyam of South India. I had completed junior and senior levels of Bharatanatyam by the time I joined her and went on to get Vidwath (masters) under her training. We used to give performances together.

On the other hand, Maharani College had a very good reputation. I was satisfied with my job and also excited that I was learning Bharatanatyam again.

Astonishment filled to the brim in heart; from a small town I stepped into the city of AWE, called Bengaluru, exploring the amazing energy of the place unknowingly I had become a Bangalorean in a very short timespan!!

***

THE DANCE STEPS AND THE JINGLE BELLS: THA-KA-DHI-NA-THA

My Ajji really wanted me to learn Bharatanatyam and practically insisted on it. She was a very strong-willed, adventurous person. Her friend Jayamma was also a widower like my Ajji. They ran a coal depot in partnership. In those days, coal was the main source of cooking in the kitchens. The other option would be to use the kerosene stove. Ajji used to sell Kerosene as well, right adjacent to her coal depot. The government would regulate the prices of kerosene back then, and she had to sell at that price only. Most of her household responsibilities were absorbed independently. While this was already a lot to handle, her financial independence had fuelled her confidence to admit me into the dance school.

Not one or 2, for a good 3 years, Ajji managed to take me to the dance school, with Appa being clueless. She would work hard at the depot from morning to evening. Weighing the heavy firewood involved a lot of physical work. Once the labourers would bring the firewood, it needed to be assorted and stacked neatly. As a lean, tall, and well-built personality, she was mentally strong as well. She was the exact opposite of my soft-spoken, mild-mannered Amma.

Ajji would finish her work on time and take me to the dance classes. In the evening, she would go home first and collect the snacks that my Amma would have prepared for me. She would feed me first before going to the dance class. After the dance classes, I would have another round of practice to show Ajji what we were taught that day. She was so strict about this that dinner had to wait until it was done. Ajji had a melodious voice and sang beautifully. She also choreographed dance movements. She taught me the choreography for a very popular devotional song called 'Krishna nee begane baaro,' which is a song dedicated to Lord Krishna.

Bashing for secret learning

I was still trying to learn the semantics of steps and the rhythm. Our dance teacher used to teach dance to seniors along with us. They were being taught some advanced dance moves, and once he was teaching 'Thodayam' dance to them. Apart from learning the lessons given to us, I would also observe their lessons without even blinking an eyelid. But we were not allowed to learn what was not taught to us by the teacher. Hence, I would wait until getting back home to rehearse those dance steps. If I had any doubts from this rehearsal, I would make a mental note and wait for the next class to closely observe and clarify them for myself.

As such, I ended up learning the Thodayam dance on my own. But I did not know that stolen knowledge shall not be displayed openly. Once, when the dance teacher went inside the house, I started displaying my talent. I told my friend, 'I also know what was taught to the seniors, see!' and she said in a surprised tone "What! You learned it already!'

As I started showing her the dance moves, our dance teacher happened to come out of the house, which I didn't notice, and I continued to enjoy my dance. The teacher's temper rose instantaneously, and I was beaten royally that day. I understood how to be sensitive to these aspects of life on that day.

That was the last day; he never taught anyone else alongside us afterwards. He would send us all into the kitchen and lock us up before teaching them. But I don't know if it was his bad luck or our good fortune; the doors were a little weak, and there was a small gap between the door panels. We would peep from that gap to learn the moves. If she moved a little extra during the dance, she disappeared from our view. And we would hilariously start trying different angles of view to see if we could spot her. I learned to dance for many years in similar conditions and situations.

Appa's 'No' to dance changes for good!

Once my dance teacher declared 'You have to perform on the stage.' By then my dance skills had improved but my fear was, at home Appa didn't even know about my dance classes and I could not share that with my teacher either, as it would lead to more troubles. I was perplexed how to solve this problem and sought help from my Ajji. She said, 'Don't worry, we will manage.' Ajji had a decent influence over Appa.

The Tharalabalu Association in Shivamogga had their anniversary programme, and we all were supposed to perform at the event. There were no separate stitched costumes for the dance, and the practice was to drape any nice silk saree in a certain way. But I did not have a saree. Amma had only one silk saree, which she would wear at festivals. It was a parrot-green coloured saree with a red border. It was the only expensive saree she had in her wardrobe. Amma came forward to offer her precious silk saree to me. She gave instructions: 'Take some special care of it. Ask the teacher to drape it on you. Don't stretch and damage the saree,' and I was on cloud 9. I still had to invest a little and buy the required ornaments and mock jewellery.

During all of this, Appa came to know about it. He was upset and started a police-like investigation into the matter. 'How did she go to the dance classes? As a little girl, she cannot go on her own. You, mother, and daughter, paired up to deceive me,' and he took out his anger on all of us for some time, including Ajji.

But in the end, maybe by God's grace, he said 'Ok fine. Take the money, go, and perform.'

Ajji had a newfound courage to pursue Appa and even attend the programme. Finally, Appa relented and attended the programme, which was graced by Tharalabalu Mutt's Swamiji, the chief pontiff.

As soon as the performance was over, Swamiji walked over to my Appa and showered his appreciation for my performance saying 'Your daughter is a blessed talent. She will be an exceptional artist in the future. You must get her trained well and encourage her.'

My Appa sincerely respected Swamiji. He must have felt, if Swamiji is respectful of the dance, then dancing cannot be as bad as he had believed it to be so far. His attitude towards my dance changed for good thereafter. Going forward, when anyone visited our home, be it friends, relatives; the first line that would come out of him was 'My daughter is taking dance lessons.'

He was highly supportive of my dance afterwards. His friends circle was quite big. Due to his influence, we could get to do many performances. The dance teacher had a newfound respect for me, when he realised that my Appa could get us performances.

We performed at numerous events and avenues. Those days the make-up for a dance performance was very different from what is used today. Colourful powders would be mixed with grease, and that sticky mixture would be applied on to the face. We had to use many chemicals to remove the make-up, and most times even chemicals couldn't help. So, removing the make-up was a dreaded task.

Choreographing for my own Ranga Pravesha

At some point during my dance lessons, my dance teacher and his family relocated to their hometown. I was without guidance for a while.

When I went to Mysuru for my studies, I started honing my dance skills under a dance teacher named Muralidhar Rao. He was an expert with recognition at the state-level. I had to restart my dance lessons from the beginning. That didn't mean my previous lessons went to waste. They equipped me with my new learning phase. As such, apart from restarting my classical dance classes from the beginning, I went on to take exams as well.

After all this, I prepared for my Ranga Pravesha, a traditional ceremony for the maiden stage performance of a dancer. The performance was self-choreographed due to my confidence, backed by my long experience in dance. I also selected the music band. My friend Nagaratna used to sing very well, so I asked her to sing. I knew someone who played the Tabla (a kind of drum), and I requested him to play the Tabla. It was to be accompanied by another similar musical instrument, Mridang, which I was unaware of. Out of sheer excitement and enthusiasm, I proceeded with my maiden performance. Since I had made some name for myself in Shivamogga, I also had invited a lot of guests.

There was a Kannada professor called Shrinivas Adiga in DVS College of Shivamogga. I had studied in the same college since my chosen language was Sanskrit, and as such, he had never taught me at the college. Professor Shrinivas was a learned NatyaShāstra scholar. With his help, I shortlisted some pieces from Kannada poetry to perform on stage and to represent the concept called 'Navarasa,' or the art of blending the 9 distinctly complex expressions in the dance choreography. I embedded those epical chapters into my performance and invited the professor as the chief guest of the ceremony.

With much adventure, the programme was organised and attended by a lot of well-wishers. The Ranga Pravesha proved to be a huge success.

Dance master in tears

After many years of this event, I became a dance teacher. Now, I had the responsibility of planning the Ranga Praveshas for my students. Anupama was my first student to do a Ranga Pravesha. She was a 12th-standard student then. I was an associate professor of English at Maharani College, Bengaluru, and had earned state-level recognition in dance. It was 1992, just before I met my guru, Swami Rama.

The Ranga Pravesha was organised at the prestigious venue of Ravindra Kala Kshetra. I was to direct her as well. When this programme was taking shape, I invited my dance teacher from childhood as a tribute, to him as my teacher.

On the day of the programme, a car was sent to pick him up. During the interval of the dance performance, we were honouring the guests on the stage. He was emotional and in tears even before the speech he made on the stage. He started his speech with, 'I need to confess my mistakes in front of all of you; it is time for me to address my guilt and let these tears flow.' I was not at all expecting this and had forgotten the episode he mentioned. He continued, 'This girl was learning dance from me since she was in the second standard. I have done injustice to this girl, this child; he was unable to stop his tears.

I could not understand what he meant by it. Why he was speaking that way, what injustice he did to me: being unable to understand what was going on, I just looked on. I did not have any kind of negativity towards him. In my mind, he was my dance guru, and there was only respect and affection associated with him.

'If I had taught her well that day, she would have really learned a lot. Because of the injustice I did, she had to go and learn from another teacher. Worried that she was very quick to learn and would learn everything, I used to lock her up in the kitchen when I was teaching others. But she has the grace of Lord Nataraja (the lord of dance) himself. She has surpassed me in calibre, as she stands in front of me here today as a Guru herself. For her student's Ranga Pravesha, she has invited me as the chief guest. I am truly honoured' his cheeks were drenched by then with the free-flowing tears.

The backbone to my dance: my Ajji

If I have achieved anything in the field of dance, it is because of my Ajji. Apart from taking me to the dance classes, she would also choreograph. In those days, the word 'choreography' was not used. She would finetune my dance steps at home. She also sang very well, like my Amma. She also used to sing company drama songs effortlessly. Those days, every company drama used to have the song 'Krishna nee begane baro,' even when there was no link to the storyline of the drama. These songs played on the loud music would make their way into the compositions, which we would choreograph.

She would vocalise that song so melodiously that it would seem very close to classical singing. After I returned from dance school, she would teach me the choreography of this song in the corner of the coal depot and under the Kerosene lamp. Only after I learned those steps would I get my dinner. She was strict but also very committed. She was the reason behind my love for Lord Krishna. Even before I joined the dance classes, I used to try dancing to Krishna's songs under her guidance.

Sometime later, the dance class venue was shifted to Shivamogga's Karnataka Sangha (an association). I was in the 5th or 6th standard by then. Karnataka Sangha was quite far from home. And Ajji would take me by hand to the classes. I was so engrossed in the dance that even while walking to the classes, I would ask her to hold my left hand so that I could use my right hand to emulate some of the dance moves. She would mutter in a low voice, 'Don't dance on the road, keep quiet,' and I would stop for some time and start my notional dance practice again.

Until we reached the venue, this continued. After the class, while returning to the coal depot, the same routine repeated. At home, I would dance hiding behind the curtains. If the radio was playing some song, I would be dancing to that too. Dance had taken over my very existence. The dance seemed to be a connection since many past lives.

And the one who seeded my interest in dance, my Ajji, was an admirer of the artform. She cried after watching me perform for the first time. The troubles she went through for me are inexplicable and she was very positive in life.

After completing my student life, I entered the professional life of a lecturer. Question of my marriage was bothering my Amma; my father had already left his mortal body. My days were busy being spent in dance and literature. I was stubborn not to get married because I had thought that marriage and dance career do not go hand in hand.

At that point of my life I was not wise enough to understand the hard realities of life, neither the inevitable part of karma in life. Certain events both good and bad, happen contrary to our expectations in life. Eventually my stubborn efforts not to get married, ended in a happy note and I entered married life in 1988, with Yogacharya Sri Pattabhiram.

***

7

MY GURU PARAMPARĀ

My Gurudēva, Swami Rama, used to say; "Himalayan rishi tradition is my Guru lineage." As someone who is on this spiritual voyage, eternally surrendered at his lotus feet, do I not belong to this rich tradition too?

As one of the greatest Yogis of the 20th century, Gurudēva Swami Rama says - "My guru Paramparā (lineage) is the one which is eternally active, bestowed to us by the Himalayan Rishi lore. Though it may seem like a melee of many traditions, at first glance, there is only One in reality – the great Satya Paramparā (The tradition of the Ultimate Truth), which includes all and excludes none. And this Truth is not bound by the rules of any time or space, nationality or religion and will always remain the same. It is permanent, eternal, and this Truth is at the heart of our Sanatana Paramparā, which is over 5000 years old."

The Himalayan Rishis have gathered the knowledge and energy of all the spiritual traditions from around the world, in an encapsulated form in this One tradition. These Rishis are the forces behind all the traditions that have emerged anywhere in the world. They focused purely on the direct experience of Truth and made it available to the entire humanity; not bound by any religion, nationality, geo-proximities, time, and caste structures.

Why do we even need Spiritual Traditions?

As seekers, at some stage in our lives, we find ourselves on a deeply immersive journey which can be dark and directionless. There are no milestones to count in this journey, as it is a pathless path and a mapless map. These are usually in the purview of direct spiritual experiences. But, without direct experience, there are times when we feel insecure and anxious. It can be a scary experience as the follower may feel directionless. It is important to have the right guidance at such times, and when the right guidance is provided, the very feeling of insecurity will be replaced by immense hope. We realise the importance of the Guru Paramparā here. Because, in the spiritual journey, Guru is a Shakti Swaroopa (manifested energy) who has travelled ahead of us, surpassing all the boundaries. Their experiences and guidance are the beacons for us to follow.

The spiritual heritage of the Himalayan Rishi lore!

This tradition is a tradition of our Himalayan Sages, which is timeless; it is as old as the Vedic times and continues to exist among us even today in this modern world. Their sole purpose is to help humanity with a clear map to realise the true self. Delivering the benefits of this Vedic knowledge and sharing the importance of meditation in one's life is the purpose of our Rishi lore, the Sages from The Himalayas.

Geographical spread of the Rishi Lineage!

The influence of our Rishi tradition has crossed the might of the Himalayas. The mountain ranges of Bharatha Khanda, such as Vindhya, Sahyadri, and the Deccan plateaus, are also known to have been witness to the Mantric practices of these Rishis. South India, which currently comprises Tamil Nadu, Karnataka, Andhra Pradesh, Telangana, and Kerala, continues to be an epicentre for spiritual charging. To go by Swami Rama's words, at the end of the journey, all of these traditions have a deep connection with the caves of the Himalayan Rishi lore and their teachings. Disciples get funnelled through to the Himalayan Tradition one way or another. Similarly, many Siddhas (accomplished beings), Yogis, transit through these caves and carry the messages to the world at large.

At the end of it all, the Himalayan Guru lineage is the same as the Vedic Rishi Paramparā.

Shedding some light on the Vedic Rishi Paramparā

Through the oral knowledge transfer, and the ancient scriptures one can establish that 'Narayana Guru,' an immortal and ancient Rishi, established our Himalayan Rishi Paramparā. He is known to be the universal consciousness itself and a Rishi of the highest order. The spiritually charged Badrinath Temple's courtyard is said to be his ashram. The Vedic and Tantric scriptures evidence this clearly.

Rishi Sanath Kumar and his 3 Rishi brothers, Sanaka, Sanandana, and Sanatsujata, are the Aadi Gurus (Primordial Masters) in this tradition. They are the sons of Lord Brahma. Originating from Rishi Sanathkumara, this unbroken rishi tradition has continued through Sages such as Vasishtha, Shakti, Parashar, Govindapada, and Shankaracharya, and also counts Sages such as Atharva, Angeerasa, Vyasa, Dakshinamurthy, Chyavana, Dadhichi, Dattatreya, Hayagreeva, Parashurama, Haritayana, Agasthya, Atri, Markandeya, the list of our Guru-gan just goes on. These are sages who saw the mantras in their meditation and shared them with the world in a capsule form of organised syllables. Their deep knowledge encompassed the intricate science behind the physical body (Deha Vijnana), the science behind the Praana or the life force (Swara Vijnana), the science behind the Sun and the Moon, called the Surya Vidya and the Chandra Vidya, respectively, etc., which are great gifts to the mankind.

Swami Rama says the supreme knowledge of the Yogas and Meditations is found in the Tantra Shāstras and Agamas, whereas the Vedas and the Upanishads only introduce these. Its theory, language and gestures are all very mysterious. For example, some of the scriptures of the highest order in our tradition are Sanaka Samhita, Sanandana Samhita, Sanatkumar Samhita, Vasishtha Samhita, and Shuka Samhita. These scriptures are not available to us today, but there are thousands of scriptures that base their content on the above. i.e Parasurama Kalpa Sutram, Tripura Rahasya, Nitya Shōdashikaarnava, Rudrayaamala, and Soundarya Lahari. The Puranas have also grown as branches of the Himalayan rishi Paramparā itself.

Once Swami Rama visited Sringeri on a pilgrimage, as the roots of the Himalayan Rishi lore are deeply connected with Bhagavathi (divine mother). The Shree Meru chakra, consecrated by Sri Adi Shankaracharya, proved the link between the Rishi lineage and the temple itself. I went through a direct experience of it myself, with the grace of Swami Rama.

Sri Shankaracharya, behind Sringeri Srigalu!

I was fortunate to visit Sringeri once and to visit Sri Sharadamba, the supreme deity, with my entire family. The group included myself, Pattabhi ji, my mother-in-law, Sādhana (our daughter), and a couple of friends. We all went to the temple and got to seek the blessings of Sri Sharadamba. Next, the plan was to meet the supreme pontiff of the mutt, Sringeri Srigalu. So, we reached Srigalu's residence nearby. There was a long line of visitors already ahead of us. We reverently waited in the queue to seek the blessings of Srigalu. It was a very long queue, and it would take roughly 60 to 75 mins to complete the visitation. I was not really excited about standing in the queue for such a long time, as there was a lot of work to complete and very little time on hand.

But somehow, we stayed firm on receiving the blessings of Srigalu, and we waited in line. After waiting for a while, we were in visual proximity to Srigalu, but there were still 15 to 20 more people ahead of us in the line. Srigalu was in clear sight for me by then. I was observing him as he gave Akshatha, sacred rice grains soaked in vermilion, to the seekers as his blessings, but he would give it with his hand held a bit high up. Seeing this, I was contemplating whether it could be considered rude to throw Akshatha towards devotees, as I didn't really appreciate it. But my awareness said, 'Since he has to meet and bless so many people in a day, it is normal to do so, and it is for us to understand these subtleties.'

I was watching Srigalu, and along with it I was chanting my Srividya mantra that I was initiated into. At some point when I was busy watching Srigalu, I had the divine sighting of Sri Shankaracharya, standing behind Srigalu, with his hand in a blessing posture and with a divine smile on his face, looking at me.

It was not an imagination. I was not even thinking about Shankaracharya, but I was concentrating on my mantra. And I was just absorbing my surroundings, a long line of people in front of Srigalu, and he was blessing everyone. But what I saw was incomprehensibly amazing experience beyond my guess!

In that defining moment, with the grace of Sri Shankaracharya, I got to experience the divinity of our Guru Paramparā. And my thought process, body language, and emotions changed magically. My concentration improved, and I craved to see Srigalu from an even closer proximity, with all respect and devotion. I was mesmerised and in awe of Guru Paramparā, and I garnered even deeper appreciation than before. Eventually, when I reached Srigalu to receive his blessings through the Akshatha, my heart was filled with nothing but infinite devotion towards the guru.

Sringeri deity is called Sri Sharadamba (Bhagavathi), and she is also referred to as 'Bhārathi.' She is the mother deity whose grace is nurturing the Bhārathi tradition. She showered me with her blessings by giving me a glimpse of Mahaguru Shankaracharya. Along with it, she also gave me a pleasant realisation that Bhārathi is not any different from the pontiffs, as she physically manifests as Srigalu.

Finally, what we need to understand about the Himalayan Rishi Paramparā is that it is a spiritual path of Advaita, the non-duality, which is the ultimate truth. And the messages from the Paramparā are clear; experience your Atman. Understand yourself. It leads you to the ultimate truth, which is eternal, and delivers you as Immortal. Immortality going even beyond Death!

***

8

MY 'MASTER,' BHOLE BABA SWAMI RAMA

Swami Rama is recognised across the world as a saint, a humanitarian, and one of the greatest Yogis of the 20th century. He is also aptly referred to as the Himalayan Sage, by most people. He established the 'Himalayan International Institute of Yoga Sciences and philosophy' in the USA; and 'Himalayan Institute Hospital Trust' in India, apart from hundreds of Yoga centres across the world.

In the cave monasteries of the Himalayas, he learned the nuances of various Yoga Shāstras from advanced yogis and sages. While he attained his higher education from a top university in Europe, he was also mentored by some of the foremost spiritual leaders of the world, such as Sri Ramana Maharshi, Sri Aurobindo, Sri Ravindranath Tagore, Mahatma Gandhi etc. These luminous souls contributed significantly to the making of Swami Rama. To fulfil the purpose of his life, as directed by Bengali Baba, he went to the United States of America, where he took up the mantle of bridging the gaps between the spiritual wisdom of the East and the scientific prowess of the West.

Swami Rama was born in 1925, in the Himalayan region of Gadhwal, in North India. He grew up in the caring protection of Bengali Baba from his childhood and went on to pursue his higher education from Bengaluru, Prayag, Varanasi, and completed his academic pursuit at the Oxford University.

When he was only 24 years old, he was installed as the Shankaracharya (supreme pontiff) of the holy Karaveera Peetha in south India. As the Shankaracharya between 1949 and 1952, Swami Rama brought revolutionary changes to the rules and customs of those days, which enabled people of all strata to participate in the temple's activities and festivals that were restricted back then. Even more so, Swami Rama empowered the women by liberating them to pursue spirituality and meditation. After leaving Peetha, he assisted deep research in the field of parapsychology in Moscow and helped as an adviser in the field of medicinal science in London.

Swami Rama's free thinking was a result of his direct experiences through the spiritual wisdom deep within. Hence, he also trained his disciples in the same manner. 'I am a messenger. I transmit the knowledge of the Rishi Paramparā. My mission is to introduce you to the Guru within you'.

The head of Menninger Foundation (Topeka, Kansas, USA), Dr. Elmer Green, had requested Swami Rama to advise on a research project. Under this project, called 'The Voluntary control of involuntary states,' he played a catalyst in the experiments that revolutionised the way modern science perceives the correlations between the mind and the body. In the controlled environment of a research lab, the scientists were left in awe when he debunked the common belief that the mind does not have any control over the involuntary functions or responses of the body by demonstrating unbelievable control over both.

Apart from this, he also authored over 100 books pertaining to health, meditation, and yoga etc. Swami Rama left his body on November 13, 1996.

2025 is the centennial year of his birth. He is an eternal ambassador of the Himalayan Rishi lore.

***

VENERABLE BENGALI BABAJI

Writing anything about Bengali Babaji's background, such as his birth, adolescent years, education, job, family, etc., will be an adventure, to say the least, because the details of his personal life remain as hazy as the Himalayan mountains, which were his home. His early life is as mystical as the Himalayan ranges itself. He avoided public places, and his life was that of a nomad, constantly moving from one place to another. He preferred staying under the trees, in dilapidated houses or temples, deep in the forests or mountains, on the banks of the Holy Ganga river, etc. Babaji is reverently referred to as 'A Sage from the Highest Peak' by all of Swami Rama's disciples.

The available information on Babaji is as follows: He was born in a small village called Medhinipur in West Bengal, India. Some sources say that Babaji and his parents were visited by an accomplished yogi of the Himalayas, who initiated them into a Mantra.

Justin O'Brian, senior desciple of Swami Rama, captures the details of some of the tragic and heart touching episodes from Bengali Babaji's life, which also sheds light on the mystical origins of Babaji. Babaji used to be a Judge in the District High Court. He was known to be the only judge of Indian origin in the British Judges Bench panel, at that point.

The Indian freedom revolution was reaching its peak, and Babaji's son, who was involved in the revolution, was arrested for his role in the assassination attempt on a British general called General Dyer, which eventually led to his death by hanging. Babaji commanded deep respect among his colleagues at the British Judges Bench, due to which many of his colleagues suggested that he write a public apology letter, declaring his son's act as a crime - in exchange for life imprisonment for his son instead of a death sentence. It was one of the most difficult decisions Babaji had to take in his lifetime. He stood firm, saying, 'The responsibility of my son's action lies with him. As a Judge, I will not be apologising for it. Anyways, you Britishers should not even be in our country, which ruffled many feathers within his ranks and beyond. The angered Judges, in the most inhumane way, pressurised Babaji to sign his own son's death warrant. Having signed the death warrant, Babaji is said to have broken the pen in half before tossing it and walking out of the courtroom, never to be seen again by anyone. Babaji's wife could not bear losing her son and passed away a short while thereafter. Babaji had turned his back on societal life, and the Himalayas gave him his new abode. His sacrifices did not go to waste. This entire episode added fresh fuel and reach for the raging freedom revolution. But Babaji decided to dedicate the rest of his life to the lotus feet of his Guru Mukti Baba and to the service of his family deity 'Chinnamastā Devi.'

There is another side to Babaji, which is demonstrated through the beautiful bond shared between him and his disciple, my Guru, Swami Rama. After the passing of both his parents, Swami Rama grew up in the loving shelter of Babaji; however, along came ample doses of disciplining through teachings on the virtues of love, patience, and many life lessons.

The eternal love showered by Babaji not only helped Swami Rama forget about the loss of his own parents but also prevented him from getting drawn to worldly attractions. Like the mother chooses to tolerate all the naughtiness of her child while continuing to shower her love and care, a Guru also helps his disciples to scale to newer heights, and this is clearly witnessed in the loving bond that existed between Babaji and Swami Rama. In the end, Babaji left his body after transferring 15 years of his life to his disciple through a mysterious tantric way, which is a stage beyond comprehension for most people, almost a super-human level.

Living in a cave, Babaji used to come outside only once a day, at dawn. He would spend an hour or so outside and return to the cave. Likewise, he only got up from his seat twice a day. He lived on the milk of sheep or cows. He seemed eternally meditative and spoke very rarely. His preferred method of communication was silence through meditation. Swami Rama reverently referred to him as 'Master' and firmly believed Babaji to be one of the greatest enlightened yogis of the Himalayas. He made it his life's mission to mentor the qualified souls who were looking inward for answers and the ignorant ones whom he would protect and guide with great empathy. Most of his disciples share their experience that if someone sought his help, they were never sent back empty-handed. He firmly believed that fame and pride are the biggest pitfalls for spiritual practitioners and can push them into an abyss.

When Babaji wanted to cast off his physical body in 1945, Swami Rama succeeded in changing his mind by guilting him by saying, 'When a Guru leaves his disciple incomplete, he goes to hell – say our scriptures.' It was almost 9 years later, in 1954, that he realised he was in the wrong to tie down his Guru in a physical form. Of course, Babaji takes it upon himself to protect Swami Rama in all the critical situations of life ahead, promising to eternally protect him before leaving his body.

Swami Rama is truly blessed to have gained a Guru of such calibre and magnitude, and it is a double-blessing for us to have become a part of this illustrious Guru Paramparā.

***

10

MUKTI BABA – MY GREAT GRAND MASTER

In the Samayāchārā Tradition of Sri Vidya, the relationship between the disciple and the Guru is made in 3 tiers, as in Swaguru (my own Guru) – Parama guru (Guru of my Guru) – Parameshthi Guru (Guru of my Parama Guru). Situationally, when the need arises, there is a fourth Tier of Guru called Apara Parameshthi Guru as well. As such, my Himalayan Guru Lineage can be represented as captured below.

- Swaguru, Swami Rama - Bhole Baba
- Parama guru, Bengali Baba
- Parameshthi Guru, Mukti Baba

In his autobiography 'Living with the Himalayan Masters,' Swami Rama refers to his Guru as 'Master' and his Parama Guru as 'Grand Master.' My thoughts of writing about them were sometimes met with great internal turmoil, whether I possessed the basic qualifications to even know of them. But in the world of infinite love, deep devotion, and faith, that question dissolved in no time.

In Swami Rama's own words, 'I want to tell the whole world about these Rishis because humanity needs to know that such great beings exist. And the scientists need to know about them so they can research so many amazing topics that are mysteries to mankind along the way.'

At this juncture, it is important to share about the Rishi lineage, my personal connection with my Great Grand Master, Mukti Baba and the role he played in guiding me in my journey in this tradition.

During my frequent visits to Swami Rama's ashram in Rishikesh, one of the days, he said, 'Bete, when an opportune moment arises, I will show you the photos of my Master and Grand Master.' I remembered this promise after Baba had taken Samadhi and left his physical body in 1996. But this promise was fulfilled very soon, in a matter of a few months.

We visited Delhi for some work and happened to visit Baba's Himalayan Trust Hospital campus at Jolly Grant. Pattabhi Ji, Dr. Ashok Bhat, and I travelled as a trio, and we were lucky to have met one of Baba's close disciples. He took us to his humble abode within the campus and opened the doors of his pooja room, where 3 photos were aligned in the order of the lineage – and this is where I got to see Mukti Baba for the first time. I was totally mesmerised and frozen in my spot. Instantaneously, Dr Ashok Bhat pulled out the camera hanging around his neck and clicked a photo with a blinding flash. This unanticipated move made our host agitated, and he insisted that the photo be erased immediately. He felt that it should not be made public because it is against the wish of the masters. Somehow, we managed to convince him to let us keep the photo and made a hasty exit. Whether we were impolite or disrespectful in doing so, I will leave it to the judgement of the readers. The way I see it, Baba never missed his promises, and this was his way of fulfilling his commitment to me. It is meant for us, undoubtedly!

After many years, in 2017, when Pattabhi ji left his physical body, I was in a state of deep depression and visited Swami Rama's ashram in Tadakeshvar Mahadev Temple located in the Garhwal region of the Himalayas. Swami Rama and Bengali Baba showed the depth of their affection towards me by gracing me with a visit. I had set up the photos of Mukti Baba, Bengali Baba, and Swami Rama in an array and sought their approval by asking, 'Is it ok?' Bengali Baba nodded in affection with a beautiful smile, thus unveiling the compassion of Himalayan Guru Paramparā to me.

Swami Rama has already captured a lot of information about Mukti Baba in his autobiography. He is among the great Rishis in this unbroken Himalayan Guru lineage. In Swami Rama's own words, "He looked very old but very healthy. He would get up from his seat once in the morning and once in the evening. His height was 5 feet 9 or 10 inches. He was slim but very energetic. He had bushy eyebrows, and his face glowed and radiated deep calmness and tranquillity. He had a perennial smile. He lived on Yak's milk most of the time and sometimes barley soup."

In his autobiography 'Living with the Himalayan Masters,' in the chapter called 'My Grand master in sacred Tibet,' Swami Rama has penned a beautiful and loving tribute to Mukti Baba. He captures in detail his visit to Tibet in the year 1946 and the bond he and his Parama Guru Mukti Baba shared, which makes for a heartwarming episode. The vivid details in which he explains how he learned the science behind 'Parakaya Pravesha' will surely leave the readers with goosebumps.

I must also share a couple of facts about my Guru lineage and the Srividya Samayāchārā tradition at this juncture. As stated by Mukti Baba - Himalayan Rishi lineage, while it is the same as Adi Shankaracharya's path, it remains a very different spiritual Paramparā that does not fall under any structured traditions of this land. Explaining his learnings about Srividya from Mukti Baba, Swami Rama says the following: In advanced practices, the student learns how to concentrate on different parts of the Sri Yantra, and a few rare students learn to travel to the centre. This Yantra is considered to be a manifestation of the divine power, and the Bindu, or point in the centre, is the centre where Shakti and Shiva are united.

The methodical technique of becoming one with the Bindu, only our lineage teaches. In the event someone has achieved it, they are bound to be from our Himalayan Rishi lineage only.

I was very fortunate to have a visitation of such an elevated Rishi. I was meditating on Panchadashee Mantra - which was blessed upon to me by my Srividya Sriguru Sri Sathyanandanatha of Mysuru, who belonged to the Sri Vidyaranya tradition of Srividya – when Mukti Baba blessed me with a visit and smiled at me, a smile which is forever etched in my memory.

The last days of Mukti Baba in his physical body are described as follows by Swami Rama in his autobiography: 'He bid goodbye to his close disciples and disappeared. Some people say they last saw him sitting with garlands of flowers around his neck, floating on the Kali Ganga, a river that flows through Tanakpur' in the Himalayas.

***

11

SRI VIDYARANYA BHĀRATHI TRADITION

It was a blessing to have received the mantra initiations and Deeksha by Sriguru Sathyanandanatha, belonging to the unbroken Guru lineage of Sri Vidyaranya Bhārathi tradition. It feels like the good karmas from my past life that descended from the universe onto this planet Earth. I had received initiation into Shāmbhavi Deeksha from the Himalayan Sage Swami Rama in 1992, and when he took samadhi in 1996, he had appeared in a dream to instruct that 'My wish is that you shall learn the Dakshinachara tradition of Srividya, and I am sending you to a Shastri in Mysuru.' With his guidance, my learning under Rā Sā Gurugalu commenced. By doing so, I was graced with an opportunity to understand, experience, and learn about the perpetuity of the Himalayan tradition.

I had an unforgettable experience that solidified this belief. I had many questions lingering in my mind, 'What is Sri Vidyaranya Bhārathi tradition? How is my Himalayan guru, Swami Rama, connected to this southern tradition? Why had he directed me to practice in this tradition? What is expected out of it? Where are the roots of this Bhārathi tradition?' etc. During this time, on one of the days, as I was finishing my mantra meditation, I had a serene vision. I saw the luminous figure of Sriguru Sathyanandanatha standing in front of me. Draped around his waist was a shiny red silk Dhoti, Angavastra (a hand towel) on his shoulder, and Vibhuti (the holy ash) adorned his forehead. He had an old scripture in his hand, of which half was covered in a red silk cloth. The remaining piece of that cloth was fluttering in the wind. With a smile on his face, he was looking at me with a singular focus. As I was looking at him, he slowly elevated from the ground and started flying in the sky. The way his Angavastra and the silk cloth of that book were dancing with the wind was very pleasing to the eyes, to say the least. In a sudden change of landscape, I saw Gurugalu floating above the ice-capped mountains of the Himalayas, and he disappeared.

These are the kinds of experiences that are exclusive to Tantra Sadhana. It inspires and reinforces the practitioners' faith in the practice. It makes the disciple realise that the Guru is eternally protecting him, and that realisation strengthens the disciple in the path. There are so many symbolic layers in these images. In that moment of silence, I had all the answers to my questions.

If I have to delve deeper, in Srividya practice, if a Guru has to vocalise everything for his disciples, it is considered the defeat of the vidya itself, and it is considered a lack of maturity on the Guru's part by the tradition. Hence, the answers I used to receive were in silence during meditation.

The Bhārathi Tradition and the Sri Vidyaranya tradition of southern India are directly connected to the Himalayan Rishi lineage. Sri Vidyaranya, who was the supreme Pontiff of the Sringeri Sharada Peetham, was a disciple of Sri Bhārathi Theertha and the originator of Kaadi Mata in Srividya. He was a devout follower of Sri Bhuvaneshwari, one of the Dasha Mahavidyas. He was the inspiration for the creation of the legendary Vijayanagara kingdom (SriVidyanagara back then) near Hampi, in the shape of Sri Chakra. Rā Sā Gurugalu writes in his book 'Srividya Shōdashika' that we belong to the Householder's path of Srividya path. Sri Vidyaranya was instrumental in building the Vijayanagara Kingdom, which forms an important chapter in the annals of the history of Karnataka.

**

12

THE PROXIMITY OF THREE GURUS

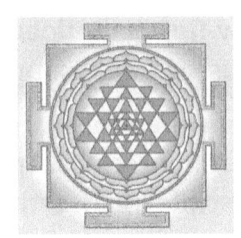

I have already mentioned that in Sri Vidya, the guru lineage is identified in 3 stages. Svaguru (my Guru), Parama Guru (Guru of my guru), and Parameshthi Guru (Guru of my Parama guru). As such, in the Dakshinachara tradition, my Guru lineage is as captured below:

- Svaguru - Sriguru Sathyanandanatha
- Parama Guru - Sriguru Pundareekakshanandanatha
- Parameshthi Guru - Sriguru Brahmavidyanandanatha

And behind them stands the entire lineage of gurus, which disseminates spiritual knowledge without any discrimination to everyone, as deserved through their cycles of birth. While some may find it unbelievable, it is the reality.

Svaguru, Sri Sathyanandanatha

His name for the outer world was Dr. Ra. Satyanarayana (shortened as 'Rā Sā' within his close quarters), an adept in the fields of musicology, Dance, Spirituality, Yoga, Tantra, Mantra, and Tattva Jigjnasa (a process of arriving at the fundamental truth). He was very popular as a scholar in multiple fields and respected, the world over. He was accoladed with many national and international awards. He was also accorded Padmashree, one of the highest honours for a civilian, by the Government of India.

His 'SriVidya Shōdashika,' a three-part anthology, demonstrates his wisdom and intellectual superiority. The speciality of these anthologies is that he has managed to take a topic such as Srividya, a topic of oceanic depths and breadth, and simplify it and make it comprehensible. His contributions of over 20,000 pages worth of published content on various topics mesmerise me, and I am left in awe of his sophisticated thinking, keen interest, and super-human level of scripting capabilities. A layer he hid from the world was his prowess in Srividya Tantra. Not even his closest friends knew he was an accomplished master in Srividya.

In a chapter within Srividya Shōdashika, Rā Sā Gurugalu writes, 'I am blessed with the inheritance of Srividya Upasana from my familial roots, and by the grace of the unbroken lineage of my Gurus.' Apart from this, Gurugalu has also documented his life experience of witnessing his maternal grandfather, Sri P. V. Sheshagiriaiah, who did ardent Sādhana of the Beeja mantra instilled Sri Chakra in solitude, leaving his body through his Brahmarandhra (an invisible portal at the top of the head) during his deep state of meditation.

Now, the mother of Rā Sā Gurugalu, Srimathi Varalakshmi, was even a step ahead. Having taken the initiation into the 'Bala Tripura Sundari Mantra' at a very young age from the Supreme Pontiff of Sri Sringeri Sharada Peetham - Sri Guru Chandrashekhara Bhārathi - she was deeply spiritual and the mantra would become Ajapa-Japa, a spontaneous chanting even in the sleeping state. After a while, she was initiated into the 'Hamsataraka Mantra, and she reached a spiritual state called Atmabhaava, being one with the eternal Atman. Rā Sā Gurugalu was initiated into the Hamsataaraka Mantra by his mother at the age of 12. With great love and affection, he used to say, 'She was not only the architect of my life, but also the god personified.'

But when it comes to his guru lineage, he was saddened that he could not find much information about his Parmeshthi Guru, Sriguru Subrahmanyanandanatha. His disciple, Sriguru

Brahmavidyanandanatha, happens to be Parama Guru for Rā Sā Gururgalu. He was also a blood relative to Rā Sā Gurugalu and a scholar in Veda Shāstras. He left his body, attaining Mahasamadhi, as an accomplished soul in 1954. He was an aggressive sadhaka of Srividya. He was adept in Lambika Yoga. He recreated 'Sri Chakra Navavarana Pooja' in a novel way, a Vedic and tantric ritual; Rā Sā Gururgalu documents it in his memoirs.

Svaguru of Rā Sā Gurugalu is Sriguru Pundareekakshanandanatha. He was also known as Yajnanarayana Somayaji. He lived in Bheemana Katte, near Theerthahalli in the Malnad region of Karnataka. He was adept in Shaiva Āgama and Shakta Āgama. He attained the siddhis of hundreds of mantras from the Mantra Shāstra by doing penance in various spiritually charged places. In the Malnad region, he is still referred to as the Walking Lalitha and the Talking Lalitha, which equates him to the divine mother.

In Tantra Shāstra, there are 6 paths:

1. Gaanapathya - Supreme deity, Ganapathi.
2. Shaiva - Supreme deity, Shiva.
3. Vaishnava - Supreme deity, Vishnu.
4. Saura - Supreme deity, Sun god.
5. Kumara - Supreme deity, Subrahmanya.
6. Shaakta - Supreme deity, Bhagavathi.

He had expertise both in the right hand and the left hand practices of Tantra, which shows the epitome of individual attainment par-excellence. Rā Sā Gurugalu used to mention how his Guru Pundareekakshanandanatha received initiation into a mantra of 'Bhavanopanishad,' a text of Srividya Shaakta Tantra, in silence just through a simple gaze of Sri Chandrashekhara Bhārathi, the Supreme Pontiff of Sringeri Sharada Peetham. He was then initiated into and trained by Sri Guru Brahmavidyanandanatha in Srividya Tantra and Mantra Shāstras.

Rā Sā Gurugalu has penned a few critical insights about Sri Pundareekakshanandanatha. He mentions that his Guru transferred the knowledge of Srividya to various mediums such as verbal, touch, and gaze. Secondly, he initiated Gurugalu into Maha Shodashee Vidya without any verbal communication, just by willing it. Lastly, he blessed Rā Sā Gurugalu by gracing him with a boon, which means any information / wisdom related to Srividya would manifest on its own, when he desired it.

Srividya is a highly mystical, secretive vidya, and the following will prove it. Due to ill health, Sri Pundareekakshanandanatha had to leave his body at the age of 60. His Guru, or my Parameshthi Guru, Sri Brahmavidyanandanatha, transferred all of his disciple's Srividya wisdom to Rā Sā Gurugalu to ensure the wisdom is not expunged. Along with the siddhis, Gurugalu also had to absorb the illness. It seems like Rā Sā Gurugalu absorbed the illness from his Guru as a small service to his Guru and cleared 'Guru Runa' (debt due to the Guru). Words fall short to explain how he would speak of his Guru - with all his joy, respect, and devotion.

He used to say, 'How can I pay back to my Guru in my next life for all his kindness and grace when he has already blessed me with Jeevanmukthi Vidya, the boon of liberation!'

***

Section 2

- Ten steps towards Bhole Baba
- If Swami Rama wills, there can be a shower of dollars!!
- Shield of Pirouetting Shri Chakra
- Accept me as your Guru only when you are convinced of my power and siddhis!!
- Baba visits Bengaluru – 1992
- Guru's Disembodied Love
- Beyond the Veil: Two Supernatural Experiences with Swami Rama
- A Guru's Promise – A serpent headed Rudrākshi
- Yogananda paramahamsa in the train!

13

TEN STEPS TOWARDS BHOLE BABA

"Only if you believe in my Powers and Siddis should you accept me as your Guru."

Gurudēva Swami Rama told me this a few days before initiating me into Shāmbhavi Deeksha in Srividya. Which Guru gives so much freedom and courage to his disciples? It was this courage that enabled me to wholeheartedly accept Him as my Guru without any hesitation. The belief was so strong that in the very first instance itself, the great wise one initiated me into Srividya's sublime Shāmbhavi Deeksha in the presence of Lord Shiva himself!

This sacred initiation took place in 1992, and from that moment, Baba has been my constant companion, a Sreeguru, a mother, a friend, and a guide, nurturing my spiritual growth. He has led me into the elevated realms of Srividya, and even though his physical presence was with us for only 4 years, in the Srividya tradition, this is a profound blessing. Even after transcending His physical form, He continues to manifest and guide me, ensuring my spiritual journey remains unhindered and progressive.

Swami Rama, also known as Bholebaba, is a living embodiment of Shiva, radiating boundless love that transcends all comparisons in this material world. This is the Maha Guru that I have had the privilege to witness and the one I am leading you towards. In His physical form, He is a person with long hands, mischievous eyes, and a profound knowledge that belies His childlike heart. Yet, when you delve deeper, you will discover a vessel brimming with the elixir of limitless love. I invite you to take a step towards this great spiritual guide. Let the transformative journey begin.

***

14

IF SWAMI RAMA WILLS, THERE CAN BE A SHOWER OF DOLLARS!!

Those 2 eyes were noticing me from behind the glasses. I wondered why he was looking at me. As I continued observing, his gaze moved in the same line and stopped at a point. It dawned on me that he was looking at someone in the men's row. I bent down and took a peek. He was looking at my husband, Pattabhiji. I wondered, 'Does he know that we are husband and wife? And why is he looking at 2 of us among the hundreds gathered here?

***

It was 1992. A conference on 'Shiva Yoga' was organised at the JSS Institute in Mysuru.

An acquaintance of Pattabhiji, Professor Krishnamurthy, informed us about the 'Shiva Yoga' conference at Mysuru, which would be inaugurated by Swami Rama. With all innocence, Pattabhiji asked him, 'Who is Swami Rama?' It was a time when the mode of information and communication were not this powerful and widespread. We hardly had access to the happenings of the world. So we both were oblivious about Swami Rama despite he being so popular. It was a media-limited world.

Prof. Krishnamurthy informed us, 'Swami Rama is the most popular and wealthy Swamiji in America. He is very passionate about yoga, and since you have an organisation with the intention of propagating yoga worldwide, financial aid is essential for such a massive project. Getting to know your work and vision in the field of yoga might definitely make him happy. Since this Swami is rich and intends to support yoga sadhakas like you, who knows, he might take an interest in your work. If Swami Rama wills, there can be a shower of dollars to further your vision. This might solve your financial concerns. Pattabhiji nodded in agreement.

After a few days, Pattabhiji received a call from the organisers of the 'Shiva Yoga' conference requesting him to deliver a lecture on Patanjali's Yoga Sutras. Guruji accepted and started preparing for it with dedication. After a few days, we were informed about the unfortunate event of Guruji's lecture being cancelled. Due to internal miscommunication, the organisers invited 2 speakers to discuss the same topic, and they apologised for the inconvenience.

Despite this fiasco, Pattabhiji decided to attend the conference and asked me to join him. We both ended up attending the conference together and what happened next was quite intriguing!

Until then, I had not been aware of Swami Rama; I attended the conference just to accompany Pattabhi ji.

"Look, that is Swami Rama," a well-wisher gestured towards a man clad in a kimono (A Japanese-styled Buddhist garb) and donning oversized sunglasses.

I felt a sense of curiosity; why was he wearing such large sunglasses? Was it to shield his eyes from others' view, perhaps suggesting their significance?

On further observation, those 2 eyes were noticing me from behind the glasses. I wondered why he was looking at me. As I continued observing, his gaze moved in the same line and stopped at a point. It dawned on me that he was looking at someone in the men's row. I bent down and took a peek. He was looking at my husband, Pattabhiji. I wondered, 'Does he know that we are husband and wife? And why is he looking at 2 of us among the hundreds gathered here?

As I grappled with this ambiguity, the stage programme continued. It dawned on me that Swami Rama's speech was next.

'Man - citizen of 2 cities inner and outer...' is how Baba started his keynote speech on that day.

That was the most exceptional speech by any standards that I have heard so far. The audience was electrified. The speech was a balance of power and humour. Somewhere in the middle of the lecture, Baba made a joke, 'Indian Women are murderers.' Observing the belligerence among the audience, he went on to explain why. 'Indian women love their husbands a lot, and they express this by preparing and serving scrumptious food. Indian husbands quickly consume such delicious food, beyond necessity, and quickly befriend diabetes, followed by high blood pressure. And quickly completing their worldly journey' was what he meant when he said, 'Indian Women are murderers.' The audience was spellbound throughout Swami's lecture.

Pattabhiramji had decided to meet Swami Rama after the inaugural address, but soon after his speech, Baba disappeared. We both started wandering inside the JSS Institute campus in search of him.

We stumbled upon a small room, and within the closed doors, we could vaguely hear the voices of Swami Rama and a few others in a conversation. I turned towards Pattabhiji and said, 'Swami Rama is inside; go and talk to him.' Since Pattabhiji felt very hesitant, I gently pushed the door and peeped inside the room. I could feel Swami Rama, who was seated inside, gaze directly at me. Perplexed, I retreated immediately. Meanwhile, hundreds of people had queued up to meet the Swami on the other side of the same building, and we joined them. We both doubted the possibility of meeting him amongst all these people, and we wondered whether we would get a chance to talk to Baba.

I was shaken out of my reverie by a loud, piercing voice. I turned in the direction of that voice; I was shocked to see a gorgeous elderly woman adorned in diamond jewellery crying loudly in front of Swami Rama's room. Vehemently sobbing, she asked, 'Swami, Will my life come to an end without seeing you? When will you give me the fortune to touch your feet?'

I found this act to be childish. I found her behaviour was uncalled for; if she had waited patiently, Swami Rama would have come out of the room. At that time, my uneasiness at the sight of such strong emotions stemmed from a lack of awareness of such a mental state. Swami must have heard the commotion because he immediately stepped out of the room and rushed towards her. He gently lifted her, who was by this time at his feet, and comforted her affectionately. Her face lit up with a sense of fulfilment.

As soon as Swami Rama stepped out of the room, the atmosphere turned celebratory, and hundreds of people erupted into loud cheers. People rushed forward to seek his blessings. At the other end, Swami Rama's driver readied the car for his departure. Throwing angry glances toward the disorderly crowd, Swami Rama abruptly stopped on his way towards the car, turned around, and started walking towards us. I started to wonder where he was off to. He halted in front of us, swooped Pattabhiji towards him and hugged him tightly. To see my husband embraced by the 6.'1" towering personality of Swami Rama was like seeing a swallow nestled in a huge tree. He glanced towards me with a familiar smile and said, 'I am very happy that both of you are in this activity, but why did you come so late? I was waiting for you; if you hadn't come I would have made you come and meet me.' Failing to understand what it all meant, I stood there dumbstruck. My head was reeling with a lot of questions; though we met him for the very first time, why did he say he was waiting for us? I noticed Pattabhiji asking, 'Could you spare 5 minutes for us?' Swami Rama replied, "Why 5 minutes? I will give you ample time; come and meet me in the evening' and waved at us.

If Swami Rama wills, there can be a shower of dollars!!

Swami Rama with Pattabhi Ji in Bengaluru

***

15

SHIELD OF PIROUETTING SHRI CHAKRA

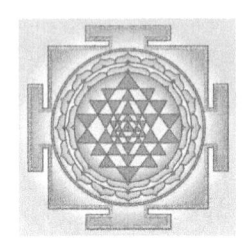

It was midnight, and we stood clueless at the Mysuru bus stand.

Casually looking around, my heart skipped a beat when I saw a person dressed like a Sadhu with knotted hair sitting next to the driver, holding a trident in hand.

I experienced fear and, simultaneously, a surge of anger towards Swami Rama because of his earlier statement, 'Your protection is my responsibility henceforth.' I questioned whether this unusual encounter was his way of providing protection.

Out of the blue, I noticed a light above the Ambassador car we were seated in.

***

Let's meet in the evening," Swami Rama suggested. Following his suggestion, Pattabhiji and I arrived at the renowned hotel where Swamiji was residing. The receptionist said, "Swamiji's appointment calendar is fully booked; hence, meeting him may not be possible." Nevertheless, we decided to wait, hopeful that an opportunity might arise.

While we were waiting in the lounge, Prof. Shivram, a close friend of Pattabhiji and a disciple of Swami Rama, noticed us and asked what we were doing there. After we explained our situation, he happily escorted us to Swamiji's room. However, at the entrance of Swamiji's room, Mythili, overseeing the appointments, informed us, "The meeting slots are fully booked until 4:30, and after that, Swamiji goes for a walk and doesn't meet anyone."

We continued to stand there, unsure what to do next. The friend's words, 'He is an American Swamiji; his donations will be in dollars.' echoed sarcastically in my mind. While pondering whether to continue waiting or return to Bengaluru, Mythili received an update that Swamiji had cancelled his stroll, and suddenly, the possibility of meeting him opened up. After a few minutes, Mythili showed us the way in.

In those days, I wasn't a firm believer in Swamiji; Therefore, when I stepped into Swamiji's room, I did so without feelings or expectations.

'Aaj aao' (Come in), a voice reverberated when I knocked at the door.

Since Pattabhiji was wearing belted sandals, he took a while to remove them. So, I had to step in first. The room was spacious but dimly lit, which initially caused a bit of disorientation after being in a brightly lit area for so long.

'Andar aao' (come inside), he called again.

Since I was alone in that spacious room, I walked further warily.

As my eyes adjusted to the room, I noticed Swami Rama seated on a sofa. Unsure of how to proceed, I found myself in a dilemma. Should I seek his blessings by touching his feet or just remain where I was and wait for Pattabhiji to join us? I was in a total fix, contemplating the appropriate course of action. Thankfully, Pattabhiji entered the room, and I sighed with relief.

Swami Rama gestured towards another sofa and instructed us to take a seat. Usually, I would have complied, but on this particular day, I acted impulsively without realising it. I walked straight to Swami Rama, touched his feet, and sat at his feet. That moment was serene, and the silence heavenly.

As we sat near Baba's feet, he placed both hands on our heads. For the first time, I found myself immersed in the state of yoga samadhi!! Pattabhiji became wholly immersed in devotion, his tearful eyes fixed on Guru's feet.

"Both of you are my son and daughter. Now, I am connecting you to the Rishi Paramparā. From now on, we will fully take care of you."

I couldn't comprehend and continued staring at him, "I will initiate you today through Mantrōpadēśa after Bhūtaśuddhi. Be here around 7 p.m.," he said

Hearing Swami Rama's words, I felt anxious, especially when he mentioned "Bhūta," which means ghosts. Thoughts raced through my mind - would he attempt some form of black magic? What did he have in store for us? We had come here because a friend mentioned the possibility of donations in dollars, and now I couldn't help but think that this was a lesson we needed to learn. "Oh God, please protect us this time. I promise I will never even sleep in this direction again," I thought, restless and apprehensive.

The situation suddenly changed. It felt as if Swami Rama had somehow read my thoughts because moments later, he informed us, "No, I will not initiate you both today. Instead, I would like you both to visit my ashram in Rishikesh and stay with me for a few days." This unexpected turn of events brought me a sense of relief. At that moment, I wasn't aware that Swami Rama could intuitively read my feelings and concerns.

I was anticipating that Pattabhiji would broach the topic of donations to our yoga trust, but in the presence of Swami Rama, he seemed lost for words. When I gave him a subtle hint, Pattabhiji spoke about our Trust and its activities and handed over a file with all the details. Swami Rama glanced at it briefly and then swiftly tossed it over a nearby table, saying, "You will attain all this - fame, name, men, material success; only if you have done some Sādhana, tell me what Sādhana have you done?"

Time passed, and Pattabhiji remained silent, not responding to Swami Rama's words. The atmosphere was charged with a sense of expectation and introspection. Unable to bear the awkward silence, I felt compelled to break it by sharing about Pattabhiji's remarkable achievements in yoga. I recounted how he had left his home with just 2 pairs of clothes and no money, embarking on a quest for higher knowledge in the Himalayas, trusting in divinity at every step. I shared about his journey from the Himalayas to Kanyakumari, where he worked tirelessly to create awareness about yoga among common people. I also recounted Pattabhiji's visit to the Horanadu Annapoorneshwari Temple, where, lost in meditation, he had experienced a profound Kundalini awakening. At that moment, I shared everything I thought was relevant and that would give Swami Rama a glimpse of Pattabhiji's spiritual journey.

Swami Rama was listening to me intently, but as soon as I mentioned Kundalini's awakening, Baba said, "Enough, stop it!" once again, he placed his hand on Pattabhiji's head and blessed him. At that point in time, I did not realise that it was a gift of Shakthipatha to his loving disciple. We left after thanking him.

As soon as we returned to our hotel room, Pattabhiji fell ill. He was utterly exhausted to the point where he couldn't take a step. However, we had to return to Bengaluru due to an unavoidable commitment. Despite his condition, I managed to get him ready, and we made our way to the Mysuru bus stand.

To our dismay, the bus stand was crowded with people due to the Pithru Paksha Navarathri season. Every bus we approached was fully occupied, and no matter how long we waited, we couldn't find a single bus with empty seats. As the clock struck midnight, we were still stranded at the Mysuru bus stand, facing a seemingly endless wait. We stood there clueless, realising that if this situation continued, we might have to stand there until dawn.

Suddenly, we heard someone shouting, "Bengaluru, Bengaluru!" and saw an Ambassador car with people already seated inside. We quickly adjusted ourselves to fit in. I helped Pattabhiji get into the back seat while I sat in the front seat, beside the driver. As the car was about to depart, I casually glanced to the side, and my heart skipped a beat when I saw a person who appeared to be a sadhu. He had matted hair, holy markings, and vermilion on his forehead, and I noticed a trident beside him. His entire presence was intimidating, and I wondered how we would manage to travel with him to Bengaluru.

On one side, I had to assist Pattabhiji, who was not feeling well. Due to an entire day of running around, I was exhausted, and my body was crying for sleep, which was the necessity of reaching Bengaluru due to unavoidable commitments. On the other hand, I had to travel with this person who appeared like a black magician, and his mere presence induced fright in me. All compounded, I experienced despair and a surge of anger towards Swami Rama because of his earlier statement, 'Your protection is my responsibility henceforth.' I questioned 'Is this the way of providing protection? We had travelled all the way from Bengaluru just to meet you. How are you treating us? I can't comprehend your words or actions! What does this all mean?'. I was visibly angry and irritated.

Out of the blue, I noticed a light above the Ambassador car we were seated in. I stared at it. The more I focused, the more I realised that beyond that light, there was a pirouetting golden-coloured radiant Meru Shri Chakra!! This Meru pulled all my attention towards it; I continued to observe it. It looked like it was visible only to me, and no one else in the car saw it. I don't know when I slipped into sleep; I woke up to the voice of Pattabhiji saying, 'Jyothi, wake up, we have reached home!' it must have been around 3 a.m. I stepped into the house wondering, 'Was I immersed in the Guru's illusion, or had the illusion that enveloped me dropped off?'

***

16

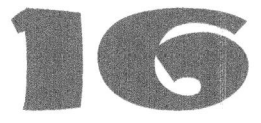

ACCEPT ME AS YOUR GURU ONLY WHEN YOU ARE CONVINCED OF MY POWER AND SIDDHIS!!

As the days in Rishikesh neared the tenth mark, our anticipation of meeting Swami Rama grew stronger. Doubts about our chances of meeting him crept into my mind, prompting me to write a heartfelt 10-page letter to Baba. In my imagination, I envisioned myself handing him the letter and swiftly embarking on a journey to Delhi, catching a train to Bengaluru. With this scenario in mind, I carefully tucked the note into my pocket.

Suddenly, I heard Baba's familiar and affectionate voice calling me, "Beta." Hastily, I searched through my pocket for the letter. Baba continued, "Let's meet tomorrow."

***

A few years before I met Swami Rama for the first time in Mysuru, I was working an English professor at a college where Shyam Sundar, a Kannada professor, was my colleague. Then, during his free time, he would translate Swami Rama's book titled 'Living with the Himalayan Master' into Kannada. Occasionally, he would share interesting insights about Swami Rama with me, and I would listen to him silently. Swami Rama was in Bengaluru for the release of this book, and I was also invited to the event. However, I chose not to attend since such topics didn't interest me then.

Years later, I had the opportunity to meet Swami Rama in Mysore, and his presence had a tremendous impact on me. The experience was so mesmerising that it sparked a strong desire to learn more about him. I began searching for the book 'Living with Himalayan Masters,' translated by Shyam Sundar, but could not find any copies. I tried contacting Shyam Sundar, but he had been transferred to a different college. Determined to read the book, I set out on a mission to find out Shyam Sundar's current whereabouts. After obtaining his address, I met with the professor and shared my experience meeting Swami Rama in Mysuru. He felt delighted and said, "You are really blessed to meet him." I expressed my eagerness to read the book, and that's how I landed on a copy of the Kannada version of Living with the Himalayan Masters.

On that very night, at around 10 p.m., I delved into the book's pages. Hours passed unnoticed, and when I finally set it aside, it was already 3 a.m. I had devoured the entire content in one immersive session. Throughout the reading journey, I experienced a range of emotions—from bursts of laughter to moments of tears streaming down my cheeks. As I reached the book's final page, I realised that I was in a different world; I had transcended into a realm beyond this world. The book had a profound impact on my perception of Swami Rama. I started seeing him as a Guru, to whom nothing was impossible in this universe. From that moment onward, I started counting the days, hours, and minutes until that divine moment of meeting him would arrive.

Nearly a month after reading the book, I found myself in Rishikesh at Swami's ashram, Sādhana Mandir, eagerly awaiting an opportunity to meet him. During that time, a ten-day International Yoga Conference was in progress; Baba's disciples from around the world had gathered, and it seemed like he wanted us, Pattabhiji and me, to be a part of this gathering. Therefore, he invited us to visit his ashram, coinciding with the conference. In addition to Baba's lecture, the conference featured speeches by other eminent speakers on Yoga. Alongside this conference, Baba was extremely involved in overseeing the construction of a hospital and various

Accept me as your Guru only when you are convinced of my power and siddhis!!

other developmental projects in Jolly Grant, Dehradun. He was on a very tight schedule and tirelessly working to fulfil his commitments.

Finally, we got to see Baba; it was late in the evening. As soon as Baba's eyes fell on us, he asked, 'Who are you? And what is your purpose of visiting?' I was bewildered by this inquiry. Anger welled inside me because, for a month, I eagerly looked forward to meeting Baba; as soon as I received an invitation from him, I got my leave approved with incredible difficulty. I had waited patiently for days, anticipating our meeting with Baba, but he failed to recognise me; this was frustrating.

In the heat of the moment, my anger overtook me, and without realising it, I blurted out, "We're here because you invited us!"

Baba must have sensed the anger in my voice, but he simply said, 'Haan, haan, haan...' which implied 'Have Patience.'

I fell silent because I realised the way I spoke wasn't appropriate.

Alas, and I didn't realise it, by then, Baba had initiated a 'game,' and I wasn't allowed to meet him for the next few days.

During the next few mornings, as he was about to depart, I would run and stand before him, asking, 'Swamiji, when can I meet you?' Without giving me a chance to inquire further, Baba glanced at his watch as though in a rush; he would then get into the car and say, 'Bete (child), I have a lot of work; I must leave now, shaam ko milenge (Let's meet in the evening).' In the evening, I would wait for his arrival near the garden, and he would depart, saying, 'Bete, I am exhausted; let's meet in the morning.' This routine continued. However, amidst this waiting, I had an opportunity to deliver a lecture on Indian Classical Dance. I also got to meet several of his senior disciples from different parts of the world and learn more about Baba.

After failing to meet Baba for days, I gave up on my attempts because I initially believed he wouldn't let me leave without meeting him since he had invited me here. However, as time passed, my confidence in this belief diminished.

He stated, addressing me, 'Accept me as your Guru, only when you are convinced about my power and siddhis!' These words of Baba got me thinking. I wondered which Guru imparts such confidence and freedom to their disciples. My eagerness to know about Baba increased twofold. I felt deep within that he was not an ordinary man, and I wanted to build a deeper connection with him.

Days went by quickly, and it was almost time for us to return, yet the prospect of meeting with Baba seemed like a faraway land. Since our return tickets were not confirmed, we decided to travel to Delhi and catch a train to Bengaluru. Pattabhiji, who was a silent witness to this tussle between Baba and me, noticed my emotional turmoil and, at this point, intervened and suggested, 'Why don't you write a letter to Baba pouring all your thoughts? Perhaps we can give it to him before leaving. If not this time, we might get to meet him in the future. We can always come back later. His idea was appealing, so I took some sheets of paper and poured my heart out about all I wanted to ask him. It ended up being 10 full sheets of heartfelt letters. I slipped the letters into my sweater pocket, thinking when I came across Baba, I would hand him these notes and then depart.

Finally, I came across him, and immediately, my hand slipped into the pocket and caressed the warmly nestled letters; I was about to pull it out when Baba said, 'Child, let us meet tomorrow.' For a brief moment, I was stunned. I pulled myself together, mustered some strength, and said, 'Baba, I understand you are under a lot of work pressure, and I do not wish to burden you further. I have written everything that I want to share in these letters. Could you please read it?'

He gently took it, slipped it into his pocket, and said, 'Tomorrow morning, freshen up and be ready by 7 am. I will arrange for someone to bring you to me. I will initiate you to The Path. Since you love everything traditional, I will traditionally initiate you.' I was unsure if he even listened to me. All I could say was, 'OK, Swamiji.' I went silent and wondered how in the world he would know what I liked.

After this incident, on my way back, I stumbled upon Pandith Usharbudh Arya, who we all know today as Swami VedBhārathi. I took the liberty of narrating the whole incident, from writing a letter to the next day's initiation. He burst into a loud, heartful laughter and said, 'Perhaps you didn't realise, Jyothi, writing and handing that letter to Baba is as good as offering it to Ganga. He will not go through it.' I felt disappointed, thinking all that hard work had gone to waste. However, the thought of meeting him the next day brought a sense of relief.

A few minutes later, I felt maybe I hadn't grasped the underlying meaning of Panditji's statement. It felt way more mysterious than it appeared. I turned towards him and gently enquired. 'What did that statement mean?' he said smilingly. 'There is no difference between Guru and Ganga!!' A Guru doesn't have to read through the letter to know its content; he knows while the disciple writes it.

The memory of the day I was initiated fills me with exhilaration—the day Swami Rama initiated me into a more profound spiritual journey. As dawn painted the sky in golden hues, the cool breeze from the sacred Ganga infused my being with the essence of spirituality. Unknowingly, every fibre of my existence pulsed with devotion. Stepping into the dimly lit room adorned with traditional decor and a gentle ghee lamp, I felt enveloped in a profound spiritual ambience.

Baba came before us, adorned in a white jubba and pyjamas, a departure from his usual red kimono. His face, serene as the Ganga, exuded a divine radiance that enveloped us in love. As the initiation commenced, we immersed ourselves in the sacred rituals, progressing steadily towards the heart of the initiation ceremony. Upon reaching the core of the ritual, Baba proclaimed,

"Shiva bears witness to this whole initiation process. I bestow upon you the Shāmbhavi Deeksha. Sākṣāt Shiva himself will be present here!"

At that moment, a surge of energy coursed through my entire being! My eyes welled with uncontrollable tears; I transcended into a higher vibrational state in the profound moment. It marked a pivotal turning point where I could sense a profound shift in my life's purpose, all under the grace of Mahaguru. I was reborn on that day.

***

Shashtra says that our first birth is a gift from our parents in the form of a physical body, but the Guru blesses us with a second birth when he initiates us to the Path, the beginning of our spiritual journey. After that, he nurtures and protects us as a father, mother, Guru, friend, and guide.

Tva mēva mātā ca pitā tvamēva |

Tvamēva bandhuśca saka tvamēva |

Tvamēva vidyā draviṇaṁ tvamēva |

Tvamēva sarvaṁ mama dēva dēva |

> Shāmbhavi Deeksha - Shāmbhavi Deeksha is the highest initiation given by the Guru to his disciple in the Samayāchāra Path of Śakta tradition. It symbolises the love of the Guru and the sign of the disciples' spiritual advancement. In the word Shāmbhavi, 'Sham' means auspicious and 'Bhava' means 'happen.' The sacred initiation cuts off all the shackles of ignorance and leads the sadhaka towards spiritual progress.
>
> When Shiva's consciousness awakens in the heart of the aspirant, the entire universe unveils as the manifestation of Shakti of Shiva. The duality of existence vanishes; all differences of perspectives are removed. Then, the practitioner is able to experience the entire universe as one nest by the Highesh Grace descending upon him.

***

17

BABA VISITS BENGALURU – 1992

My scooter halted right at Corporation Circle! I had to push it to the roadside and stood there, feeling utterly helpless. The only thought racing through my mind was, "Baba, what should I do now?" I was supposed to introduce Baba, and here I was, stuck, with Baba and the entire audience waiting for me. What could all of this possibly mean?

***

"Children! Organise a programme and invite me; Bengaluru people are waiting for me!"

Baba said this to Pattabhiji and me after our initiation at his Sādhana Mandir Trust in Rishikesh. Our eyes lit up with the possibility of Baba visiting Bengaluru. As we began planning, numerous questions arose about the date, time, flow of events, duration, and more. Pattabhiji sought guidance from Baba on how to organise the programme; however, Baba dismissed his queries with simple instructions: 'You are already familiar with event organisation. Just initiate the process, and everything will fall into place. I have a Doctor's conference scheduled in Chennai, and after that, I will attend your event in Bengaluru.

After returning to Bengaluru, we enthusiastically started planning the event. Some of Pattabhiji's Yoga students eagerly joined us upon learning about Baba's impending visit. We planned to host 2 events: a morning session at the Institute of Engineers and an evening Lecture by Baba, open to the general public at Town Hall.

As the days passed, we completed all the preparations for the event. However, the only hiccup was the lack of information about Swami Rama's exact schedule. Despite our efforts, we couldn't get any updates from the Rishikesh ashram or the conference organisers in Chennai. This uncertainty left us feeling underprepared and internally restless, as we were eager to ensure that Swami Rama's visit to Bengaluru would be pleasant and seamless.

All our worries melted away like a piece of ice the moment Baba landed in Bengaluru; everything seemed to fall effortlessly into place. Baba's words, 'People are waiting for me,' proved true beyond measure. More than 500 people registered upon announcing the event, and about 200 had to be turned away due to space constraints. This happened in the 1990s when advertising and marketing avenues were non-existent, yet we saw a packed auditorium, a testament to Baba's immense popularity and power to attract people!

On that beautiful morning, Swami Rama demonstrated incredible feats that had already captured the world's attention. He began by stopping his heartbeat for a few minutes, leaving everyone astonished. Later, he mesmerised everyone by exhibiting different temperatures on each side of his body. His right side registered 98 degrees Fahrenheit, while his left side measured 78 degrees Fahrenheit. Even doctors were unable to explain this extraordinary phenomenon!

Later, Swami Rama proceeded to demonstrate another unbelievable task. At that time, cancer was a major concern in the medical field, with extensive research ongoing to understand it. During the event, Baba asked a group of doctors to examine what appeared to be a tumour on a specific body part. After their examination, he questioned them, "Where should I move this tumour?" Initially appearing on his thigh, he then shifted it to the upper part of his body, leaving everyone present astonished. The Doctors repeatedly tested and examined the phenomenon. Then, assuming the Shavasana posture, Baba peacefully, as described by Pandit Rajamani, released the tumour to nature. Upon re-examination, doctors found no trace of a cancerous tumour in his body. This remarkable display left everyone with the same question: "How is this possible?" Doctors pondered the medical possibilities, while spiritual seekers were intrigued to learn more about yoga. The event concluded as planned around 1:30 p.m.

Indeed, this wasn't Baba's first demonstration of his Yogic Siddhis. He had previously showcased his extraordinary abilities at the Menninger Foundation in Topeka, Kansas, in 1969. This event is well-documented and renowned worldwide for its profound impact and revelations.

In another experiment, Baba increased his heart rate to 300 beats and stayed in that state for about 17 seconds in the presence of scientists and specialist doctors. This whole feat was meticulously documented by Minneapolis physician Dr. Daniel Feruguson and his colleague Dr. Elmer Green. This rate is 5 times faster than normal and akin to a heart-stopping phenomenon. His simple yet profound statement, "I can make my heart listen to me," gained popularity.

Swami Rama's demonstrations of yogic siddhis were not merely limited to physiological feats but extended to remarkable displays of control over external objects and energies. From exhibiting different temperatures in his hands to moving objects with the power of his gaze, Swami Rama's mastery over various yogic powers is well-documented and serves as a profound testament to his spiritual prowess. One of Baba's profound proclamations emphasised the significance of these displays in front of sceptics and believers alike. While a non-believer's disbelief might hinder their understanding beyond the surface, a believer's witnessing of these siddhis often leads to a deeper spiritual awakening and a newfound path towards spiritual growth.

***

I was responsible for introducing Baba during the evening programme. Alongside that, we organised a dance performance by my students. Since everyone had left for the venue early, I planned to finish up some tasks at home before heading there. Opting to use my scooter, I aimed to arrive just before the stage programme commenced.

Whether it was fortune or misfortune, my scooter abruptly stalled right in front of Corporation Circle. Despite numerous attempts, the engine refused to kick start. I had no choice but to push the scooter to the roadside and search for an auto-rickshaw. The stage programme was on the verge of starting, and I stood there feeling utterly helpless, uncertain of how to reach the venue. The only thought racing through my mind was, "Baba, what should I do now?" I was supposed to introduce Baba, and here I was, stuck, with Baba and the entire audience waiting for me. What could all of this possibly mean?

After precisely 15 minutes, my scooter's engine roared to life. Without wasting another moment, I raced towards Town Hall. Upon arrival, I found that the programme had already commenced. Aware of the importance of keeping the audience engaged, Pattabhiji had taken the initiative to address them in my absence. As I approached the stage, he called out my name and handed me the microphone.

Baba visits Bengaluru – 1992

Smt. Jyothi Pattabhiram (Guru Sakalamaa) introducing Swami Rama at the event in Bangalore

Now, when I look back on this incident, I feel it was all Baba's play. Perhaps he must have sensed that if I reached the venue on time, I would be the only one speaking, and Pattabhiji may not get an opportunity at all. Since he desired both Pattabhiji and me to address the gathering, he must have delayed my arrival.

As I stood in front of the gathering to introduce Baba, I felt compelled to quote one of Kabir's verses on the significance of the Guru, which I had heard numerous times in Swami Rama's lectures. Kabir says, 'Both the guru and Govind (God) are in front of me. Whom should I bow down to first? I bow down to my guru, as through him, I have found Govind. For me, these lines encapsulate Baba's role in guiding us towards Mother Divine and in this manner, I introduced Gurudēva with utmost reverence. My speech would have lasted not more than 5 minutes.

Gurudēva's turn came to address the gathering, and with a solemn gaze at the crowd, Baba remarked, "It was a sweet introduction, but personally, I don't feel entirely comfortable. While I agree that the Guru is worthy of the highest praise and is indescribable, I'm not sure if these lines suit me!" and then he continued his address. That's how Baba is: direct and simple.

His talk revolved around the concept of "Citizens of 2 Cities - Inner and Outer World," offering detailed insights into Yoga and its profound impact. Towards the end, there was a question-and-answer session where members of the audience could pose their queries.

One youngster asked Baba, "What is Karma, and how do we manage it?"

Baba explained what Karma is. In his answer, he said, "Act of donating generously, sharing resources and knowledge is the quickest way to get liberation from bondage." However, this young man in the audience took offence and raised his voice in disagreement, questioning, "How does sharing money lead to liberation?" expressing his doubt about its correctness.

Baba immediately responded, "My dear gentleman, could you get up?" Now everyone's eyes were on this chap, "How much is your monthly income?" Baba questioned him, but he remained silent. "It's ok if you don't want to answer it. But how much of it do you donate for a cause?" to which he said, "I don't engage in such acts!" Baba immediately said, "There is no point in explaining about liberation to someone who doesn't believe in sharing. First, you start from there; now, please sit down."

The guy got cold feet, I guess.

A dance piece presented in honour of Baba, praising the noble Guru in the classical dance style, Bharatanatyam, concluded the programme on a grand note.

***

18

GURU'S DISEMBODIED LOVE

Baba, I never longed for a Guru in my life, nor did I actively seek a spiritual guide. I mean, I never thought of it as a necessity in my life!! You walked into my life as a divine blessing!! Now, realising your profound impact on my life, how could you do this to me? Aren't Yogis supposed to live hundreds and hundreds of years? How can you leave me and go, Baba? I cannot excuse you for this, Baba!!

"Bete, are you crying?" felt like Baba's voice, and I was momentarily frozen.

***

Guru's love, care, and protection persist even beyond the physical form. The physical body is merely a vessel; the connection remains eternal because Guru's love is divine, pure, and boundless. In fostering the holistic development of their disciples, a Guru will go to great lengths to support their growth, persistently reminding them of life's ultimate purpose and occasionally manifesting in subtle forms to communicate, instruct, and steer them. Conversely, when proximity isn't necessary, the Guru can maintain a sense of distance from the disciple.

Allow me to share an incident that unfolded after Gurudēva Swami Rama transcended his physical form—a profound testament to Baba's sublime love.

It was the second half of the 1990s, to be precise, 13th November 1996. Pattabhiji and I were in our Ramanagar ashram, which was nothing more than a thatched and humble dwelling. The purpose was significant - we had arranged for a homa to be performed by a Sadhu who possessed Agni Siddi. His fame stemmed from his ability to sleep on the Agni kuṇḍa following offerings to the fire god. For most of us, merely sitting near the kuṇḍa during these rituals is challenging due to the intense heat, yet this Sadhu was known to rest on it. Such was the power of his Agni tattva siddhi! This event drew thousands of curious individuals, we had arranged food for all.

The homa proceeded smoothly, and after the rituals concluded, I made arrangements to return to Bengaluru by taxi with my mother-in-law and daughter Sadhana. Pattabhiji opted to remain at the ashram and attend to the pending work.

It must have been midnight when we finally reached home, exhausted from the day's activities. As I reached for the lock, I noticed a letter wedged in the latch. The words "Swami Rama no more" hit me like a tonne of bricks, instantly turning my world upside down.

How could a great yogi and our beloved Gurudēva leave us? I was left in shock, unable to move, and had to sit down to process the news.

It took me a while to gather my thoughts, and then I remembered Pattabhiji. Knowing that there was no means of communication like phones, television, or radio at the ashram, I realised he wouldn't have received the news. I found the taxi driver still waiting for me, so I asked him to return to the ashram, inform Pattabhiji about Swami Rama's passing, and bring him back to Bengaluru. After a few hours, the taxi driver returned, but Pattabhiji was nowhere to be seen. The driver mentioned that he had informed Pattabhiji about the sad news and was instructed to return with him. However, Pattabhiji remained silent for a few moments before saying, "No, I will return tomorrow," and then retreated into his room and locked the door behind him.

My night was consumed by thoughts of Baba.

The morning felt heavy with grief as admirers of Swami Rama began arriving at our home. His sudden passing away had deeply affected many of us, and the air was thick with sorrow and memories. Each person who came shared stories of how Baba had touched their lives. Despite the constant flow of condolences and visitors, I struggled with accepting the reality of his absence. However, I had to put aside my personal turmoil to attend to my daughter Sadhana's needs. As I mechanically prepared breakfast, tears filled my eyes, and I couldn't shake the feeling of being orphaned without Baba. Knowing that he had a way of understanding my innermost thoughts, I engaged in a silent conversation with him as a final attempt at solace.

***

Baba, I never longed for a Guru in my life, nor did I actively seek a spiritual guide; I mean, I never thought of it as a necessity in my life!! You walked into my life as a divine blessing!! Now, realising your profound impact on my life, how could you do this to me? Aren't Yogis supposed to live hundreds and hundreds of years? How can you leave me and go? I cannot pardon you for this, Baba!!

I was ready to battle it out with him if fighting could bring my Baba back.

"Child, can you hear me?" I heard a disembodied voice—it was Swami Rama's voice!

I tried to locate the voice. Surprisingly, no one was around. It looks like no one else noticed this voice. Perplexed, I remained silent, unsure what to make of the experience.

"Child, are you crying?" I heard that voice again. Slowly, I realised Baba was trying to communicate with me. With tear-filled eyes, I tuned my ears to his voice.

"Why are you crying?"

'.......'

"Why do you think I have gone away from you?"

'......'

"I feel sad to see you crying, my child. Do you really want to see me?" he asked, his tone soothing as if comforting a weeping child.

"Yes, Baba," I said in a trembling voice. Baba directed me to the meditation room. "Sit with your back straight. Can you see me now?" he guided me in a meditative tone. "Yes, Baba," I said, and I was in his celestial presence there.

"Do you see what is in front of you?"

"I can see my own body but in the form of light," I said.

"Tell me, what is the difference between your body and the body in front of you?"

I said," Baba, my body is made up of bones, muscles, blood, etc, whereas the body in front of me is filled with light alone!"

"Hmmm," I could sense a tone of contentment for getting the drift of his hint.

This whole lesson was being taught in complete silence.

Baba responded," Yes, I have fixed this realisation of inner light as the goal of your life. Out of my love for you, I am giving this gift to you today!"

It was as though rough waves crashed and dissolved in the tranquil shores of my mind. Instantly, my despair gave way to a sense of peace and serenity.

'Are you contented now? Are you convinced that I have not left you?' Baba asked with a gentle smile.

I tried to take in as much of his image as possible.

Before leaving, Baba assured me, "I cannot bear to see you cry. Whenever you want to see me, you can see me in your meditation!!" He has kept up his promise ever since, even to this day.

When I walked out of the meditation room, I was no longer grief-stricken, but my heart was filled with gratitude. After that day, I have never felt Baba's absence in his physical form.

Baba used to appear in my meditation to guide and bless me until he sent me to Mysuru Rā Sā Gurugalu, after which he took a back seat. I always feel his presence day and night; there is no moment when he isn't around.

These experiences strengthen my belief that Guru's love is incomparable and immeasurable. In this entire universe, there is no love as pristine and unconditional as Guru's love for his disciple. It is indescribable, and all the words in the dictionary fail to capture its essence. It is meant to be experienced, and oh! What an exquisite experience it is!!

***

19

BEYOND THE VEIL: TWO SUPERNATURAL EXPERIENCES WITH SWAMI RAMA

"Why did you call at such an unearthly hour?" he thundered angrily while I stood there dumbfounded. Never in my wildest dreams did I imagine that praying for a friend's well-being would summon Baba, who had already departed from his physical form, back in such a formidable manner!! Even before this, Baba had once manifested on a late-night in a subtle form before Pattabhiji and me. He would vanish into thin air once his intended task was complete.

***

When our belief is profound, the very word 'Guru' transforms into radiant light. Once the bond between Guru and Disciple deepens, even in the darkest of times, while God may seem distant, the Guru will never let go of your hand. A guru does not manifest in this world in any extraordinary form or with distinctive characteristics. They will appear as ordinary individuals. They will witness the full spectrum of experiences that ordinary individuals undergo. Yet, they grow extraordinarily while living among ordinary individuals in the most ordinary ways. The Guru's life is exemplary because it shows that someone like us can achieve such greatness, inspiring commoners like us to follow the path of Sādhana.

When Baba was in the body, and even after he renounced his physical body, he visited me many times in his astral form. One such visitation happened during Shivarātri. During those days, we celebrated Shivarātri grandly by staying awake throughout the auspicious night, engaging in mantra chanting, Satsang, bhajans, and special talks. On that particular Shivarātri, Pattabhiji had planned a Trikala pooja for Lord Mahadeva and was later scheduled to deliver a talk on meditation. Many people had gathered, and most of them were associated with our yoga organisation. The programme was underway with a lot of energy. My daughter Sadhana was just a 2-year-old infant, so I alternated between attending to her needs and participating in the pooja and bhajans whenever she was asleep.

Around 12 am, which was the auspicious timing for the Maha Pooja, I left to attend the programme after ensuring that Sadhana was in deep sleep. However, I couldn't find Pattabhiji anywhere, so I checked with a few people around when someone informed me that during the bhajan, Pattabhiji was approached by somebody, and shortly, he left with the person, saying he would be back in half an hour while asking everyone else to continue the bhajan.

I was a little worried that he left at this hour of the night that too without much information. Back in those days, there were no mobile phones, so other than waiting for his return, I didn't have any means of knowing what had happened. Though he had said he would return in about half an hour, several hours passed by when finally an acquaintance arrived with the news that Saraswathi, who was supposed to bring prasad for Shivarātri Puja had met with an accident on her way and was hospitalised. Her condition was critical, and due to the severity of the fall, she had slipped into a coma! We were all shocked upon receiving this news.

Saraswathi was a yoga instructor in our organisation, leading the women's batch with great enthusiasm. She was known for her zeal and was adored by all her students. Saraswathi had a deep fondness for my daughter Sadhana; she made sure to cook Sadhana's favourite food and found joy in feeding her while she sat on her lap. As my teaching profession and evening dance classes consumed most of my time, Saraswathi took care of these special moments. More than anything, Saraswathi and I were good friends.

On that fateful night, Saraswathi took responsibility for preparing prasad for the festival. She had prepared 2 carriers full of prasad. While on their way to our home, her husband was riding the two-wheeler and Saraswathi was riding a pillion, holding one carrier on her lap while the other was placed in front of their two-wheeler. Due to the inadequate functioning of streetlights in those days, her husband didn't notice a speed breaker in the darkness, leading to a loss of control and causing both of them to fall. Saraswathi, due to the force of the fall, lost consciousness, and her husband immediately rushed her to the nearby hospital. A few hours after this incident, someone informed Pattabhiji, who promptly went to the hospital to be by her side. He then sent someone to inform me about the whole situation. Pattabhiji went into meditation for Saraswathi's recovery.

After hearing the whole story, I promptly asked for the nursing home's contact number where Saraswathi was admitted. I tried calling that number several times, but there was no response, possibly because it was midnight. I felt saddened as I thought about her condition. Feeling helpless and unsure of what to do, I remembered Baba's assurance to me: 'In moments of adversity, keep me in your thoughts, and I shall shield you.' Taking a seat in meditation by the front door, I chanted a mantra bestowed by Baba and pleaded, "Please restore Saraswathi to her normal state" I humbly prayed for her well-being.

Baba appeared before me even before I finished my prayer! These appearances are incredibly real, very close to physical reality. It's just like that feeling of sensing someone's presence when they come near us, even with our eyes closed. I could sense his presence as he walked through the open gate, hearing the sound of footsteps. I could even perceive the subtle sound of his clothes rustling as he moved!

As he stood before me, I observed that his face had turned red with anger, and his eyes were wide open. When Baba is angry, he embodies Rudra himself.

"Why did you call me at such an unearthly hour?" he thundered with anger while I sat there dumbfounded. I was trembling with fear.

Baba's appearance was completely unexpected; I had assumed that I just had to pray and convey the message to Baba. I never expected him to manifest in front of me. When I saw him in this fierce form, I was at a loss for words or actions and resorted to silence. After a few minutes of silence, his anger gradually subsided, and his face relaxed.

In a stern voice, he questioned me, "Do you not understand that it is inappropriate to meddle in another person's karma?"

Uncertain of how to respond, I maintained my silence.

My Guru is an embodiment of compassion!! He must have sensed my fear because I felt his heart soften when he said, 'Let me see what I can do,' and then left.

As I was processing what had happened, the phone rang. It was Pattabhiji on the other end. He informed me that Saraswathi had come out of the coma. Before ending the call, he said, "I felt Baba's presence here."

***

Allow me to recount another transcendental experience with Swami Rama! It was January, and the Sankranthi festival was approaching fast. Bengaluru is typically quite chilly during this season, and my daughter Sadhana would often catch a cold during this weather, making breathing difficult for her due to a blocked nose. As a preventive measure, we would close the windows and doors in the evening. On that eventful night, we were all fast asleep when I heard my daughter's voice saying, 'Amma, Amma, wake up!' It must have been around 11 pm. Exhausted from a workday, I struggled to open my eyes and looked at her. "Amma, can I have a glass of milk?" she asked. I was taken aback for 2 reasons: firstly, my daughter was not accustomed to drinking or eating anything at night, and secondly, the voice didn't sound like hers, which filled me with a sense of unease.

"Putta, drinking milk at this late hour might cause indigestion. Come here; I'll tuck you in and put you to sleep." I said sleepily. She didn't budge; instead, she said firmly, "No, I want some milk now. Come, hold my hand; let's go to the kitchen." She extended her hand towards me. Reluctantly, I held her hand, and she pulled me towards the kitchen. I warmed up a glass of milk, which she gulped down with ease, and then she ran to her grandma's room, saying, "I will sleep next to Granny."

After switching off all the lights, I returned to our room, and there He was, sitting on our bed, deeply engrossed in conversation with Pattabhiji. I was astounded to see Swami Rama in physical form; it seemed impossible as he was residing in America during those days! He noticed me entering the room; Baba looked at both of us and said, "I came here intending to meet you both today. I could have conveyed the matter over the phone, but I felt like having this face-to-face conversation. I thought this would help to increase your trust in me."

After guiding us about our Sādhana to be done, he got up from the bed and vanished into thin air, dissipating like vapours!

***

I revisited the entire sequence of events after his disappearance and was mesmerised by how the incident unfolded that night. Baba had manifested in Sadhana's body in astral form, evidenced by the change in her voice. Later, when we went to the kitchen, he returned to the room and engaged in a deep discussion with Pattabhiji. I don't know what they spoke about, and we are not even supposed to ask. I bore witness to a captivating performance orchestrated by Baba, revealing his exquisite ability to connect with us through diverse manifestations.

***

20
A GURU'S PROMISE - A SERPENT HEADED RUDRĀKSHI

The Sadhu, seated in Padmasana, instructed me to close my eyes.

"After 5 minutes, open your eyes and gaze at my Ajñā chakra," the Sadhu instructed me.

I followed his instructions and opened my eyes, fixing my gaze on his Ajñā chakra. To my amazement, I saw Swami Rama's face appear on Sadhu's forehead!

***

Communication between Guru and disciple can take many forms; silence is one among the many, and it is always beautiful. Guru continues the connection in physical form and beyond, be it for guidance or fulfilling promises; for a Guru like Swami Rama, keeping up his promise is second to his nature.

While initiating Pattabhiji and me in Rishikesh ashram, Swami Rama made 2 promises: when the time is right, I will show you a photograph of Bengali Baba and the second one that he would gift us a unique Rudrākṣi.

These 2 promises hold profound significance. Obtaining Bengali Baba's photograph is akin to receiving blessings accumulated over many lifetimes, as Bengali Baba intentionally limits contact with the external world. There existed only two copies of his photograph: one

A Guru's Promise - A serpent headed Rudrākshi

with Swami Rama and the other with Dr Sunanda, who was another disciple; whose spiritual journey remains somewhat mysterious due to her early renunciation of the physical form. I don't know what motivated Baba on that day; he said that he would show us Bengali Baba's photograph when the time was right. His second promise was to bestow upon us a uniquely serpent-headed Ēk mukhi rudrākṣhi, but Baba renounced his physical form before fulfilling this commitment. At times, I've reflected on this promise, wondering, "Baba left us before seeing this through. Now that he's no longer with us physically, how can he fulfil that promise? He departed without fulfilling what he promised."

As time passed, these words gradually faded from my memory, but Baba had not forgotten.

One morning, we received an unexpected call from one Mr. Kulkarni, who expressed an urgent desire to meet with Pattabhiram ji. He mentioned finding our Sadhana Sangama Trust flyer in a newspaper while visiting his sister in Bengaluru. This flyer led him to discover that Pattabhiji was a direct disciple of Swami Rama, as well as our contact details. Kulkarni promptly arranged to visit us the following day at 7:30 a.m. at our residence.

As agreed upon, he arrived at our place on the dot. As soon as he arrived, he pulled a cover out of his pocket and handed it over. Upon opening it, we were astonished to find a serpent-hood-shaped rudrākṣi inside, along with a mantra message. The message instructed us to keep the rudrākṣi in a proper place and regularly practice mantra japa. This unexpected gift left us with numerous questions and brimming curiosity!

When I asked him, 'How did you come by this rudrākṣi?' His response revealed Baba's extraordinary power (Siddi) once again!

During the meeting, we learned that Kulkarni was the secretary of a central minister. In his free time, he frequented the Himalayas as a hobby. During one of these visits to the Himalayas with his friends, while they were climbing, he saw suddenly a Sadhu appearing in front of him. The Sadhu gestured with his eyes to Kulkarni, to follow him, and as if hypnotised, Kulkarni slipped away from the group and followed the Sadhu's footsteps.

According to Kulkarni, they must have walked for a few minutes before reaching a cave. The Sadhu then asked Kulkarni to be seated, and he himself sat in padmasana. Sadhu instructed Kulkarni to close his eyes.

"After 5 minutes, open your eyes and focus on my Ajñā chakra," was the Sadhu's instruction to him. "I followed his guidance, and upon opening my eyes, I fixed my gaze on his Ajñā chakra. To my amazement, I saw Swami Rama's face, playing like a video, on Sadhu's forehead! For the outer world, Swami Rama had renounced his physical form, but there he appeared on Sadhu's forehead, fully alive." Before Kulkarni could recover from the shock of this revelation, the Sadhu asked him in Hindi, 'Aaya Samaj me?' (Did you grasp the message?)

"Hmm" was all Kulkarni could say

"Who is he?" asked Sadhu

"He is my Guru, Swami Rama" replied Kulkarni

On hearing this, Sadhu pulled out a serpent-headed rudrākshi along with a paper-piece with a mantra and a message in it. He handed it over to Kulkarni and said, "Take it to Bengaluru. You will know the rest once you are there."

The Sadhu completed his task and then instructed, "Now go and rejoin your group."

Kulkarni was wary of whether he could find his group or not. "Since a lot of time has passed, I am not sure whether I will be able to find them," Sadhu said, "Don't worry, you will find them," and sent Kulkarni off.

Sadhu's word turned out to be true, and Kulkarni managed to rejoin the group and continue his trek.

On that day, Kulkarni received a message from Swami Rama instructing him to take the rudrākṣi and the accompanying message to Bengaluru, but the details of what to do with it and whom to deliver it to were vague. Consequently, Kulkarni carried it with him for almost 6 months, taking it wherever he went. His visit to his sister's house and the subsequent events seemed like a divine play—a series of interconnected events leading to this moment. Everything fell into place, from the pamphlet slipping out of the newspaper to Kulkarni reading about Pattabhiji being Swami Rama's direct disciple. Kulkarni felt a strong inner calling to reach out to Pattabhiji and fulfil this task bestowed upon him by Swami Rama. My Gurudēva had indeed fulfilled his promise.

You might be curious about the purpose of this present. For one, any gift from Guru is a blessing, but this rudrākṣi and mantra from Baba were to expand our vibrational energy for excellence, prosperity, and wealth. This incident left a powerful impression in our minds. It was the beginning of never-ending dedication and love towards my Gurdeva.

***

21

YOGANANDA PARAMAHAMSA IN THE TRAIN!

"You should not be squandering away the grace of your Guru like this for your personal excesses. You should rather try to use it to improve your Sādhana (spiritual practice) and to attain liberation.." said the monk and became silent again.

The train stopped somewhere once again, and I peeked outside to understand where we were, but my gaze was met with pitch darkness. I wondered why the train kept halting at such random places and looked back inside the compartment, only to realise the monks had disappeared. Suddenly, I was jolted out of my seat, and it slowly dawned on me that it was none other than Swami Yogananda Paramahamsa.

***

Swami Paramahamsa Yogananda (1893-1952) is a highly revered yogi who transformed millions of lives through Meditation and Kriya Yoga. His autobiography, 'Autobiography of a Yogi,' created sensational waves across the world and continues to be popular. Under the tutelage of his guru, Sri Yukteshvar Giri, he established 'The Yogoda Satsang Society of India' and brought the divine light of spirituality to people across the world. Swami Rama (1925-1996), from the Himalayan Sages Tradition, continued this divine mandate of spreading our Eastern spirituality in a different time period through the latter half of the 20th century. Both are revered as the foremost sages witnessed by the 20th century, who spread ancient wisdom from the spiritual scriptures and practices of India globally.

While Swami Paramahamsa Yogananda and Swami Rama belong to different yogic traditions, an esoteric experience in my life demonstrated to me how they are so deeply interconnected and in communion.

This incident happened almost three decades ago. Both Pattabhi Ji and myself had taken a late-night train to Hyderabad. We had to conduct a series of programmes on meditation the following day. The train left Bangalore station somewhere around 10 PM that day, and we finished our dinner in the train itself and were getting ready to catch the much-needed sleep, given the packed schedule of the next day. But the train had come to a halt. I looked out the window, and darkness was all that was staring back at me. I assumed it to be a small railway station without electricity. The train started again and slowly picked up pace.

By then, I noticed three young monks had entered our train cabin. They must have been around 30 years of age, and one of them seemed a little older, and the other two seemed to be his disciples. The cabin was very quiet, as if it were paying tribute to the middle of the night. After a brief period of silence, we started to converse. When they inquired about us, I was brief in my response, saying, 'We are direct disciples of Swami Rama, and with his grace, we are on our way to host some programmes on meditation in Hyderabad.'

The senior monk was seemingly charged up upon hearing Swami Rama's name and said, 'Oh, you are direct disciples of Swami Rama! I have heard so much about him, but meeting a direct disciple is a first for me. Could you please tell us more about him?' It must have been about 11.30 PM or so by that time, and after a long day of discourses, Pattabhi Ji was very tired. He responded, 'If you need to know about Swami Rama, please continue to converse with Jyothi. She is like Gurudēva's mouthpiece and can explain Swami Rama much better than I can. I will relax in the upper berth' and he retired to bed almost instantly.

Being sleepy, I was not excited to have a conversation at that hour of the night, but the monk would not give up easily. 'Jyothi Ji, please share something about Swami Rama. I am very curious,' the monk insisted. Upon hearing Baba's name, I felt that my exhaustion had vanished, and I was no longer sleepy. It felt like I had a newfound energy to share my experiences with Swami Rama. Though not as many as now, there was no dearth of stories to share. In my excitement, I had spoken for over 2 hours, and the monks were quietly listening and absorbing everything.

The time was 1 A.M the conversation was coming to an end after I had exhausted most of my experiences. The deserted train compartment seemed to have pushed every other passenger into a deep sleep. 'I have shared all my experiences with my Guru Swami Rama,' I tried to conclude the conversation.

Long pause and silence! The senior monk had gone into deep contemplation, and I kept wondering what he must be contemplating or what I said, which could have pushed him into silence. I was clueless and edgy at the reaction I was receiving.

He took a long sigh and said, 'I have been hearing your experiences for the last 2 hours. I have a few thoughts I would like to present, but I hope you wouldn't mind,' and I nodded in acceptance.

'Swami Rama is a Yogi par-excellence, recognised and revered the world over as one of the foremost Gurus. Such great sages usually would not accept disciples like you. If he has accepted you as his disciple, he must have considered you very important to him. The stories you shared about your experiences with Swami Rama demonstrate the amount of love and affection he has bestowed on you and the guidance he has provided. But you have not understood him at all,' the monk summarised. I was unable to understand his criticism and naturally sought an explanation, asking, 'Is it? How? Why do you think so?'

'Looking at the way in which he accepted you as his disciple, I felt so. Why else would he put up with your naughtiness, immaturity, pranks, etc.? Because there is a rare bond that exists between you two. He has been bestowing all his grace due to that bonding. It would have happened only because of your karmic connection from your past life. You must have done a lot of service for your Guru in the past life. The benefits of which he is returning to you now. But do not be under the impression that this will continue to remain the same way. At some juncture, your good karmas are bound to get exhausted, and as a result, your connection to your Guru will also come to an end. Don't let this divine connection end in such a manner. Use his grace only to enhance your spiritual practices!' he explained in a way I could comprehend.

While sharing my experiences with Baba, I shared a specific episode with them. As a Bharata Naatya (an ancient form of Indian classical dance) teacher, I had conceptualised a mega dance festival, and during my meditation, I had asked Baba to help me meet the budgetary goal of Seventy-Five Thousand rupees, which would be equal to approximately 7 or 8 lakhs in today's value. With Baba's grace, the funds were organised very easily, and the dance festival was executed with absolute grandeur. I had taken these things very casually and was naïve to understand the seriousness of these matters.

Against this backdrop, he said again, "You should not be squandering away the grace of your Guru like this for your personal excesses. You should rather try to use it to improve your Sādhana (spiritual practice) and to attain liberation. From now on, ponder a few times before asking for blessings such as these," and he became silent again.

The train stopped somewhere once again, and I peeked outside to understand where we were, but my gaze was met with pitch darkness. I wondered why the train kept halting at such random places and looked back inside the compartment, only to realise that the monks had disappeared.

My eyes were scanning the entire compartment and all the exit doors, but they were not to be seen anywhere. I was trying to comprehend what had happened, wondering where they could have gone in a matter of barely two seconds.

With a growing sense of anxiousness, I returned to my seat. All attempts at getting some sleep failed miserably as I kept thinking about the monks. For some reason, I recollected the face of that monk, and he seemed way too familiar.

His facial features were exactly like Swami Yoganada Paramahamsa (Yogananda ji) from his younger days, probably as in his early thirties. His attire, the chest-long curly hair, and those piercing eyes! I was jolted out of my seat upon this realisation. It was not that easy to accept that the one who had spoken to me earlier was none other than Yogananda Ji.

By then I had already read the highly popular book, 'Autobiography of a Yogi.' The book had found a permanent place on my desk, and I had seen his photo on the cover of the book almost on a daily basis. I wondered; how could I not recognise him when the monks were engaging with me?

It took some time for my mind to settle down, but only after having a realisation on why he had blessed me with a visit.

He had visited me that way to guide me onto the right path, to make me understand the importance of my Gurudēva Swami Rama, and to educate me about the seriousness that we need to have towards our Guru.

In doing so, he had awakened me at an hour when the whole world seemed to be asleep.

***

Messages from the Himalayan Sages: Timely & Timeless

Section 3

- A Journey To Satyaloka- The Real World
- Part 1: Chinnamastā means a severed head
- Part 2: Chinnamastā means rebirth

22

A JOURNEY TO SATYALOKA- THE REAL WORLD

Rishis are happy in the world they reside in. If you were to pray for their appearance, they might grant an audience, but if you are convinced they do not exist, then why should they appear before you? It is only after facing innumerable difficulties, ill health, and loss of mental strength that you begin to accept that there is a power beyond your imagination; life would be ever, that is all!!

***

My Mother had excellent storytelling skills. She would regale me with stories of the Rishis, various Gods, and other great sages; that was how I came to know about them. Though I grew up listening to these stories, I never believed them to be of any relevance to the times we lived in. I was convinced that the elders were merely rehashing the stories they had listened to when they grew up and that this modern age has no use for these Rishis-Munis from the past. I even believed that most people had the same opinion as mine. This very limited frame of thinking about the Rishi-Munis in itself is meaningless.

Right from childhood, I had a very inquisitive and questioning mind, but after joining college, I began to change; effect of reading a lot of Western Literature, my outlook towards life began to change, and my very thinking process underwent a change. My mother let go of her desire to see me married as she was convinced that I would not listen to her. But then, Life had something else in store for me. Coming in contact with Swami Rama made me realise that I am part of a very great Himalayan tradition. I learned that this tradition encompassed all the Rishis-who look out for the good of humanity as a whole and continue to strive for our betterment. With a lot of compassion, they continue to reveal the secrets of Sādhana to generations of humanity, and this is why they are so significant in our lives. They keep guiding us, and this awareness also turns into experience!

So now you must be wondering what about those who are not part of this tradition? Swami Rama states that every other tradition or practice comes under the Himalayan tradition, the ultimate all-encompassing tradition. It is likely that some of you might feel offended by such a profound statement, but then it is the truth. This is one tradition that is not bound by tradition, caste, language, religion, skin colour, or geographical boundaries. Here, I would like to remind you of his words: 'This is the eternal and continuous process towards Truth.'

***

Among common people, the image of a Rishi is one who is clad in saffron with a long flowing beard, his knotted hair tied in the shape of a bun, a rudrakshi mala hanging from the neck, whose forehead is adorned with vermilion, ashes all over the body and forehead, has a Dandakamandala in one hand and is forever in meditation! They think of Rishis as being unpresentable and of no value to the present time; the mind keeps rejecting their lifestyle as being impractical in today's age. These biases prevent us from understanding and recognising that the Rishis are forever amongst us. It is time we imagined Rishis in a contemporary way, for example, as one wearing regular jeans and a T-shirt!! The old image of a Rishi is so ingrained in us that even if a Rishi were to appear, we would ignore him as someone in a fancy costume. This fictional situation has been hilariously portrayed in the Kannada movie 'Nārada Vijaya,' wherein the Sage Nārada comes down to Earth, roams around the streets of Bengaluru, even visiting the Vidhana Soudha, where the state government's administration is carried out from, all the while telling people that he is Sage Nārada himself only for onlookers to simply ignore him. We have conditioned our brains so much that even if the Guru, out of love and compassion, were to show us Lord Shiva Himself, we still would not believe him! It is for precisely this reason that the Guru does not undertake such feats without a specific purpose. Only those who are eligible for such Divine experiences get to experience it.

In English, Rishi means seer. However, this does not capture the true meaning of who Rishi is, as compared to Sanskrit. A Rishi is not one who merely sees but one who sees that which even the Sun cannot see. A Rishi is one who sees through his inner eye, who has understood the mysteries of the universe with his inner eye.

Rishi is a Tapasvi as well. Tapa (endurance) is an integral part of Tapasvi. One who endures is a Tapasvi; here to endure does not mean mere physical endurance but also mental and emotional endurance. Just as a Caterpillar has to endure many hardships to turn into a Beautiful Butterfly, a Tapasvi needs to endure much struggle and hardship to attain the inner transformation. A person who can give up, endure much struggle and hardships, and yet perseveres in his/her mission becomes a Rishi or Rishika if it is a woman.

Gold, in its naturally occurring state, is nothing but a stone. In the depths of the Earth, which is covered in mud and various impurities, its lustre is never visible. When the stone is cleaned, and the impurities are melted in the fire, the Gold attains its lustre. Fire is an enabler. Similarly, the Human Body also needs to burn its impurities, but without an inner fire, no cleansing can happen. Only when he endures, while the inner fire burns these impurities, does a Human being shine with the lustre of gold, as a radiant being.

A person who has crossed these limitations and stands at the peak of such purity is a Rishi. There is nothing that he cannot see; Nature listens to him. I am reminded of an incident narrated by Swami Rama about his Guru and an Avalanche. Once, when Swami Rama was trekking in the snow-covered Himalayas with his Guru, Bengali Baba, an Avalanche got triggered and was hurtled down towards them. Just as Swami Rama began to think that they would be trapped in the Avalanche and die, Bengali Baba said," Fear not. I'm with you!" Just as the Avalanche was about to cross their path, Bengali Baba instructed the Avalanche to stop, and there it froze! Swami Rama witnessed that once they crossed over, the Avalanche continued, leaving no trace of their path. When the Guru wishes, he can control all the five elements at will, but he will never go against nature just to display his powers. This very incident is proof that he is forever mindful of Nature's freedom. Only when one has such control over oneself can one become a Rishi.

Fourteen Lokas (realms of Existence) and we, in this Universe

A Rishi is beyond everything; there is nothing that is impossible for a Rishi. Rishis are content to reside in their World. Now you must be wondering what world these Rishis inhabit!? If I Am to answer this question, you must understand the Fourteen different realms that exist. According to the Puranas, Vedic Cosmology and the Atharva Veda, there are Fourteen Realms of existence. Most importantly, these are divided into two halves: Urdva Loka/Unnatha Sthana/Vyahruthi and Adho Loka/Pathala. This egg-shaped Universe has 7 Urdva Lokas and 7 Adho Lokas. Bhooloka, Bhuvaraloka, Swaraloka, Maharloka, Janaloka, Tapoloka, Satyaloka (BrahmaLoka) are the 7 Urdva Lokas, while Athala, Vithala, Sutala, Rasaathala, Thalaathala, Mahathala, Pathala are the 7 Adho Lokas. Below these is Naraka Loka. All these Lokas are present in this material world, itself.

Where are these 7 Urdva Lokas, you must be wondering? Satya Loka is at the top, and it is also the place where Brahma resides. He is the creator, the root of all creation; all knowledge in the universe resides here. Those who reside here never die, suffer no ailments, are always healthy, suffer no pain or sadness; only peace, stability, contentment, and calmness prevail here. This is the place where Yogis and Rishis, who have cut off their connection with the physical world; having attained the higher spiritual knowledge through generations of penance, are in a samadhi state encompassing knowledge of the Divine, reside.

Tapoloka is below Satya Loka, the place where Tapasvis' reside. Tapasvis' being eternal, Angels, Celestial beings, highly knowledgeable, can move to Satya Loka with relative ease. The Great Fire that causes immense destruction cannot destroy them. This is also the place where the 4 Kumaras, namely Sanatha Kumara, Sanaka, Sanandhana and Sanathana Kumara, reside. Having gained immortality and glowing like pure crystals, they are like forms of energy for whom the journey to Satya Loka is easily achieved.

Slightly below Tapoloka is Jnanaloka. Great Rishis, Enlightened Beings like Rishi Markandeya, reside here. Those who reside here have overcome the attractions of the Physical World and are in total control of their emotions.

After this is Maharloka, situated above Dhruva Loka of the well-known Dhruvathare, the abode of saints; their stay in this world is equivalent to one Brahma Dina / Cosmic cycle. They have the qualifications to communicate with people from all over the world.

Then comes Swaraloka or Swarga Loka. Lord Indra rules over this world and is responsible for guarding the Universe. He resides atop Mount Meru; while this beautiful, wondrous world immersed in splendour and filled with countless riches is inhabited by Divya Purushas, Gandharvas, and Apsaras. Amaravathi is the Capital of Swarga Loka. Indra possesses, Kamadheu, a holy cow from the churning of the sea, the Three-Headed holy elephant Airavatha, and Uchaishrava, the holy galloping Horse. Higher souls travel to Swarga Loka after their death in order to enjoy the fruits of their good Karma. Here, if they are able to overcome their base desires and serve with devotion, they can progress to Maharloka, but if they give in to their desires, then they go back to their lower world.

Below Swaraloka to the east of Dhruvaloka is Bhuvarloka. This is an Eternal and Spiritual world that acts as a gateway between the Physical world and the Spiritual Realm. The Siddhas and Heavenly beings communicate with this world. There is a Saptarshi Loka, located below Dhruvaloka, whose Seven Rishis are the guiding lights for Humanity, extending a helping hand when in need. Maharishi

Vashishta, the Guru of Surya Vamsha; Vishwamitra, who was a guiding force and Guru of Sree Rama; Sage Dhruvasa who could burn the karmas of his disciples by the sheer intensity of his anger; are some of the Rishis who are in the Saptarshi Loka. The various knowledgeable residents of the Surya Loka, Chandra Loka, and Nakshathra Loka are all able to communicate with the various Worlds while still residing in their respective worlds. The Sky is at the bottom most portion, below the Urdva Lokas, and right above Earth. The Sky contains within itself Yakshas, Rakshasas, and Spirits, which can be divine or harmful, as well as a lot of small microbial living beings.

Right at the bottom of the Urdva Lokas is Bhooloka, also referred to as Prithvi. This is where humans live, along with animals, plants, and so on. It is made of Vast Oceans, Rivers, Forests and Towering Mountain ranges. It is so vast that the rays from the Sun and the Moon tend to set over it. Also referred to as Martya Loka, the world of Mortals, or Jumbudvipa, Bhooloka is the first of the 7 Urdva Lokas, and the Ado Lokas are supposedly geographically below Bhooloka. Humans are reborn in different lokas according to their Karmas, and in that sense, it could be inferred that these lokas are various states of awareness of the soul. To elaborate further, the human body is divided into various lokas; right from the skull on top to the soles of the feet, it encompasses the various lokas, which also affect the mental conditioning of humans. Yajur Veda, one among the 4 Vedas, captures this phenomenon in a very significant phrase: "Yatha Pinde Tatha Brahmande; Yatha Brahmande Tatha Pinde" (that which encompasses an atom encompasses the Cosmos; that which encompasses the Cosmos encompasses an atom) which roughly means - as is the atom, so is the Cosmos.

Now try to imagine such a vast Cosmos; where do we find our insignificant selves in that vastness in which the Rishis also reside? Rishi's are content in the world they reside in. If you were to pray for their appearance, they might grant an audience, but if you are convinced they do not exist, then why should they appear before you? It is only after facing innumerable difficulties, ill health, and loss of mental strength that you even begin to accept that there is a power beyond your imagination, but by then, it is too late for you to even pray! Under such circumstances, when you undertake a journey through self, you may experience that power. Such a journey is time-consuming, which is why the mind is considered the most ancient of travellers! There comes a point when, after having been repeatedly ground by the various Karmas, he realises that this is not his true self and yearns for liberation. This yearning prepares him to meet his Guru, and the Guru guides him through the path. This is what our scriptures mean when they say, "The Guru appears when the Disciple is ready." In this manner, a meaningful spiritual journey begins.

The Saptarishis and various other Rishis are great examples of how we can harness our inner energies when we lead highly disciplined lives. When we study and learn about any of the Rishis, we feel they are capable of performing feats that humans cannot. They appear to have the same human features that we all have, but the secret behind their super-human feats is their Sādhana. The Rishis are our Ideals to realise that if we have the resolve, then even being in this human form, we are capable of extraordinary accomplishments. Think about it: In today's world, who does society consider to be a role model or Ideal? Film stars? Cricketers? Politicians? Parents? Friends? Teachers? All burdened by their past, anxious about the future, unable to live in the present, and trapped in the cycle of Karma. How can they guide us on the right path?

The responsibility of passing on this valuable knowledge and facts about the Rishis to future generations rests with us. It is with this intention that I am sharing my experiences with you. It is imperative that you mentally prepare yourself before you read about these experiences; it is only then that you will realise their importance.

***

A Journey To Satyaloka- The Real World

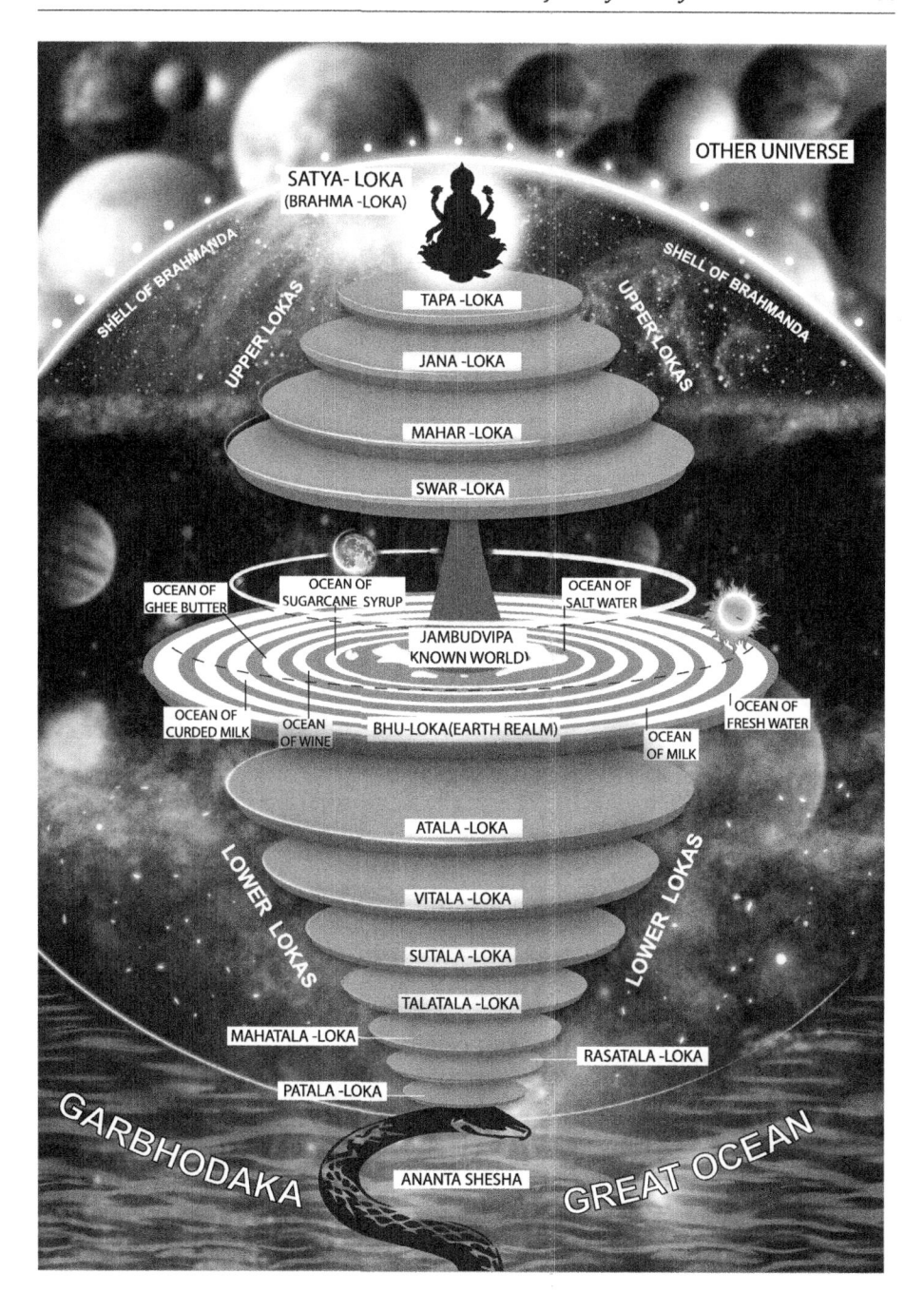

23

PART 1: CHINNAMASTĀ MEANS A SEVERED HEAD

I was sweating profusely despite the shivering chill; the time was 5-5:10 in the winter morning. It was still dark outside. Newborn morning rays were just striking the ground. No one was around to respond, even if I called out to them. It was frightening to stay outside. It was terrifying to go inside. Ohhh! What happened to Baba? Why did he have to die for me? If I step inside, there is blood! What do I do? What do I tell the police when they enquire on arrival?

***

It is a rarity to be accepted as a disciple by an adept Guru in Srividya. If one is accepted, then it is a matter of absolute blessing and fortune. Likewise, if one is initiated into mantra practice by one such Guru, then it indicates that the life of such an initiate is truly purposeful and fulfilled. Even if the initiate is unable to complete one's Srividya practices in this life for some reason, the soul will be blessed with another human life to attain that fulfilment by the grace of the Guru.

Guru Sri Rama initiated me by mantras unto the Samayāchāra tradition of Srividya Practice in 1992. At that time, he had told two points, as I have shared with you elsewhere.

First, he said, "I am now linking you to the Rishis of our lineage and bringing you under their protection." Second, he initiated me into the foremost of Srividya practices – the Shāmbhavi Deeksha (initiation). This is one of the rare amongst Sri Vidya practices. At the time of initiation, he had said "I am initiating you in the very presence of Shiva!" I had not realised at the time that it would be the holiest of moments in my life.

Later, as you know in 1996, after leaving his mortal body, Swami Rama directed me to learn and practice Sri Vidya in the Dakshināchāra tradition under Sri Rā Sā Gurugalu, hailing from Mysuru. After many years of practice in the Dakshināchāra tradition under Rā Sā Gurugalu, one day, he taught me the Panchadashi mantra and said, "With this, I have completed passing all the knowledge that I needed to pass on to you. There is nothing beyond the Panchadashi mantra to be taught. You may now move forward and continue your practices. Now you may return to your Guru." I felt the skies break over me. I asked, "What does 'may return to' mean?" He replied, "You may now return to your Guru Swami Rama." I composed myself and beseeched him, "Gurugale, why are you speaking like this today? Does the relationship between the student and preceptor ever conclude with the teachings? How much love you have showered on me? Why are you suddenly saying this? You have always blessed me with all that I needed in life. I never perceived Swami Rama and you as separate." I tried to reason with him. But Gurugalu was very grim. He seemed fierce and said, "No, dear! Enough. You may now return to your Guru." I pleaded with him and said, "Why so, Gurugale? Why should I not stay with you? What mistake did I do?"

"Being with 2 Gurus is like being a harlot," he said. How intensely I felt after I listened to that. A thunderous whip! I did not cry in front of him despite being choked in pain. For the first time, and perhaps the last, I left without a word of farewell, picking up my bag and stomping away hurriedly from there. Gurugalu did not even stop me. I was supposed to return to Bengaluru, but I did not feel like it. I got down in Chennapatna itself and took an auto to the outskirts of that town where our ashram was. I called home in Bengaluru and said, "I am going to stay here tonight" I could not sleep the whole night. I was confused and distressed. The question nagged me to no end as to why Gurugalu spoke thus with me.

The next day, I got up as usual early in the morning.

Gurugalu had asked me to keep practising panchadashi. Thinking I should at least do that, I went to my room at Gurunivasa and sat for meditation. About 5-10 minutes might have passed. Tears burst out, overwhelming me, and I spoke my heart out to Swami Rama. I was completely upset and lamented, "Gurugalu said so and so….. I never differentiated between the two of you. I never had felt that the two of you were separate. Yet, why did Gurugalu push me away like this? I don't understand at all, that too, using such demeaning words! You only have to show me what I need to do. I am unable to comprehend anything. Why am I in this circumstance? After Gurugalu showered me with so much love, taught me everything, and blessed me with all requisites in life, how could he utter such words at this juncture in my life? How am I to comprehend this? How am I to accept this? I do not understand. I am deeply shocked. I sobbed as I conveyed each of my words. I looked at Swami Rama's photo on the wall and thought, "I know that you are listening to all that I am saying now. I have no doubt."

All of a sudden, Baba projected into this reality from the photo and stood in front of me. It was winter, and there was quite a chilly breeze. I was the only one at Gurunivasa. No one was around. Not many were there at the ashram. Gurudēva was standing right in front of me in his white kurta pyjama, just as in the photo. Instantly, he cut off his head with his right hand as if it were a sword! The blood just splashed forward! Baba started laughing loudly! His laughter echoed through the skies! Hah hah hah hah....! Even as I was watching, his severed head fell to the floor. The head continued to laugh! Blood meandered mellow from the body continuously. In a few minutes, the room was filled with blood. The whole scenario felt gruesome. The loud cackling laughter – hah hah hah hah, ripped across the room, and a stream of blood gushed forth silently from Baba's body.

I felt choked and dizzy. When I poised myself a bit and saw, his head that had fallen near me was still laughing!

The room was flooded with blood. Unable to bear it, I somehow leapt across and ran out of the room. I went to the garden and sat on a chair petrified and completely out of breath. I was sweating profusely despite the shivering chill; the time was 5-5:10 in the morning. It was still dark outside. Newborn morning rays were just striking the ground. No one was around to respond, even if I called out to them. It was frightening to stay outside. It was terrifying to go inside. Ohhh! What happened to Baba? Why did he have to die for me? If I step inside, there is blood! What do I do? What do I tell the police when they enquire on arrival? Even if I tell, will anybody believe this? They will convict me of murder. I was overcome with fear and sorrow. I was riddled with queries. I sat still, without moving a limb, for almost 45 minutes. A little light trickled through in the sky. What to do? Even if I wanted to return, my tote bag was in that room. My purse and money were all in that.

Slowly, I gathered up some courage and paced myself as I treaded forward very slowly towards that dreaded room when I moved the door, Woah! There was nothing! No blood, no head, no body, there was no sign of anything there. Yet, I could not stay there. Without having breakfast, I hurried back to Bengaluru.

After returning home, I called Gurugalu in Mysuru around 10:30-11 AM since I knew he would be a little free at the time, having finished his daily worship. It was as if he was waiting for my call! He answered instantly. I explained all that had happened and then said, "Please forgive me. Being upset, I left without a word of farewell yesterday" I kept thinking he would nicely reprimand me for being delusional and say that I was hallucinating, and yet I had explained all that I had experienced. But Gurugalu started laughing mirthfully, listening to me. He was amused for quite a while. It was a distinct moment of rapture for him, too. After a while of cheerful laughter, he said softly, "OK, Good. Continue with your Panchadashi practices. After a few more days or whenever you feel like it, you may come here."

Hmmm, now what is the meaning of all this?

"This is Chhinna-masthā."

***

24

PART 2: CHINNAMASTĀ MEANS REBIRTH

"I am dying! My time is over! I am grieving deeply in my heart!"

I reached Mysuru Gurugalu's residence in such a desperate state. He was sitting there as if he awaited my arrival.

Gurugalu graced me with life – a resurrection!

He sat still with his palm over my head for over 45 minutes. I was inanimate. Tears flowed out effortlessly in a continuous stream from my eyes. It was a state of non-being. Isn't death so? Death is not just the annihilation of ego but also the end of life as I knew it. My former existence never returned. "The old me is not there, gone away forever so that I became a good instrument in the hands of the tradition." I became a tool in the hands of the Paramparā (lineage)!

***

In fact, it was a particular incident that led to me being in this condition today. There had been a preceding event too.

By then, Pattabhiramji was no more. On one end, the agonising loneliness of losing my life partner and feeling orphaned, and on the other end, the overwhelming responsibilities of Swami Rama Sādhana Dhaama, the ashram. This is not fate; this is reality. This has to be accepted. I took residence at Swami Rama Sādhana Dhaama to fulfil my responsibilities. The construction work of some buildings was happening in a full-fledged manner there. I was under regular physical stress since it was mainly my obligation to supervise. In general, I was under some duress. Amidst all this, I had a strange experience. I constantly felt somebody's presence with me all the time, but I could not see anybody when I turned to see who it was. I would wonder for a moment as to what is happening and then continue through the rush of my day. But, after that, the event that ensued left an indelible mark on me.

One day, I was cleaning up the photo of Swami Rama in the pyramid meditation centre of our ashram. Suddenly, I saw a peculiar lizard behind Baba's portrait. I had never seen that kind of a lizard at our ashram until then. Unusually black and uncommonly large. I stood for a bit, looking at it, surprised. Later, I composed myself. I kept Baba's portrait aside on the chair near me and turned. That lizard was nowhere to be seen.

There was no way that kind of a lizard could hide so easily over the wall or any crevice, yet it had vanished! I finished cleaning up the room and was almost stepping out of the room as I closed the door when I abruptly remembered my Paramaguru– Baba's Guru – Bengali Baba. I swiftly realised the meaning behind the vanishing lizard and the feeling that somebody was constantly with me!

For almost 45 days subsequently, I realised Bengali Baba blessed me with divine protection to alleviate my sufferings and remove my sense of being orphaned in time. I started frequently seeing that big jet-black lizard. It would be still on the wall or door, as if in meditation, for about 6-8 hours. This way, Bangali Baba mutely made sure I realised his presence.

On one such day, I was seated for meditation. The ashram was pin drop silent. All of a sudden, a piercing raucous angry voice said, "Sit straight," as if it came from the skies above.

I was stunned aback as I was sitting in my meditation posture and straightened my back an inch further in my stance. My spine was straight, including the very tip. My body and mind were extremely alert. My consciousness was concentrated at the focal point of the thousand-petalled lotus of the sahasraara chakra. I was seated absolutely still and insensate. My breathing was feeble at the mooladhaara chakra. These happened spontaneously without my efforts. Even before I realised what was happening, my head was severed.

Behold!, it was Chinnamastā!

I remembered my previous experience with Baba and thought my head also must have rolled somewhere alongside. No! My head was separated but still in the space about half a foot above my neck! It was completely cut at the Vishuddha chakra, floating in the air, suspended above my neck with some empty space that shining like a column of white light. While I watched this process, my head gradually retook its place over my neck! My chanting practice that was stunned to a stop in fear, resumed.

Later, I completed my chanting and meditation as usual. I got drowned in the mundane work that demanded my attention. I came to have lunch with a sādhaka (spiritual practitioner) in our ashram. I was about to finish the last morsel of my food when the morning events flashed like thunder across my mind. I just dropped my hand down. I could not eat at all. Now, my head was completely severed, and it was suspended above my neck over an empty space that shined like a column of light. There was no face, no mouth, how do I eat?

My hands froze. The sadhaka with me panicked and shook me, calling out "Amma, Amma."

"I am conscious, dear," I said, conveying my meditation experiences from the morning that day.

I said, "I can completely sense the absence of my neck right now. Once you check!"

"Everything is normal, Amma," he replied.

But I did not feel anything normal. I could not feel my neck. I distinctly felt space between my shoulders and my head. How do I eat?

"Amma, please compose yourself. There is nothing wrong. Everything is alright. Get up. Wash your hands. Rest for a bit," he said in an attempt to pacify me.

"No, dear. This is something very serious. I have to do something about my head," I rambled.

Somehow, I got up and started walking so cautiously like I was balancing a few pots, one above the other, over my head. If not, my head might roll off due to imbalance. In fact, I started feeling maybe it's time for me to leave this body. I just said what I felt, and he panicked even more.

"I'll get the car here. Let's go to the doctor," he said. My voice had completely changed by now. In a feeble voice, I said, "Doctors cannot help me. My time has come. I am dying. I am very sad. I am in a deep depression."

"No Amma. Nothing has happened to you. You are healthy. You are alright. Please come out of this" he requested. I steamed out in anger "you cannot understand this. You won't understand..."

Not knowing what else to do, he suggested, "Amma, shall we go to Rā Sā Gurugalu?"

That's when it seeped into me: "Ah, yes, I could go to my Guru." We immediately boarded the car and went to Mysuru to see our Gurugalu. Throughout the journey, I babbled, "I am dying slowly. My time is over. I am feeling intense agony. I am in deep pain! I wonder how he must have driven the car listening to all this. Finally, we reached Mysuru. Gurugalu was seated as if he were awaiting us.

As soon as we went, he casually asked, "How are you? How come you came so suddenly, out of the blue? Is everyone alright at home? There was silence, and then I asked, "Gurugale, do I look alright to you?"

I felt my head would roll off even if I spoke a little loudly. I was sitting in the chair in front of my Guru. With inquisitive tenderness, he asked, "What, what happened to you?" I replied, "Gurugale, my head was separated from my neck a few hours back. I can clearly sense an empty space in between. Whatever I do, my head won't return to its former state. I have realised I am dying! So, I came to see you." Gurugalu became very grim then.

He said "yes" and looked at me. He pulled his chair towards me. "Now, close your eyes," he said. He knew what had happened to me. He abruptly smacked the crown of my head, downwards. At that time, I felt my head come back to its place on my neck, as it was before. In reality, although my mortal body was intact after my experiences in the morning meditation, my subtle body was still discordant, having been slit at the neck. I had constantly been sensing that gap in my subtle body since then. Gurugalu did not move his palm from my head, even a bit, for 45 minutes. I was not myself in the interim. This long process had resurrected me. I received another birth from my Gurugalu.

Few months after this, another incident occurred.

I already had thyroid issues and was undergoing treatment, but I never felt its seriousness in my body. The problem required immediate surgical intervention, and despite looking minuscule in the initial presentation, it had quickly enlarged onto a drastic-sized mass internally. The doctor had to remove it with a lot of effort. He was very shocked and exclaimed, "How did you live with this in your throat?" He shared the reports with my daughter Sadhana, who is also a doctor. She explained that the tumour mass was quite risky and was at such a stage that it could have turned cancerous at any moment. I was flummoxed listening to them since I had not even experienced discomfort or pain until then. But, by the time the surgery was over, my voice was gone!

I clearly realised that all this happened as a consequence of some actions (bad karma) from my previous births. Some bad deed related to the speech was troubling me, not allowing me to talk. I had to write and communicate everything. How much can one really write? This continued this way for 2 years. Eventually, I became very solitary. I could never voice myself. I did not believe my voice would return, and neither did the doctors assure me so. My state of mind was such that I did not want my voice anymore. My Guru was with me!

That is enough for this life. I started meeting him more often. But I could not utter a single word. Gurugalu constantly cared for me. He would place his hand over my throat and heal me every time I went there. He cleansed all that karma from me. What and all did my Guru not do for me? He has done everything! Now, my voice has returned to a great extent, although not to absolute normalcy like before. Likewise, I was also blessed with the capacity to speak again. Another aspect of my experience is that Divine Mother Chinnamastā, who pleases quickly, came back to my life this way in order to accelerate my Sādhana and drive me on the path forward. Mortally, I was operated on by the doctors, yes, but Divine Mother had already worked on my subtle body much before in order to heal me, together with Guru's love and compassion. I do have to mention in great reverence and gratitude, Bengali Baba's presence, who brought the Grace of Chinnamastā in my life by his blessings. It is also imperative to mention that Divine Mother Chinnamastā is his family deity.

***

Who is this Mother Divine Chinnamastā? One might wonder what her special qualities or energies are. To comprehend this, one must understand what the 36 tattvas (or principal existences) and the Dasha Maha Vidyas (10 Great Wisdom Goddesses) are.

As per tantra Shāstra (study of the technique by which one may reveal the divinity residing within oneself), the universe is made up of 36 tattvas. The 36 tattvas in the descending order are:

1. Shiva (absolute consciousness),

2. Shakthi (manifest dynamism),

3. SadaShiva (all-encompassing),

4. Ishvara (omniscient),

5. Shuddha Vidya (pure knowledge),

6. Maya (veiling power),

7. Kala (nature of attributes),

8. Vidya (knowledge),

9. Raaga (attachment),

10. Kaala (time),

11. Niyathi (limitation),

12. Purusha (the existential principle),

13. Prakruthi (the creative principle),

14. Ahankara (ego),

15. Buddhi (intellect),

16. Manas (mind),

17. Chakshu (eyes),

18. Srotra (ears),

19. Ghraana (nose),

20. Rasanaa (tongue),

21. Tvak (skin),

22. Vak (speech),

23. Paada (movement),

24. Paani (grasping),

25. Paayu (excretion),

26. Upastha (reproduction),

27. Gandha (smell),

28. Rasa (taste),

29. Roopa (visual),

30. Sparsha (touch),

31. Shabdha (auditory),

32. Prithvi (Earth),

33. Jala (water),

34. Tejas (fire/light),

35. Vayu (air), and

36. Akasha (space).

The Dasha Maha Vidyas are

1. Kali,

2. Tara,

3. Tripura Sundari,

4. Bhuvaneshwari,

5. Bhiravi,

6. Chinnamastā,

7. Dhoomavathi,

8. Bagalamukhi,

9. Mathangi, and

10. Kamalathmika.

To approach Chinnasmatha, one must first understand the 14th tattva - ahankara, the 6th Dasha Mahavidya - Chinnamastā, and the interplay between the 2. It is very difficult to get rid of the principal entity of ego within us. It is a subtle entity that surpasses arrogance. It is impossible to liberate oneself without getting rid of one's ego. This ego must be dissolved in order to experience the 5th tattva, " the Shudha Vidya," and to realise the inner self. Ego is the darkness of ignorance. It is quite impossible to remove this by human effort. But for Srividya practitioners, this dissolution of ego is a shielding protection bestowed by the grace of the Guru and Mother Bhagavathi. Beyond the Shuddha Vidya are the Ishvara tattva, Sadashiva, Sakthi

Part 2: Chinnamastā means rebirth

and Shiva tattvas, and to practice and surpass each of these tattvas and wade into the realms beyond tattvas, where there are no more tattvas, and to receive the Anugraha of Parama Shiva, one needs the absolute anchor of this tattva.

The link between this ahankara tattva and Mother Chinnamastā – one of the Dasha Maha Vidyas, is very exceptional. Chinnamastā is a tantric path of eliminating the ego of the practitioner and having a new life – a rebirth. Doesn't the word Chinnamastā itself mean "severed head"? Isn't this a death? But what kind of death is it? A death that gives the elixir of life!

As the practitioner is born again, he is completely drenched in the grace of the Guru and Mother Divine. The path of Chinnamastā is the quickest way to get rid of the ego that blocks the path towards liberation.

She is also known as Prachanda Chandika. Decked with diamonds as Indrani – the consort of Lord Indra. She is an aspect of Mother Durga. She is lustrous like diamonds and has a lightning bright form. She is a tremendously powerful form of the Mother Divine that can grace a seeker with Her vision in a trice.

Chinnamastā is the power of lightning as well. It is not an ordinary energy to manifest. It can radically transform the practitioner. The electricity we use is one aspect of her energy. In a subtle sense, it is an energy that breaks away the ignorance and anchors as the power of inner sight within the practitioner.

In introspection, Chinnamastā Is the kundalini shakthi in itself. She activates the Kundalini by enshrining the Kundalini energy at the eternal beyond the Sahasraara chakra after causing it to surge up from the bottom of the spine.

There is a secret in the practice of Chinnamastā Sādhana. The adept yogis and yoginis in this path of tantra make their consciousness exit from the Sahasrāra chakra through the path of the Sushumna Nādi as they approach the time of their death.

The prana, or life force of the ignorant masses who are unaware of this tantra, exits from other points or holes in the body. This causes the soul to lose its way and endure much strife in its later journeys. Hence by the propitiation and meditation of Mother Chinnamastā, one can directly (without the involvement of any lower chakras) activate one's Kundalini shakthi by raising it directly to one's third eye or the ajñā chakra (the seat of Mother Chinnamastā).

The visual form of Mother Chinnamastā

A naked headless form, holding the head in the right hand. A sword in her left hand. The tongue extending from the head is voraciously swallowing the central bloodstream that is flowing out of the open neck.

The essence of Mother Chinnamastā

The visual and word implications of Chinnamastā with a severed head verily signify liberation. She is terrible to witness. Yet, Her very face beams with the intoxication of bliss. Her presence in the aspirant is a direct experience beyond the limits of philosophical understanding to stay in the space of reality in life.

Swami Rama writes beautifully about Mother Chinnamastā. The senior disciple of Swami Rama, Pandit Rajamani Tigunait explicates Chinnamastā thus in his book "At the Eleventh hour" that presents conversations he had with Swami Rama.

'Mother Chinnamastā is the protector of the yogis. She is the mother who bestows the fruits of the yogic practices or yoga siddhis. For this, she persistently asks for the yogi's heads! If you offer your head or blood to her companions, she is capable of providing the practitioner with emancipation that is beyond death. For one to fulfil this practice, one may need over 2 lives. Only the senior yogis, who have overcome the fear of death and suffering, may try to practice this Sādhana. Death is no obstacle for this practice but is an ally in this path towards receiving Mother Chinnamastā's grace and blessings.'

Mother Chinnamastā is feasible. The text 'Shakthi Sangama Tantra' elucidates this very clearly.

Furthermore, Mother Chinnasmatha is the deity of the family of our Bengali Baba. The Chinnamastā siddhi is one of the many achievements of Bengali Baba's practices. He had accomplished the Chinnamastā Sādhana. Babaji was renamed "Dharmadas" as twice born after being initiated into monkhood at the temple of Mother Chinnamastā.

Swami Rama says that at the time of initiation, the Guru of Sri Rama Krishna Paramahamsa – Rishi Totapuri, was also there, and he rained blessings on Babaji. Bengali Baba had the power to resurrect the dead, which is demonstrated in the narratives of the life of his monk disciple Bhaval Prince.

***

Messages from the Himalayan Sages: Timely & Timeless

Section 4

- Sage Agasthya's messages
- Temple Cat and the Nurturing Mother
- Animā Siddhi Agastya Entered My Throat
- Mere gaze granted mystic moon knowledge.
- Chandra Vidya and Tithinitya practice

25

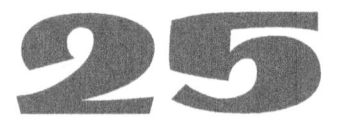

SAGE AGASTHYA'S MESSAGES

A potbellied, dwarf-like physical appearance does make Sage Agastya stand out among Rishis. It is not his physical attributes, though, but the fact that he is a Siddha beyond the realm of imagination, with profound knowledge and his immense contribution to mankind, which makes him stand apart among all the Rishis.

Listening to the tales of Sage Agastya, you may be able to grasp his psychic powers, and the heights of his attainments by way of the distance he covered to travel to reach the southern parts of India.

His Sādhana. His achievements, and his contributions are beyond what an ordinary human being is capable of; they are of a divine nature. The numerous tales of Sage Agastya, such as using his Tapa Shakthi to stop the egotistical upward rise of the Vindhyas, freeing the world of the tricks of the Demons Vatapi and Ilwala who threatened to trap it, helping the Gods to destroy the demons, by swallowing the ocean in which the Demons were hiding after the death of their master demon Vritra enlighten us about his capabilities.

Sage Agastya and South India have a huge connection. He came down and stayed in South India to guide people on the spiritual path. There are many shrines dedicated to Sage Agastya and his miracles, that are household names to even this day in Tamilnadu and Karnataka. The Lalithasahasthranama and numerous other hymns have been passed on to humanity by Him. Even now, he guides us in our spiritual journey through the various Sādhanas; as proof of it, various accounts of meeting him are narrated here. Presenting a few chapters of his Glory.

***

26

TEMPLE CAT AND THE NURTURING MOTHER

We were inexplicably pulled towards this place by an unknown force. Despite our best efforts to reach the place we had initially planned, destiny led us in a very different direction. We were unaware that such a place existed until we stepped out of the car and looked at this magnificent temple!!

***

This incident unfolded when I was deeply immersed in Sri Vidya anuṣṭāna under the guidance of Rā Sā Gurugalu. Following our lineage's custom, the dissemination of knowledge occurred in profound silence!!

We were inexplicably drawn to this place by an unknown force. Despite our best efforts to reach the place we had initially planned, destiny guided us to this tiny remote village nestled in the interiors of Tamil Nadu. The existence of such a temple was that revelation, a temple to be unveiled. As we stepped out of the car, we saw the magnificent temple of Sri Lalitha Tripura Sundari and Meghanatha Swami in a remote village with a countable number of houses in Thirumeyachur!! The view that came into sight left us in awe.

Until that day, I had never encountered such an ancient and majestic temple dedicated to Sri Lalitha Tripura Sundari anywhere in Karnataka. This temple in Thirumeyachur was not just a structure but a powerful and mystifying entity, a testament to the sacred principles of the Āgama Śāstra.

The temple premise was bustling with people, possibly because of the festival on that day.

We entered the sanctum precisely during Maṅgaḷārati. After having a blessed darshan of the goddess, I received prasada and stepped out. I started observing the temple architecture. In one corner stood the Lalitha Tripura Sundari temple; at another corner, the Meghanatha Swami Temple.

I, along with two of my disciples, was entering the inner Sanctum of the Meghanatha Swami Temple when I noticed a White Cat following me wherever I went. Initially, I assumed that since food was plentiful in the temple, it was only natural that cats would also be present. But then this cat was insistent on following me, walking around me in circles, even standing along with me when I stood in the queue for the Prasada. It kept looking at the Prasada in my hand and my face alternately as if trying to say something to me. We stepped outside the temple, went towards a shaded area and sat down; the cat followed us diligently and sat beside me.

Generally, we consume the Prasada, maybe share a morsel with the cat, and then leave. On that day, something unusual but interesting happened. After feeding a morsel to the cat, I was about to consume the Prasada when I felt a change inside me. I started feeding the Prasada, with a lot of motherly love, to everyone there. Everyone around me was surprised!! I even fed the cat while it was constantly gazing at me. Just as I finished feeding the Prasada to everyone, the cat disappeared right before my eyes!

Sitting beside me, did Bhagawathi herself awaken my motherly, nurturing self, inspiring me to share with others? That day, she gave a very clear instruction - "Share with everyone."

What was I to share; she would not go to such great lengths for me to merely share the Prasada? If so, what else I am supposed to share with others?

This was our first visit to the Sri Lalitha Tripura Sundari temple!

***

27

ANIMĀ SIDDHI AGASTYA ENTERED MY THROAT

As soon as I began chanting Nīlapatāka Devi japa, Rishi Agastya appeared before me. With his Aṇimā siddhi, an ability to reduce one's body to the size of an atom, he shrank his body to one or one and a half inches. As I continued observing, he directly entered my throat and positioned himself at its base! I could feel his presence in my throat, leaving me anxious and uncertain about what to do next.

***

Gaurav, his friend, a few of my disciples, and I were en route to Kanyakumari when we learned that the Lalitha Tripura Sundari temple was on the way, so we decided to seek Devi's darshan. Since it was a Friday, the temple was crowded, and we entered the sanctum precisely during Mangalārathi, a sight to behold. It was a glorious aarathi; my eyes were fixed on Bhagavathi.

The goddess is not just an idol but a mandala of life force; to fill in her image in our psyche, we have to gaze at the Bhagavathi throughout the ārathi. When we witness the celestial beauty of the idol in the light of Mangalārathi, it leads us to internal Dhāraṇa, a single pointed focus. That is precisely why we should observe the ārathi with open eyes. For the next 10-15 minutes, the ārathi continued uninterrupted. I was utterly absorbed in marvelling at the exquisite idol of Devi as each form of aarathi was lit in succession by the priest. Due to the crowded inner sanctum, we had to adjust our positions and crane our necks to catch a glimpse of the ceremony. Amidst the crowd, a saffron-clad sanyasi ahead of me in the line drew my attention. His messy hair, matted locks, and grey beard indicated that he hadn't bathed or washed his face for days.

At first, he kept looking back, and then suddenly, he turned away from the ārathi and started staring in my direction; I first assumed he must be looking at someone behind me. But then I realised that he was staring at me! As I became aware of him staring at me, I could not concentrate on the ārathi because he was now effectively blocking my view of the Devi. He seemed to smile, revealing his crooked teeth, but it was more like he was teasing me. I did not acknowledge his smile; his weird behaviour made me wonder if he was mentally disturbed. I tried to, once again, focus on Mangalārathi, but he continued to stare at me, drawing my attention to him. He was now rubbing his forefinger from the tip of his nose to his forehead while continuing to gaze at me. He then turned around to watch the Mangalarathi, and after about 2 minutes, he once again looked at me, rubbing hard his forefinger from the tip of his nose to his forehead as if trying to convey something to me in his own coded language. Once again, he smiled at me while continuing his action with his forefinger; each time I looked at him, he would smile. His behaviour perplexed me, making me wonder if he was trying to say something to me. Amidst this, the Mangalarathi drew to a close.

In the ensuing melee of the devotees rushing to cup their hands around the ārathi, the sanyasi was nowhere to be seen. After collecting the Prasad, I came outside the sanctum sanctorum to a pillared hall adorned with paintings of various chakras and giant photos of the Devi in various forms. Out of curiosity, I began to observe these photographs and realised that these pertain to the Sixteen Tithinitya Devis of Chandra Vidya as part of Srividya practice. After studying each of these 16 images, I was about to sit and meditate under one of the images, and I saw the sanyasi sitting near one of the pillars. He was sitting and looking at me; in fact, he was gesturing at a photo on the wall and looking at me. I became curious and studied the photo, and it was an image of Rishi Agastya! Though in my heart, I instantly realised that the sanyasi was Rishi Agastya himself, my mind refused to believe it. I moved on, though now I started wondering what was happening; what was the sanyasi trying to convey through his various signs? Why did I come across the images of Tithinitya Devis and Rishi Agastya? Without getting any answers to these questions, I stepped outside the temple. The disciples accompanying me had a lot of questions, so we sat in the temple courtyard to discuss them. We sat down in the afternoon before we realised it was already evening. By the time we left from there, it was about 6- 6.15 p.m. Since it was winter, darkness had set in early.

We had to reach our Hotel as soon as possible, so we left immediately; since we were unfamiliar with the place, we had to depend on Google Maps to guide us. Unfortunately, the Driver's phone switched off as its battery had no charge. Everyone was tired after having travelled the whole day, and so slept off. I closed my eyes and rested my head on the seat while the driver drove on, hopeful of reaching the highway shortly. Even after driving around for half an hour, we were still in the same village, eventually reaching a dead end. The driver applied the brake abruptly, and I opened my eyes to realise we had reached a dead end. There was a stream on the right, and we could hear the sound of flowing water. I also saw a garden in front of me with a statue in the middle. The car's headlight fell directly on the statue; that is how I spotted it. When I approached the statue, I noticed it was of Rishi Agastya in a Padmāsana pose. I joined my hands in front of his statue with profound reverence. After taking in the surrounding landscape, we boarded the car, and in a few minutes, we reached the highway and proceeded to Kanyakumari.

My visit to the Garden with Rishi Agastya's statue was his way of telling me that "The sanyasi you met at Lalitha Tripura Sundari temple was indeed me." I was now convinced, but what was he trying to say to me? What did those signs mean? With these questions swirling in my mind, I reached Swami Rama Sādhana Dhama, our ashram in Ramanagar. A few days after reaching the ashram, one evening, I sat down at my usual place in Guru Nivas for meditation; those days, I was teaching my disciples Matruka Chakra practice. As I meditated, concentrating on Vishuddha Chakra, the light dimmed inside and outside of me, and I sensed something profound happening. Rishi Agastya appeared in front of me!!

This was a period when I was trying to understand and unravel the mysteries of Thiti Nitya Upasana in my own way; I would merge Matruka Chakra's meditation with the chanting of Thiti Nitya Devi's mantra. Rishi Agastya, a 4.5-foot-high rishi with a round belly, appeared before me. He was observing me intently, and my heart was frozen in silence! He waited until I came upon to chant Nīlapatāka Devi japa (Neela meaning blue), Rishi Agastya, with his Aṇimā siddhi, an ability to reduce one's body to the size of an atom, shrank his body to one / one and a half inches. As I continued observing, he directly entered my throat and positioned himself at its base! I could feel his presence in my throat, leaving me anxious and uncertain about what to do next. I continued to chant the Nīlapatāka Devi Japa; by the time I had chanted it thrice, my Vishuddha Chakra, the entire throat portion, turned blue. The rays from the Vishuddha Chakra, both inside and outside my throat, began to glow blue in colour due to the blue light.

My throat was illuminated with blue rays like the throat of Neelkanta Shiva. But my Tithinitya Japa continued, irrespective of what was going on. As soon as I finished Nīlapatāka japa, Rishi Agastya came out of my throat region and stood before me. He held Kamandala in one hand and Bramhadanda in another. He simply nodded, indicating, 'Your practice is going in the right direction.' Words were not his forte of communication.

***

Animā Siddhi Agastya Entered My Throat

28

MERE GAZE GRANTED MYSTIC MOON KNOWLEDGE

Chandrashekar Bharthi Swamy appeared in life form and sat before me in Padmasana. With his razor-sharp eyes, he delved deep into my eyes. I lost track of time in this state.

***

An incident occurred much before my first visit to Tripura Sundari Temple. Those days, I was immersed in studying 'Matruka Sambodha,' which is mentioned in the Shiva Sutras.

During one of my visits to Rā Sā Gurugalu, he asked me, 'Are you able to grasp Matruka Sambhoda?' I said, 'Gurugale, Matruka Chakra is truly a wonderful subject. While reading it, I feel I can grasp it, but later, when I ponder it, it feels like I haven't understood anything. I feel confused.' Gurugalu said, 'Oh, is it so?' and then peered deeply into my eyes.

I wasn't sure what, but I felt some form of communication from Gurugalu. After this, when I resumed reading 'Matruka Sambhodha,' I noticed that sentences that I found mysterious and incogitable after meeting Gurugalu were simple and easily understandable!

I must mention another incident which happened way before this. I was deep into my meditation in my room in Bengaluru. During those days, I was observing the Mahāṣōḍaśi mantra Japa. Suddenly, out of the Guru Paramparā photographs, Chandrashekhar Bhārathi Swami floated out of the picture in Padmāsana posture and sat in front of me in the life form!! With his razor-sharp eyes, he delved deep into my eyes!! I looked at him curiously and was unsure how long I had been seated in that position. After some time, he disappeared. I strongly felt some rare knowledge was transmitted through his gaze that day.

My mother was a devout follower of Chandrashekhar Bhārathi Swami; she was blessed by him on multiple occasions during his lifetime. This familial connection deepened my familiarity with his name. In fact, since I hail from Sagar, a place close to Sringeri, I remember accompanying my mother to Sringeri on multiple Occasions. On one of those visits, my mother bought for me a small picture of Sharadha Devi and I stuck it on the wall near my study area. She was a form of Dhārana for my studies then. So when Chandrashekara Swamiji appeared in front of me that day, I felt familiar with him. I must mention here that transmitting knowledge through gaze or signs isn't an uncommon way in our tradition. I remember my Mysuru Gururgalu sharing how Chandrashekar Bhārathi Swami initiated our Paramaguru Pundareekshananda even as he was being carried in a palanquin on the streets of Sringeri!! As per Rā Sā Gurugalu, Srigalu looked at Pundareekshananda with his piercing gaze. Right there, they communicated!!! And Pundareekshananda grasped the given mantra immediately. This is also why Chandrashekhara Bhārathi Swami is our Parameshti Guru, according to tradition.

A few days after this incident, I met Mysuru Gurugalu and detailed the whole experience. Gurgalu surprisingly asked me, 'Is it? What did Chandrashekar Bhārathi Srigalu tell you? I said, "He didn't say anything; he just looked deeply into my eyes." He pleasingly said, 'Why does he need any words? He can convey everything in silence; he is such a phenomenal person. You are blessed, with Guru's Grace. I am pleased with your Sādhana."

It is not regular to receive praise from Gurus, no matter who it is. But Srigalu's visit was a rare occurrence, especially when I was practising a mantra initiated by Rā Sā Gurugalu. A visit from Paramaguru is considered a sign that both the disciple and his Guru are proceeding in the right direction. I asked 'But, I couldn't decipher what Chandrashekhar Srigalu was trying to convey, Gurugale;' to which he said, 'Someday it will get revealed, then come and share with me as well!!'

So, going back to that day, after seeing Chandrashekhar Bhārathi Srigalu, I completed my meditation, got up, and started strolling inside my room. A colossal bookshelf was kept to the left of the table where we had placed his photo. I started walking towards it, thinking, 'Gurugale, why did you visit me today? I didn't understand your message. Could you please guide me through this?' I have no clue why I walked towards the bookshelf and unconsciously pulled out a bulky book from there!! It was a collection of lectures on Adi Shankaracharya's "Soundharya Lahari" by none other than Kanchi pontiff Sri Chandrashekara Saraswathi ji, known for attaining jīvanmukti while in physical body. I realised that Chandrashekar Bhārathi Ji directed me to read this book.

Holding that bulky book in hand, I wasn't sure where to start or which chapter to read. So, I closed my eyes, sought guidance from Shrigalu, and opened the book. When I opened my eyes, there it was: 'Lalāṭuṁ lāvaṇyam,' the 46th Shlōka of Soundarya Lahari. In this Shlōka, Sri Shankaracharya compares Bhagavathi's forehead to the moon, saying her forehead is as lustrous as the moon. A detailed explanation by Kanchi Srigalu followed the Shlōka. I lost sense of time reading paragraph after paragraph. While reading, I started drawing the moon one after the other according to the description in Shlōka. As I continued to deliberate on these, the essence of 'Chandravidya' suddenly touched me. In a very mystical way, Chandrashekhar Bhārathi Srigalu revealed the mystery of 'Srividya Tantra' also known as 'Chandravidya' through Kanchi Srigalu.

Over the next few days or weeks, I dived deep into understanding Chandravidya; in due course, a question started bothering me: 'How do I teach this to others? A knowledge bestowed on me from an ethereal plane, that too in silence, how can I teach such a supreme esoteric experiential learning through mere words?'

After a few days of reflection, practice, and anuṣṭhāna, I met my Gurugalu again with this question in my mind. After explaining my understanding, observation, and experiences, I asked him, 'Is my understanding, observation, and experiences in the right direction, Gurugale? Please guide me.'

He looked at me and smilingly said, 'This is Chandravidya,' he leaned towards me, placed his forefinger on the tip of my nose, and rubbed it from nose to Sahasrāra and from Sahasrāra to nose. He continued, 'It just goes up to the top and from top to down; he showed the moon's waning and waxing symbolically.' Just like the Sadhu at Lalitha Tripurambhika temple in Tamil Nadu. He had similarly rubbed his nose!! There it was, 'The missing link'!!

I had never mentioned that sanyasi whom I saw in Tripurambhika temple to my Gurugalu. But my Guru knew it all. The communication between Rishis is unimaginable; such a beautiful, spiritual exchange between Gurus led to an unveiling of the mysterious knowledge of Chandravidya to me. It was possible because of Guru's Grace.

This is one of the many episodes in which Chandrashekara Bhārathi Swami bestowed ethereal experiences that led to a deeper understanding of Chandravidya. Rishi Agasthya was crucial in directing me in this path. I am eternally indebted to the Rishi Paramparā for its love and grace.

***

29
CHANDRA VIDYA AND TITHINITYA PRACTICE

It is lunar science related to the Mystical moon, also known as Somavidya. The first reference to this science is found in the tenth book of the Rigveda and is later elaborated in the Upanishads and Tantric texts.

Further reference to it is:

Eight tantra scriptures by the name 'Chandra Kalastaka' meaning a set of 8 scriptures on Chandra Kala. Namely –

1. Durvasa Mata
2. Kularnava
3. Brahaspatya
4. Kuleshwaree
5. Kalanidhi
6. Chandrakala
7. Bhuvaneshwaree
8. Jyotsnavatee

These texts are a combination of both Kadi and Hadi Vidyas called Kahadi or Mishra Marga. Therefore, Sri Vidya is called Chandrajnana Vidya.

In this Vidya, Sridevi Bhagavati wears 16 digits of the Moon, of the Shukla paksha, that is the 15 days after the New moon of Amavasya, as her splendour and spiritual glory in the name of Tithinitya Kalas. The 16th kala or digit of the moon resides in the centre of the Chandra Mandala- the orb of the Moon. It is known as Sādakhya Kala, which is free from the waxing and waning of the digits of the Moon. This is what Srividya is. The 15 Nitya Devis or deities are equated to the supreme Mantra of Srividya by the 15 syllables of Panchadashi Mantra in Chandravidya. Vidya means Mantra of female deity.

Another very noticeable quality of this system of Sādhana is the Mayukha-s; the 360 rays of rapturous radiance of the moon, in Srividya. These 360 rays radiate from the feet of Sri Bhagavathi being responsible for the creation (Srushti) of the Brahmanda (Macrocosm) and Pindanda (Microcosm). Hence, she is addressed as the creative matrix of this Universe (Lokas - realms of existence).

When we mention the name, Srividya, it invariably gets connected to the Sri Yantra or Shri Chakra of the Deity Bhagavathi Lalitha Tripura Sundari. Tithinitya Sādhana gets linked to Sri Chakra in its second āvarana or enclosure by the name Sarvāsha-paripooraka chakra.

The 16 petals in this chakra are the radiance of 16 Nitya Kala Devis, namely –

1. Kamakarshini - Kameshwari Nitya Devi

2. Buddhyakarshinee - Bagamalini Nitya Devi

3. Ahankarakarshinee - Nitya Klinna Nitya Devi

4. Shabdakarshinee - Bherunda Nitya Devi

5. Sparshakarshinee - Vahnivasinee Nitya Devi

6. Roopakarshinee - Mahavajreshwaree Nitya Devi

7. Rasakarshinee - Shivadhooti Nitya Devi

8. Gandhakarshinee - Tvarita Nitya Devi

9. Chittakarshinee - Kulasundari Nitya Devi

10. Dhairyakarshinee - Nityanitya Devi

11. Smrutyakarshinee - Neelapataka Nitya Devi

12. Namakarshinee - Vijaya Nitya Devi

13. Bijakarshinee -Sarvamangala Nitya Devi

14. Atmakarshinee - Jvalamalini Nitya Devi

15. Amrutakarshinee - Chitra Nitya Devi

16. Sharirakarshnee - Lalita Mahanitya Devi

All these deities relate to our individual bodies (Microcosm) at the subtle plane during this esoteric science Sādhana.

Tithi Nitya practice involves, ultimately, very advanced practice of Pranopasana and all the practices are directed to Samayāchārā seekers. Its practice is secretly associated with the foundational principle of Matrika mandalas existing as Surya (Sun), Chandra (Moon) and Agni (Sacred Fire) - 3 Mandalas. Hence, this practice turns out to be centred around Sanskrit Varna Mala or 16 alphabets – vowels configuration with 16 digits of the Moon, as existing in Chandra Mandala or the orb of the Moon. The rest of the alphabet sout of these 50 Aksharas is related to Surya and Agni Mandalas. It symbolically represents the body and eyes of Srividya Bhagavathi, Sri Chakra, Srividya Panchadashi Mantra and Bala Tripura Sundari Mantra, etc.

The source for this Chandra Vidya wisdom are Vasista Samhita of Sage Vasista, Sanandana Samhita of Sage Sanandana, Sanatkumara Samhita of Sage Sanatkumara, as taught by my Srividya Guru Sri Rā. Satyanandanatha.

***

Chandra Vidya and Tithinitya practice

Section 5

- Sage Durvasa: Ocean of Snow Inside a Volcano
- I shalt slit thee, this very moment
- The secret of the wombed face, unveiled!
- Unveiling Chandrakala namaskar in the presence of Rishi Durvasa!
- What is Chandrakala namaskara?
- The benevolent son of Sage Atri

30

SAGE DURVASA: OCEAN OF SNOW INSIDE A VOLCANO

Easy to anger and prone to curse, Sage Durvasa is a character of profound complexity. Anyone familiar with the Puranas would be well-versed of his tales, often marked by bursts of anger and subsequent curses. This son, born to Sage Athree and Sage Anusuya, holds significant prominence in the Puranas; there is hardly anybody of significance who has not been the subject of his anger and curse; even Lord Shiva and Goddess Saraswathi have fallen foul of him. Among the very few who pleased him and were the recipients of his blessings, Kunti is the one who comes to mind instantly.

It is generally assumed that Sage Durvasa is akin to a volcano; the many stories we have heard of him are responsible for this image. A vast ocean of knowledge exists within this volcanic personality, and it is lost on us when we take the stories about him at face value. It is a great tragedy that humanity has failed to understand the importance and effect of those curses in determining the story's outcome, for you to understand the different dimensions of this Sage.

Durvasa, who is not only seen as a burning ember but is also an affectionate Guru capable of maternal love, as Srividya Bhagvathi Herself, who is the very manifestation of compassion.

You should read about these experiences.

Contemplating Sage Durvasa's experiences with an open mind is key to perceiving their true meaning. May you be blessed with this perception, which will enable you to expand your knowledge, deepen your understanding of these stories, and evolve spiritually!!

***

31

I SHALT SLIT THEE, THIS VERY MOMENT

"*Amma*, he seems to have a slightly dark complexion. Small snakes are crawling around his neck. His body is laden with ash. His hair is in matted dreadlocks. He seems to have travelled from somewhere far away. I mean, maybe from a different realm altogether. Traces are visible all over his dreadlocks of travels through the forest. Leaves of trees, twigs and blades of grass are pressed into his matted hair. As if he has woken up out of a volcano and come straight here, sparks of fire are spewing from his skin. He seems like the personification of raging fire *Amma*."

Perhaps Guruma had already sensed this because there was a sudden, obvious change in the atmosphere! A gust of wind blows and the doors open wide with a bang, the effects of this changed environment was already on them.

***

The time must have been a little past 1:00 am. Back in the day, we used to sit for long hours through the night at the ashram's Guru nivas, engaged in deep conversations. It was the time when Gaurav was taking the initial steps on the path of spiritual practice (*Sādhana*). With every step, he was faced with conflicts. Every day after dinner, our conversations would last for about 3 to 4 hours. On a couple of occasions, our conversations had also been stretched to the wee hours of the morning. This was one such midnight!

Gaurav and his friend were seated in front of me. They both hail from Punjab. It must have been around 1:30 am at midnight. Unexpectedly, the trees began swaying back-and-forth. A gust of strong wind. Naturally, we were distracted by the sudden winds that had taken over with no warning and then resumed our conversation. The door next to where I sat was blown ajar due to the strength of the winds. Since the door had magnets attached to it, it couldn't have been opened by the wind so easily. It seemed as if someone had put the effort to push the door open. As a result, we glanced towards the door in silence. We looked at each other's faces with curiosity in our eyes, and then we went back into our conversation. I was explaining the legacy of our sages to them.

Suddenly the expression on Gaurav's face changed. It looked like he was trying very hard to pay attention to my words. Gazing back-and-forth towards the door, he kept trying to focus at my conversation. "What happened Gaurav?" I interrogated. Keeping his gaze fixed at the door "*Amma!*" he responded. I looked at his face perplexed. "Someone has come here *Amma*, he's looking at me right now." he responded.

It would be best if you read Gaurav's side of the narrative, in his own words, from this point on.

***

"Who is he? How is he to look at?" Guruma asked.

"I do not have a clue about who he is, *Amma!*" I replied.

"Describe him to me in words," instructed Guruma

I fell into a literal dilemma from the conversation that *Amma* and I were having. My mind and emotions were in conflict about whether all this was real or not! Because the person who stood before me, although it seemed like he had a physical body, his form was not of the physical plane. It felt like an intermediate form between the physical body and the subtle energy body. Was this true? Or was it a figment of my imagination - this being who stood by the door? My mind was haunted by a myriad of questions at that moment. There he was, standing by the door, staring straight at me with piercing eyes and a gaze that didn't shift even a little. As if mesmerised by his presence, I sat frozen; I couldn't help but keep my gaze fixed on him, unable to take my eyes off him. I was unable to explain all this to Guruma. I was in a strangely helpless situation where I couldn't do a thing. The conflict and confusion in my mind also arose due to the fact that I was the only one who could see this entity before my eyes. He kept staring at me as if I had committed a sin. His gaze seemed like he could burn me to ashes at any moment. Was any of this real or just a hallucination? I stood there stunned!

I must mention another very important thing here. Swami Rama had appeared in my dreams about 3 months ago. I was asleep at the hospital; *Baba* was sitting in front of me. I saw him and said, "There is so much I wish to do in life, and yet I'm unsure if I would be able to fulfil everything I desire to do." *Baba* replied - "There is a weakness in your very statement."

"I am unable to understand the weakness in my statement. Could you please point me to it?" I responded to *Baba*. He immediately said, "You better know what your weakness is". When I woke up that day, all I could think of was Baba's words; I kept repeating the words like a mantra, "There is a weakness in your very statement" and "You better know what your weakness is!" kept resonating in my head day and night like a chant. What could be the reason behind this? What could be the reason behind *Baba's* serious demeanor? Was Baba giving me a warning? I was struggling to understand.

In such a confused state, I completely surrendered to Guruma, mustered the courage, and said, "*Amma*, there is someone there!"

My friend who was next to me said softly, "You are delusional; you are just imagining all of this" I immediately retorted, "No. No! I wish you could see him too."

After declaring that someone was there, I was literally challenged and short of words to describe the being. Even now, my whole body is gooseflesh when I remember that situation.

My heart was racing and beating out of my chest! I slowly gathered the courage and said, "*Amma*, his age must be about 28-29 years. A young man. He seems enraged. He might slit me up this very moment, if given a chance."

"Hmm, tell me more," Guruma said seriously.

"*Amma*, he seems to have a dark complexion. Small snakes are crawling around his neck. His body is laden with ash. His hair is in matted dreadlocks. He seems to have travelled from somewhere far away. I mean, maybe from a different realm altogether. Traces are visible all over his dreadlocks, of travels through the forest. Leaves of trees, twigs and blades of grass are pressed into his matted hair. As if he has woken out of a volcano and come straight here, sparks of fire are spewing from his skin. He seems like the personification of raging fire *Amma*."

Perhaps Guruma had already sensed this. Because there was a sudden obvious change in the atmosphere! A gust of wind and doors open wide with a bang, the effects of the changed environment was already on them. As she later revealed to me, that in that moment she felt her *sahasrāra chakra* awaken. As a result, she knew the seriousness of the words I shared.

"Perhaps it is the Sage Durvasa!" Guruma said. That's it. Just one sentence.

"*Amma*, in that case, what do I do now? He seems enraged by me. He is standing absolutely still with his gaze piercing right through me." I shared.

I shalt slit thee, this very moment

"All right, do one thing: take the phone and do a Google search," Guruma instructed.

I was surprised that Guruma asked me to do a Google search at such a grave moment. But I didn't question the instruction further once I saw a serious expression on her face; as guided, I opened Google and searched for "Sage Durvasa."

I was taken aback by the surprise! Piles and piles of images, like the man who stood before me. One painting caught my attention on Google; I pulled it up and showed it to Guruma, who said the man who is here would look a lot like this image in about 10 years.

"In that case, offer your obeisances to him," said Guruma. This was yet another strange scenario. My entire body was shivering and shaking like a leaf. My heart was racing beyond my control. As a result of fear, even the thought of offering respect hadn't crossed my mind.

"*Namaskar Karne ke liye bhi himmat nahi ho rahi hai, Amma*" I stated.

I felt weak in my knees. The way he gazed at me was as if I had no choice but to suffer the punishment he was to give me. No one could save me from this situation. His gaze got more sharp and edgy. In such a situation where could I have possibly gotten the courage to bow down before him?

"Irrespective of what's on your mind, just surrender to him completely. Trust that he is the truth that stands before you and offer your reverences. That's it!" she firmly instructed. I followed her words. "I know not anything about you. I am ignorant of the knowledge of sages. All I do know is that you are a very great Sage and a Seer. I offer my obeisances to you!" I said in my mind as I bowed my head in reverence.

Just then a surprise awaited me! As soon as I bowed down, he approached me. When I say he approached me, I dont mean he walked to me, his entire being floated towards me. It was as you would zoom in a video. Again, I sought Guruma "*Amma*! He just came near me now. Is he going to tell me something? What should I do now?" I asked her.

"You just bow in reverence, that's it," she said. As instructed, I bowed down again to offer my reverence, but what unfolded next was something else altogether. As soon as I bowed down, the crown of my head- my *sahasrāra chakra* instantly awakened!

Ah! What an exhilarating experience that was. It is extremely challenging to describe in mere words. For the very first time, an overwhelming experience had engulfed my entire body; the latent energy(*shakti*) at the base of my spine began to rise and made its way up to the crown! I had a vivid experience of the flow of my own energy on that day. It was as if something extraordinary had lifted me up. Blissful!

It felt as if this was not only my personal experience, but the entire environment felt this bliss along with me. It was very evident in every molecule that existed there. Even my friend who stood beside me could experience this energy flow. Along with Guruma, we were both captivated by this rare occurrence. As a result of the energy flow, the three of us had surrendered in meditation with eyes closed very organically.

Twenty minutes had passed, approximately. We slowly fluttered our eyes open; there was no one!

I saw a special sense of contentment on Guruma's face that day. When she opened her eyes "The one who had arrived is Sage Durvasa!" she said. "I have not a clue about Sage Durvasa, how is this possible, Amma?" I responded with a follow-up question. Guruma simply laughed and said, "You will know soon enough!"

When I glanced at the clock, the time was about 2:30 am. We had a plan to wake up early and leave for Mysuru the next morning. So, Guruma said "Go and sleep peacefully now, if you struggle to fall asleep, just let me know." and went towards her room.

"Ah! Finally, it's all over!" I sighed as my friend, and I walked towards our room. But the truth is, nothing was really over yet!

It was just the beginning!

***

Messages from the Himalayan Sages: Timely & Timeless

32

THE SECRET OF THE WOMBED FACE, UNVEILED!

He held me and struck my stomach. Unbearable pain. I felt my head was spinning, and I was falling into a chasm. Such was the pain. Blood gushed forth from the gash in my stomach. His face also had blood stains. "Alas! Why did this man have to cut my stomach? What did I do to deserve this? Why me?" were the questions that rose vehemently in my mind. Both my hands felt paralysed. I felt totally helpless at that moment, and it felt like this frail man had a tight grip on me. I just lay there, unable to do a thing!

***

Gaurav's narration continues -

Yes. This was only the beginning, and I was oblivious to it. I did not know that this was an experience which was beyond my senses and my mind!

After all this, when we returned to our room, I saw some ash near the bed. It looked like the ash from a beedi or cigarette. "How did this ash come here?" I thought to myself. "Did you smoke a cigarette here by any chance?" I asked my friend.

"No, bro! Why would I smoke inside the ashram," said he. Just the previous day, we thoroughly cleaned the room. I slowly climbed into bed, wondering how this ash had come into the room, especially when it hadn't been there earlier when we had left.

I reminisced over whatever had just happened. Fear was still lingering in my heart. Just then, my friend, who was standing outside came rushing in. He had felt the entire ashram and surroundings spinning. "I'm really scared. Many things that we cannot comprehend seem to be happening here. Let's leave," he said in shock. I too was contemplating on this issue.

The days we spent in the ashram were some of the most fabulous days of our lives. Guruma had begun teaching meditation and proper sitting posture. I remember vividly. During those times, Guruma used to wake us up at 5 or 5.30 am and would start her lessons. She taught us breathwork, single-minded focus during meditation and other things. As my spiritual knowledge started slowly growing, I started spending more and more time with her. In spite of Guruma's efforts, I did not have any significant experiences to write home about, and I felt quite frustrated. Maybe my efforts were not good enough, or I had probably made some mistakes. These were the thoughts that haunted me. But here, my assumptions that my efforts were not good enough were totally wrong. At that point, I did not have enough wisdom to understand this. Hence, today is a special day in my journey!

Even after all this, I was very frightened on the day these experiences happened. "Things happening here are beyond our comprehension. None of this can be understood. Guruma remains busy in her daily activities and is engrossed in the administration of the ashram. Will she guide novices and non-entities like us?" These were some of the thoughts that were haunting my mind. This could not be discussed with anybody, either!

In short, all these things were creating a lot of confusion in my mind. Under these circumstances, I decided that the next day, I would approach Guruma and tell her, "Amma, we are somehow unable to adjust and cope with ashram life. Hence, we are leaving." I couldn't sleep easy that night.

It must have been a little over 4 a.m. In my dream, I got on the bus. It was the very last seat on the Karnataka Road Transport bus.

The secret of the wombed face, unveiled!

The bus was empty, but he was there already in the bus. He was a splitting image of Durvasa, whom I had seen the previous day. He was lean, lanky, and dark-complexioned. He sported a crew-cut hairstyle. He wasn't too tall; he must have been around 5'4" at the most. As soon as he got in, he started pushing me. I was furious at this young man who was pushing me around on an empty bus. "Why do you push me?" I bellowed. He could not understand my English, Hindi, or any other language. Totally, a native of the town.

I tried to catch hold of this man who pushed me, and he, in turn, pushed me towards the end of the bus. There was an invisible force which pushed me, and after hitting the rear window of the bus, I was hanging in mid-air, and my arms and legs felt bound by an invisible rope. Even a well-built person like me could not stand strong in front of him. His push was that hard and strong. It felt like the bus itself moved backwards; that was how swiftly he pushed me.

It did not stop there. He used his hands like knives and cut my stomach. Unbearable pain. I felt my head was spinning, and I was falling into a chasm. Such was the pain. Blood gushed forth from the gash in the stomach. His face also had blood stains. "Alas! Why did this man have to cut my stomach? What did I do to deserve this? Why me?" were the questions that rose vehemently in my mind. Both my hands felt paralysed. I felt totally helpless at that moment, and it felt like this frail man had a tight grip on me. I just lay there, unable to do a thing but raging with anger deep within me!

After cutting open my stomach, he cut out my intestines and wore it around his neck like a garland. It seemed like he was cleaning it up. Nothing was clear to me. The excruciating pain was killing me. I almost blacked out, looking at him soaked in my blood. Next, he went for my liver. After that was my lungs and then my heart. He pulled out my heart and held it in front of me. Right before my eyes, I could see my heart beating lub... dub... lub... dub!!

"Alas! This should not have happened to me. Why couldn't I do anything about it?" Although these thoughts were arising in me, I could not move an inch. With immense pain in my mind and body, I helplessly watched my heart beating!

Just then, I woke up!

I opened my eyes and quickly looked at my stomach. From the outside, it looked quite normal and fine. But it was still as painful as being cut open. My entire body was exhausted. I could not move. The pain was that intense. My eyes were swollen. My arms and hands were all painful. I could feel not just my emotional pain but also the physical one.

My friend, who was in front of me, asked, "Why, what happened? Your face and eyes are swollen"!

"I'm not having any good experiences. I must speak to Guruma about this. Probably, I have been possessed by some evil, dark spirit. I just can't understand anything," was my brief response.

I couldn't even walk straight due to immense pain. My strength had dissipated. I had to somehow push myself to get ready as we had to leave for Mysuru. "What happened"? Guruma, too, asked, seeing my lack of enthusiasm. "Amma, I have to tell you something. I will do so later when we're in the car," I responded. As soon as I got into the car, I fell asleep. I would probably have slept deeply for around 10 to 15 minutes. When I woke up, we had already left the surroundings of the ashram and were on the highway. Just then, Guruma said, "Let's meditate in the car itself." At that point, Guruma taught us all about fixing our focus and meditating in a moving car. As per her words, I went straight into meditation without referring to the instances of the previous night.

We might have meditated for around half an hour. When I opened my eyes, Guruma said, "Gaurav, I have a surprise for you"! I didn't know what to say, because I was still reeling under the experience I had at dawn that day. And now Guruma herself says she has a surprise for me, which means it must be something very special I thought and was eager to know all about it.

"It is confirmed that the person who came to you last night was Durvasa!" she said. I looked questioningly at her. "Durvasa just visited me during our meditation now. It's really wonderful!" she said. She went on to describe how Sage Durvasa himself appeared to her during meditation.

I saw an egg. When observed closely, it looked rather strange because it looked like a face in the womb. A face covered by a clear, shining membrane that resembled a thin, transparent veil. The eyes were shut. Just as I was taking a closer look, suddenly, those eyes opened. Large, frightening eyes they were! They gave me a long, piercing look. A few moments later, those eyes looked away to the side, and my gaze followed in its direction. It landed on a boy around 16 years of age. He was pacing around anxiously with a heavy bag of books on his back. It looked like a field or a playground. With his booted feet, he was impatiently pacing back-and-forth and sometimes kicked the dirt, raising fine dust into the air. Just as I was looking at this scenario, the face in the womb started conversing with me, and I realised that the face was none other than Sage Durvasa. He told me. "This boy is an impatient one and gets angry easily. But you have to put up with him, that's it"!', Guruma narrated.

In this manner, when Guruma narrated the experiences that she had during the meditation that day, I was spellbound. How could I still not believe, when Guruma herself was confirming all this to novices like us?

With this, all my plans of leaving the ashram were laid to rest forever!

***

Listening to this esoteric experience in Gaurav's own words, one may have more questions than answers. What exactly happened in his dream? Who slit him to get to his heart? Why did he slit him? What is the connection between that experience and this book? etc. You would have the answers when you know the history of Gaurav's life a little more.

Gaurav was born in Chandigarh, in the state of Punjab. His father Late Major B.S. Bajwa (SM) is a martyr in the Kashmir terrorist attack. Hence, he lost his father at the age of 8 years. His uncle is Col. Parminder Singh Bajwa, retired now. His mother is Deputy Commissioner of Sales Tax in the state of Punjab. His brother Karandeep Singh Bajwa is an architect and artist, who has designed the cover page of this book and illustrations as well. He was 21 years old and had gone to a hospital for leg surgery. He was troubled by the rod inserted in his leg 3 years before and he had to go through another surgery to get the rod removed. During the pre-surgery medical tests, the doctors found some anomaly in his test results and declined to put him on anesthesia. To identify the cause of anomaly, when they carried out 'Echocardiography' test, everybody was in for a shock. Doctors declared that his heart was very weak, and emergency heart surgery was a necessity. They also had indicated that things could go wrong at any moment.

The term for his condition was 'left ventricular hypokinesia'. It is a rare condition in which one's heart loses the ability to supply sufficient blood for the appropriate functioning of the system. While a healthy heart normally supplies between 55% to 70% blood, his heart was supplying a mere 27%. Hence, the doctors had suggested to carry out a major surgery on an urgent basis. Many Doctors were consulted, but the root cause remained debatable. Some said it was hereditary, and for some it was lifestyle disease. Transplant was the suggestion given by most of them. But he bravely chose to listen to one specific doctor's timely advice to improve his lifestyle, rather than agreeing to the complex surgery. This very change got him drawn towards Yoga, and eventually to the divine city of Rishikesh. In this quest, his life changed beyond even his own imagination.

There are truths that are beyond the grasps of modern medical science. As per the predictions of the doctors then, his life would have come to an end long ago. Today he has passed 30 years of age. His heart never gave him trouble after the above incident. A karmic bond from his past lives got cleared due to Guru's grace. His curse was lifted.

Experiences such as this are rare and not easily bestowed on everyone. Gurus do not prefer to interfere in anyone's karma, for each individual soul must bear the fruits of their own karma, which is the ultimate reality. But what transpired here is quite an exception. Guru laid the path ahead for Gaurav to tread. While it was a scary experience for him, it was the special respect he was given.

***

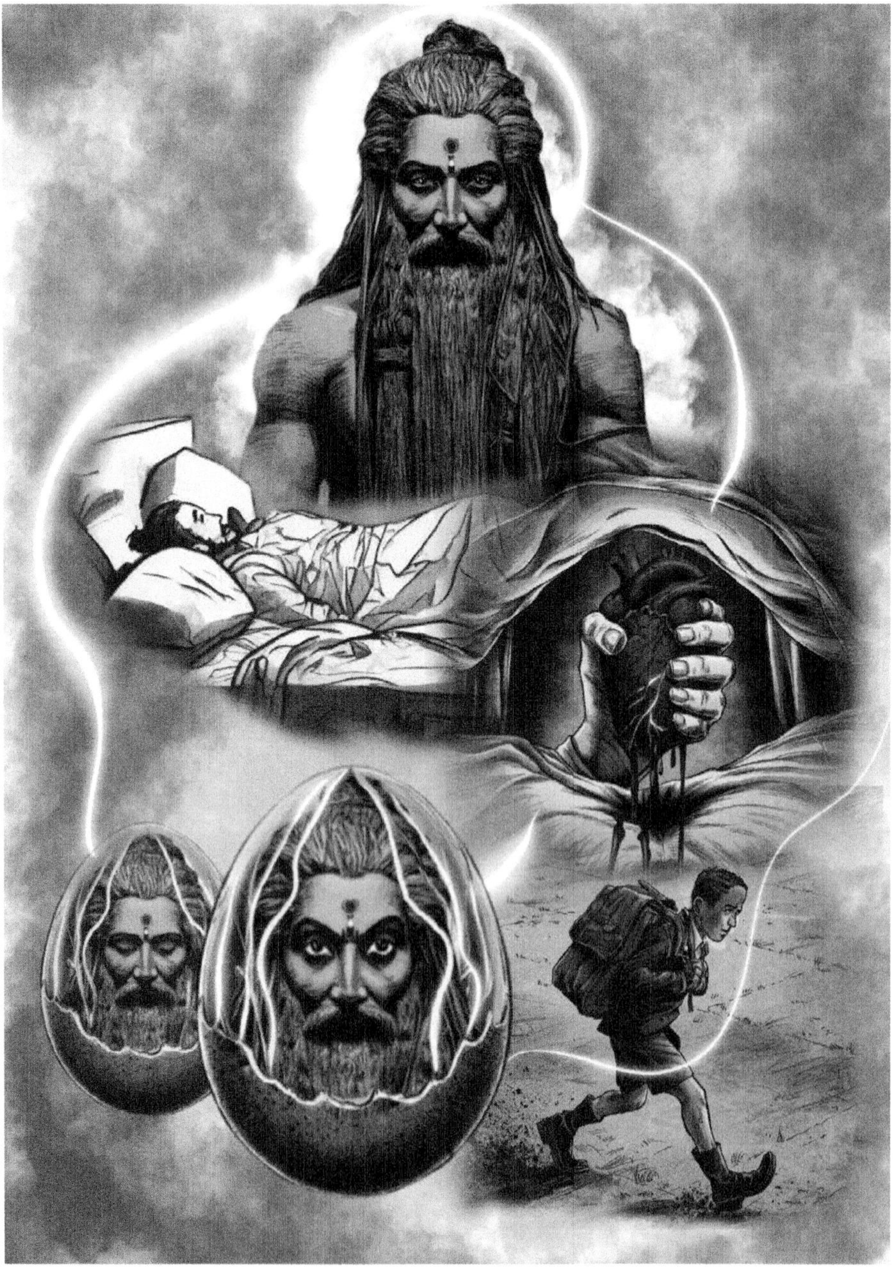

33

UNVEILING CHANDRAKALA NAMASKAR IN THE PRESENCE OF RISHI DURVASA!

At the end of the workshop, I asked Gaurav, "Share your experiences with Rishi Durvasa." Gaurav shared his experiences with the workshop attendees that day. He elucidated everything in great detail about how he saw Rishi Durvasa, Durvasa's being, his posture, and his expression. An attendee's facial temperament suddenly changed; she seemed delusional and started trembling mildly.

***

About 15-20 days were left for the International Day of Yoga. In the year 2022, I had an idea – how would it be to organise and present the Chandrakala namaskar on the occasion? I called Gaurav and said, "I have an idea that's gnawing me. If you are willing to demonstrate, I will design it. This will be a wonderful experience." He instantly replied, "I would be really happy to be instrumental in demonstrating your plans.

We had very few days at our disposal. We had to not just choreograph, but also do justice to the Chandrakala namaskara with good practice. So, I said "Lets present this on Yoga Day only if it comes up to the mark as per my visualisation. If not, lets postpone it." If we had to present it properly, we would have to work night and day to practice it. Gaurav agreed.

Besides, I was not aware of 'Chandra namaskar' until then! Lately, many have started discussing the Chandra namaskar. But there was not enough information to clarify if Chandra namaskar, like Surya namaskar, was a practice from olden times. I had practised Surya Namaskar for a long time, but the recent internet trends on Chandra namaskar had invoked my keenness. I could not find any information based on conclusive proof about this practice over the Internet. I kept browsing to collate information since I wanted to avoid presenting any redundant work in case somebody had already worked on this and presented it.

There were very many videos on the internet, but none satiated me. Bharathanatya was the art that dwelt in the depths of my heart. Over a period of 30 years, I had established myself as a dancer, choreographer, artistic director, and teacher of this art. I had invested years of hard work in honing the art, yet it was a rare moment of challenging excitement when I had to choreograph the Chandrakala namaskara! From the yogic perspective, I derived inspiration from my years of practice of yoga, music, and dance; I kept faith in Srividya tantra and the rishis of the yore. Requesting for their divine guidance, I immersed myself in the choreography of the Chandrakala namaskara.

We had very little time at hand. Amid these, I had to travel to Bengaluru for some work. I taught Gaurav whatever I could in one day and left. He presented the same to me after coming to Bangalore after just 3 days of practice. I was satisfied that I had chosen the right person for the demonstration. Gaurav was the first to practice the Chandrakala namaskara that I choreographed! We presented our offering of the Chandrakala namaskara to the world on International Yoga Day, as was our initial plan!

***

The journey of Chandrakala namaskara that started thus was now at Chandigarh. We were here for our second workshop. After the success of the launch on the International Yoga Day, we had gone ahead conducting workshops about Chandrakala namaskara.

The first workshop was in Bengaluru. The second workshop at Chandigarh turned out to be really special! Why so? I will now share it with you all.

That day, in Chandigarh. Gaurav was teaching the attendees at the workshop. Preceding this demonstration, I gave a short introduction to Chandrakala namaskara, post which we had the practice alongside mantra chanting. Gaurav had taught a mantra that had invoked Rishi Durvasa as part of the Chandrakala regime and had moved forward to the next parts of the practice. All of a sudden, one of the attendees appeared disturbed. Gaurav had also noticed this.

Noticing the changes in the attendee after the mantra chanting, Gaurav focused his attention on that attendee. However, the attendee regulated and continued with his practice. Seeing this, Gaurav continued with his demonstration.

At the end of the workshop, I asked Gaurav, "Share your experiences with Rishi Durvasa." Gaurav shared his experiences with the workshop attendees that day. He elucidated everything in great detail about how he saw Rishi Durvasa, Durvasa's being, his posture, and his expression. An attendee's facial temperament suddenly changed; she seemed delusional and started trembling mildly. Some, noticing the changes, started prodding her to see if she was okay. But she said, "Complete narrating your experiences," and hence, Gaurav went ahead with his narrative.

After the workshop got over, that attendee came to Gaurav. She said, "Today, I saw Rishi Durvasa the way you saw him. I saw him the moment I chanted the mantra. He came towards me. But I got scared. The Rishi Durvasa I beheld was akin to the one you described, perhaps a bit older, that's all. Is it possible that I saw the same being as you? Should I believe this? Or am I delusional?"!

Gaurav replied to him, "No, you are not delusional. You indeed beheld Rishi Durvasa in your vision. It's not a lie. Since Rishi Durvasa was visible to you, you are indeed blessed! So, please talk to Gurumaa; she will guide you appropriately." Thus, the attendee came to see me.

This way, we realised that the Chandrakala namaskar not only rejuvenated our body and mind but also blessed us with the grace and proximity of the rishis and munis of the yore!

***

This narrative would be incomplete if I did not explain the background of that attendee. She was a doctor who worked in the postmortem department. A job that involved regular dissection of corpses. A person who would trace the reason for death. She asked me, "Yoga explains the chakras in our body. Do they really exist? If yes, where? What are they like? But, we cannot see them internally after dissecting the body. There is no proof of their existence in the body. Hence, I have always been tormented by the query as to whether these are really true!" She, in fact, had placed these queries in front of her seniors (trainer doctors), too, but they merely dismissed her queries laughing over it, advising her not to get waylaid by such beliefs!

***

34

WHAT IS CHANDRAKALA NAMASKARA?

Chandrakala namaskara – THE MYSTIC SCIENCE AND ART OF YOGA

What to Experience in it?

At the outset, Chandra KALAA Namaskara (CKN) looks like Surya Namaskara's counterpart. Well! It is much more than being so. It is the word "KALAA" that makes a world of difference.

It revolves around the spiritual symbolism of the mystic Moon, involving chakras, Nādis, and Kundalini Energy. Its core understanding is in the phases or cycles of the Moon, which are identified as the duration of days in the Time concept. One phase of each day is called Chandra KALAA or Moon digits. KALAA are the various sizes of the Moon – digits emitting light on Earth Planet, shining in the sky. These phases are also described as waning and waxing moon cycles.

The Indian concept of the Moon is highly symbolic and spiritual in its content. First of all, Chandra, the Moon God, is, though a male figure in depiction, His energy is viewed as Chandra KALAA, the feminine aspect of creation. This feminine aspect of energy is represented as Ida Nadi in our yogic body, while Pingala Nadi stands for male energy. The merging of these two energies into the central Nadi–Sushumna in our yogic body is the ultimate purpose and goal of human life.

The esoteric dimension of Chandra KALAA is mind-boggling! Chandra KALAAs, or moon digits, 15 in number, are symbolised as Mystic Moon Wisdom, and the 16th aspect of Kalaa must be realised by the seeker by way of a tantric practice based on Vedic lore! The full moon day is an inner exploration of all 16 rays of the Mystic Moon. According to Tantra scriptures, this force of Great Energy, "Maha Shakti," operates through KALAA or waves. Chandrakala Vidya, in essence, relates to the inner experience of cosmic spanda or vibration in Bindu (point) the first waves of the cosmic sound "NAADA," and "KALAA the second wave!!

Ultimately, when practised, CKN takes you through an amazing experience that lies beyond the three states of Jagrata, Swapna, and Sushupti, and the fourth state of Turiya – the transcendental, self-luminous and effulgent dimension of the Inner SELF.

What can you expect from the practice of Chandrakala namaskara as a part of yogic discipline?

- Chandrakala is all about the rising and falling of Moon energy in terms of Kalaa or digits. It is Divine Feminine energy.
- It is the Yoga of Ida Nadi – Chandra, the planet, and as Lunar energy and the creative force.
- Chandra emits energy that is cool, tranquil, and serene. His energy is beauty personified as illumination.
- It is a combination of –
  - Asana
  - Mudra
  - Kriya
  - Gaze
  - Activation of chakras and Nadis
  - Mantras invoking the sages from the higher realms

- The flowing movements of grace, beauty, health, and harmony with the boosting power of mantra energy of the Sages in its practice sessions!
- Internalise the attitude of devotion, love and surrender by way of this Sādhana
- Resultant energy awakening, illumination, abundance, and attainment of the highest potential in you
- EXUDE all these qualities in your integrated personality.

Chandra KALAA Namaskara is the graceful amalgamation of the feminine energy of radiance, beauty, flow, abundance, opulence, creativity, and all. In one phrase – "a transformative experience of Mystic Science and Art of Yoga."

***

35

THE BENEVOLENT SON OF SAGE ATRI

What a surprise! He faced us as if he had sensed our presence before even looking in our direction. Additionally, a peaceful smile was on his face. One must witness it to feel it. To the question, "Do you live here?" He just rolled his eyes and moved his hand to hint that the geographic expanse of Ujjain belonged to him. He blessed us by placing his hands on our Sahasrāra chakra, full of love and compassion.

***

"Hey, *Karunamoorthi Athrinandan, Mera Pranam Sweekar Keejiye!*" was the way Swami Rama described and greeted Sage Durvasa.

How could Swami Rama perceive Sage Durvasa, who is typically associated with a fiery temperament and infamous in ancient scriptures for cursing individuals, as a compassionate character, even though he is seen as an angry sage akin to burning coal? It is natural for anyone who has grown-up listening to stories about Sage Durvasa since childhood to get perplexed if they hear him being described as the face of compassion. But Swami Rama's experience with him was one of pure compassion. *Baba* was very dear to Sage Durvasa. This encounter is enough to understand Sage Durvasa's profound compassion.

Yes, Gaurav's initial encounter with Sage Durvasa was indeed frightening. Despite its scary nature, it held significant importance for him. Following this encounter, Gaurav experienced sleeplessness for three days, highlighting the profound impact of the event. Before this, Gaurav had limited knowledge about Sage Durvasa and delved into ancient tales to learn more about him. Many of these stories depicted Durvasa cursing people, mirroring Gaurav's experience with the sage. Initially perceived as a curse, he realised it was a boon and a blessing, yet the fear he experienced during and after the encounter was indescribable.

One day, I was sitting and having a very casual conversation with Gaurav, and a fleeting thought of going to Ujjain came to my mind. Even the accounts of Baba's travels to Ujjain came up in our conversation.

Mahakaal of Ujjain! Among the places enlisted on Earth, Ujjain was Sage Durvasa's realm. Swami Rama also references it in his tales of interactions with the sage Durvasa. When *Baba* would share his experiences of Sage Durvasa with his disciple Pandit Rajamani, he often described him as a 'foul mouth.' Pandit Rajamani would often retort, "*Che! Che!* How could you possibly describe such a great saint in this manner?" to which *Baba* would respond very seriously, "Rajamani! You have a very tender attitude towards Sage Durvasa. I shall tell him you have a lot of affection and care for him when I see him next time." That was *Baba's* proximity to Durvasa!!

Thus, when it came to Ujjain, the realm of Sage Durvasa, Gaurav was naturally a little fearful. Having faced such intense emotions during his initial encounter with Durvasa, he frequently felt anxious about meeting him again. His mind was also conflicted on how Sage Durvasa came to be called the face of compassion; at the same time, he had a deep desire to experience 'Karunamoorthi Athrinandan.' "*Amma*, perhaps I need to put a lot more effort into the path of *Sādhana* to open myself to such experiences," Gaurav confessed. Not just that, he was thoroughly preparing himself to greet Sage Durvasa by saying, '*Karunamoorthi Athrinandan,* aapko pranaam hai' the next time he met him. "But in case Sage Durvasa appeared before you, you might just forget all these parroted words," I often teased him. But in response to that, he would only ask me very innocently, "*Amma*, are we really going to see him soon?"

"If you're feeling the urge to visit Ujjain, it must be because there's a divine connection calling you there. Otherwise, we wouldn't have such a strong desire." I said. But somehow, Gaurav never decided to book the tickets to Ujjain. Whenever I reminded him of the ticket booking, he would push it off by saying, "I'll do it, *Amma*!" But on one fine day, everything fell into place beautifully to book tickets for Ujjain.

That day, Gaurav received a call from his friend's father in Punjab. They hadn't spoken in 8-9 years. During the call, the father mentioned their annual pilgrimage to Ujjain as devotees of Mahakaal and casually asked him if he had ever been to Ujjain. After the unexpected serendipity, Gaurav politely responded that he had not been to Ujjain before. Shortly after, he excitedly told me, "It felt like a call from Mahakaal himself!" He then proceeded to book tickets for our trip to Ujjain right in front of me.

Before travelling to Ujjain, we stayed at the house of Dr Ashok Bhat and Nirmala in Delhi. They are very dear to me. I had instructed Dr Ashok to recite the Durga Saptashati about two years ago. This sacred scripture is a significant path of Shakthi *upasana* and Srividya Tantra *sadhana*. I casually checked with him about his practice of this text when Dr Bhat handed over the Durga Sapthashati book to Gaurav and said, "This is yours." This surprised Gaurav, and yet to extend his courtesy for Dr Bhat's kindness, he took the book and flipped through the pages. He landed on a page with the 'Siddhidhatri' Maa Bhagavathi image! He was attracted to that image of the divine mother, and it was imprinted on his memory.

Finally, as intended, we arrived at Ujjain. The journey was relatively smooth, and we reached around the afternoon. As we thought earlier, we had to get tickets for Bhasmārati at 3 a.m. the next day. But I felt drained that day, so I said, "Let's not go to Bhasmārathi today." We decided to just explore and walk around the temple area

The benevolent son of Sage Atri

that night. On the right is the temple of Mahakal, and on the left is the shrine of the Goddess. "Before we seek the *darshan* of lord Shiva, let's pay our reverence to the Goddess," I suggested. There were not many people outside. Gaurav stopped, stunned as he stepped inside. As you glance inside, you will notice a huge, framed image of Bhagavathi with the word 'Siddidhatri' inscribed. Gaurav said, "Amma, what sort of a miracle is this!" and looked at me for some answer. It was the same image on the page of the Durgasaptasati book that Gaurav had seen at Doctor ji's house. The exact image was before our eyes today!

Inside was a bustling crowd and a constant swing of push and pull amidst the jostling crowd. However, such scenes are frequently observed in renowned temples throughout these towns. It's a everyday affair for the security guards and policemen there to control the hustling crowd. How can they consistently give instructions politely? It may seem natural for them to use rough language since it's part of their daily routine. Sometimes, they resort to harsh words and physically guide people forward by holding their heads to manage the crowd.

In such a situation, the lady security guard naturally screamed loudly to control the crowd's push and pull. Meanwhile, standing in the same crowd, I was getting slightly annoyed by her loud yelling. However, her attention was diverted as soon as it was my turn to stand before Bhagavathi. Someone had dropped her head ornament in the shape of a crescent moon in front of the Goddess. The security guard picked it up and inquired if it belonged to anyone in the crowd. At this moment, I had the golden opportunity to stand completely uninterrupted and express my devotion to Mā Bhagavathi for about 2 minutes. I was totally lost in her magic at that moment.

After a couple of moments, the lady security guard turned to the priest, pointed to the crescent moon of the fallen hair ornament, and showed its resemblance to the jewel on Bhagavathi's crown. Though such interactions look casual or coincidental to visitors, it was not so for me. I was being guided by Guru Paramparā, Sages, and Bhagavati herself to decipher the coded meaning of seemingly normal actions. By showing the crescent moon jewel, she suggested that she was very much aware of my *tantrik Sādhana* called '*Chandra vidya*' and it was her way to bless me in the form of Maha Nitya Devi - the crescent moon on her crown symbolising Tvarita Nitya Devi. At that moment, all my fatigue due to travel and apprehensions about our present visit vanished in thin air, and miraculously, I was rejuvenated. After all these inquiries, the lady security guard returned to her duty, realising that she had given me ample time in front of the Goddess. She turned towards me, smiled, and lovingly said, "*Mataji*, this won't be your only visit here. You will be back here soon, and you can see Bhagavathi till your heart's content then!" The unique thing to note here is how sweetly she said this to me. She also never pushed me to move ahead. But the moment I moved ahead; she was back to controlling the crowd with her usual harsh tone.

On that occasion, while I was getting very irritated by the crowd's noise, pushing and shoving, Mā Bhagavathi took care of her *darshan* very effortlessly!

After all this, we wanted to sit in some place and meditate. The remarkable thing is that we found a place next to *Yajnashala* that felt very aligned; we sat and meditated for about 30-40 minutes. Along with all this, Gaurav's Karunamoorthi Durvasa chanting continued! After our meditation, we had to get past the Ganesha temple to leave the premises. Around the temple, preparations for the aarti were already underway. Devotees walked cautiously along oil-slick walkways to illuminate a lamp post that stretched a height of over a thousand metres. It is a divine sight! While we were walking, we observed several subtle details. Then, unexpectedly, Gaurav spotted a man who bore a striking resemblance to Sai Baba approaching us. He was tall, lean, and clad in a very simple *dhothi and kurta*. His headgear was strikingly attractive. He wore a white piece of cotton cloth over his head. The shine in his eyes, the radiant glow on his face and his royal gait made him a class apart! There was no one else nearby resembling him. His face exuded a serene glow. Just as Gaurav pointed him out, the man was walking towards us, with a background of aarti being performed for Lord Ganesha. It was an unusual and remarkable moment that unfolded right before our eyes.

The man who appeared in the midst of such a dense crowd came in our direction and began approaching the door to our left. Guiding me safely through the crowd, Gaurav held my hand and began navigating towards where the man went. At that moment, a realisation struck us that that was not how we had to go, but we felt very drawn to follow him. After that, with much effort, we turned to the right. Even in the thick of the crowd, that man's deep sight had befallen us! What a bewitching sight that was. In the split second that we took to process all this information, he had shifted his direction, and simply disappeared from the crowd. Later, we also went our own way.

After enjoying the aarti at the Ganesha temple, we strolled to the banks of the River Shipra and spent some time there. We experienced serene peace there. After all of this, Gaurav left me back in my room, instructed me to get some rest and left to fetch the tickets for the next morning's *Bhasmārathi*. I told him that I was not inclined to take darshan amidst the bustle of the crowd. However, he left towards the temple to check out our options.

After some time, Gaurav returned with 2 tickets. Gaurav needed an *Aadhaar* card at the booking counter to book tickets. But he did not have my *Aadhar* card, so the booking officers enquired about his whereabouts and refused to give the tickets without a valid ID. "We have come to take *darshan* of the Lord. My *Guruma* is also with me, but she is very exhausted from the travels and is resting in the room. If you trust my words, please take your time, think, and then give me the ticket." he said to convince them. They thought about it for a moment and handed him 2 tickets. He returned to the room and said, "Amma, I have 2 tickets. If you feel we are aligned to go, we can go. If you don't feel inclined to go, I won't either. You are my Mahakaal!" and kept the 2 tickets in front of me. The next day, we first went towards Kalabhairava temple and then to Bharthrihari cave.

The atmosphere near Bharthrihari cave was pleasant. Those familiar with the tale of Ujjain and Baba's encounters with Sage Durvasa in the book 'At the Eleventh Hour ' could seamlessly connect the narratives with the surroundings. The presence of the bitter neem tree and the overall ambience vividly reflected Baba's experiences during his time with Sage Durvasa. It was very sultry inside the cave. Apparently, Sage Gorakhnath travelled to Kedarnath and Badrinath from Ujjain through these caves. However, that route is said to be closed now.

Prior to this, another incident had transpired. Gaurav recounted an experience where he received the tickets for Bhasmārathi and stood in the temple surroundings. Some locals, noticing his trendy top knot and beard, mistook him for "*Jāṭādharī Baba*" and suggested, "To have an easy darshan without the crowd, visit around 8 in the morning when only locals are present." Following this advice, we arrived at the Mahakal temple around 8 o'clock. True to their words, the temple grounds were deserted. Few visitors seemed interested in seeing Mahakal at that hour; it was remarkably empty! As we prepared to enter, a guide redirected us to an easier route, facilitated our darshan, offered us *bhasma* prasad, and then departed. It turned out to be a simple and smooth experience.

Meanwhile, Gaurav's anxiousness was on the rise. We had arranged for a taxi to the airport around 1:00 pm. Gaurav, who had been quiet until then, expressed his concern that the person he came to Ujjain to meet hadn't appeared yet. "Despite everything going smoothly, Sage Durvasa is nowhere to be seen, *Amma*," he started. "*Amma*, Sage Durvasa hasn't graced me with his darshan; he seems upset with me; maybe there is a lack in my spiritual practice," he added with a frown. "Don't worry too much; there's still time. Just be patient and learn to flow with the time," I reassured him.

As we left after completing the *darshan*, we noticed the same man with the white scarf on his head from the temple courtyard receiving Dakshina from a devout woman, turning his back to us. As we moved a few steps forward, he suddenly faced us. What a surprise! He looked towards us as if he had sensed our presence. To our amazement, he greeted us with a gentle smile on his face. Witnessing that moment was truly delightful! His happy expression, eyes gleaming with love and tranquillity, embodied the essence of Karunamoorthy!

Due to this unexpected darshan, we were stunned and could not take another step forward. As I predicted, Gaurav had wholly forgotten his parroted chant and stood there in complete silence, simply staring at him. It was as if time stood still; he was frozen in his pace and stood there with his gaze fixed on the man. Karunamoorthi Athrinandan's mantra had vanished from his mind. I prompted Gaurav to offer him the Gurudakshina that we had intended to give him and bowed to him in reverence. Slipping his hands into his pockets, Gaurav pulled out a note and offered it to him. He accepted the offering, placed his hands on my *Sahasrāra* chakra, and blessed me. Gaurav also received similar blessings from him.

Gaurav asked him, "Do you live here?" He rolled his eyes and moved his hand, hinting that the geographic expanse of Ujjain belonged to him. He emphasised this piece of information before leaving. And just like that, he disappeared without a trace.

Meanwhile, a priest appeared, and we enquired about the way out. He saw me and said, "*Mataji*, the exit from here is quite a distance away, and the sun is scorching hot. If you take this path, the way out is straightforward, as this is the VIP entrance; no one will hinder you." Although his suggestion seemed strange, we took his advice and exited the VIP entrance without glitches. This was also his grace, wasn't it? The compassionate sage saw to it that we received VIP treatment, not to walk in the hot sun!

"*Karunamoorthi Athrinandana!*" No other words would better suit the man who personified the compassion we encountered that day!

***

Section 6

- Bengali Baba, the Illuminator of the path
- Have You Come For A Picnic?
- A caged, enlightened soul
- When Guru visits as a friend!

36

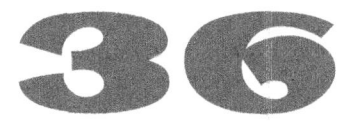

BENGALI BABA, THE ILLUMINATOR OF THE PATH

I am reminded of an experience shared by Swami Rama in his book 'Living with the Himalayan Masters,' about Guru Bengali Baba. When Swami Rama was very young, he came to know from astrologers that he would live until only 28 years old and came to know even the date and time of his death, which made him dejected. Bengali Baba consoled him, then stated, 'Since I will be sharing my lifespan with you, you will live longer. There is something beyond astrology as well!! But, since it is your fate, it is also true that you will have to face your death that day'.

Having forgotten this prophecy totally, he was crossing the mountains on that day when he slipped and almost fell in the crevice. As he was staring down at his certain death, he remembered his Guru, and in no time Bengali Baba manifested there and saved him. He fulfilled the promise made to his disciple that day.

This serves as strong evidence that when a disciple is in trouble, a true guru will always show up. As my Grandmaster, Bengali Baba has graced me with his presence whenever I was in desperate need and has handheld me to guide me in the right direction. Some of my experiences with Bengali Baba, which I have shared here, will demonstrate this truth to you very clearly.

***

37

HAVE YOU COME FOR A PICNIC?

Pitch-dark forest. Nothing apart from that is visible. There were no vehicles on the road, no people around. To add to it, tiredness, and sleepiness. The best part was that no one knew that we had lost our way except Doctorji, who was driving the car. The fun part was, after 2 or 3 hours, Doctorji softly said, "We had lost our way. While trying to get on to the right way, I dozed off too, because of tiredness. When I woke up, the car was moving. I am not sure who was driving," he declared!!

***

It was during 2013-14. Pattabhiramji was not in the best of health. Under that situation, one day, during meditation Bengali Baba came to him and said, "Come to Tungnath." He shared this information with me. We followed Baba's call and set out. Dr. Ashok Bhat and his wife joined us in Delhi and 5 of us proceeded toward Tungnath.

Being one of the 5 Kedar temples, Tungnath was the lord of the peaks. It is considered one of the Shiva temples at the highest altitude. Situated in the Rudraprayag district of Uttarakhand, it is at an altitude of more than 12000 feet above sea level. Surrounded by the Garhwal Himalayan range, darshan at Tungnath is a unique divine experience. The temple is situated a little below the Moonstone peak of the Himalayas - 'Chandrakala Shikhar'. A trek of about 4 kilometres from Chopta leads to this temple. This trek of 3 to 4 hours is through steps, and for people who cannot travel by foot, pony rides are available.

Before Tungnath, we first went to Swami Rama's ashram in Rishikesh. We intended to meet Baba's disciple, Maithili, and get information and direction for our onward journey. She had come from Jolly Grant to Rishikesh to witness the Ganga Aarthi and was to return. Just as we got all the information about Tungnath and were to leave, Dr Ashok Bhat's wife, Nirmala, went inside to purchase some photographs and books. By then, I finished my purchases and came out.

It was around 2.30 pm. With his back towards us, someone was talking to the security guard at the gate that leads to the main road. Doctorji and others were talking to Maithili near the garden. Maithili took leave of them and turned towards me, waved goodbye, and walked into the ashram. Others were still standing around talking to each other. Just as I slowly walked toward the gate, the person at the gate turned around towards me and said, "Namaste." I returned his gesture while observing his glowing, happy face and wondered if I knew this person but failed to recognise him. He was lean, slightly dark-complexioned, and middle-aged. The divine glow on his face was captivating. Just as I was in thought, he suddenly said "Mein Yog hoon! Mein Anand hoon!" (I am Yog, I am Anand) and started clapping his hands and dancing in circles! I did not know what to do and just looked at him.

As Doctor and others were coming towards me, he continued dancing and moved out of the gate, turned left, and disappeared. On seeing him, Doctorji and others enquired about him with the security guard. "I also do not know. He said he was from Kamliwale ashram," answered the security. Since that ashram was a short distance away, we assumed it was true. When I turned around, I could see Maithili in the distance, watching all that was happening. We waved goodbye to her and walked towards the car.

Since we had a long journey towards Tungnath, Doctorji proceeded towards the petrol bunk to refuel. Just then, the phone rang. I was handed the phone as Maithili wanted to speak to me. "Hello," I answered. "After you left, I sat for meditation, and Bengali Baba visited me during that time. He wanted me to convey to you about the person whom you just met," she said.

"Who was it?" I asked curiously.

"The person you met at the ashram is none other than Bengali Baba!" she said.

I had never thought of this possibility and was delighted. He had come to see me in the guise of that person! When I disclosed this to the others in the car, everyone was thrilled. This was the first time I had met Bengali Baba.

When we reached Rishikesh exit gate, it was a little over 6 pm. Since it was a forest range, the gates were closed at 6 pm. Doctorji was driving the car, and Pattabhiji was seated alongside him, dressed in an ochre kurta. Narayan, Nirmala, and I occupied the rear seat. Narayan alighted from the car, approached the forest officer, and requested, "Guruji must reach Tungnath by tomorrow. Would you please open the gate?" The officer looked at all of us and opened the gate.

We crossed the gate and entered the forest area. Somewhere in between, we stopped to have dinner and continued our journey. In the darkness, we lost our way. During those days, we did not have Google Maps or other such support. It was not easy to get directions. Enquiring someone was not even an option, as we were inside a thick forest in complete darkness. To add to it, we were tired and sleepy. The best part was that no one knew that we had lost our way except Doctorji, who was driving the car. The fun part was, after 2 or 3 hours, Doctorji softly said, "We had lost our way. While trying to get on to the right way, I dozed off too, because of tiredness. When I woke up, the car was moving. I am not sure who was driving," he declared!!

Have You Come For A Picnic?

All of us who were sleepy till then suddenly froze after hearing what he said. But there was lots of clarity in his voice. He did not seem confused or disoriented. "It was true that I fell asleep. It is also true that the car was running smoothly, too," he said with confirmation.

It was past midnight. Finally, we reached a big building and stopped the car. When we enquired with the security there, we understood that it was a colonel's house and a lodge. However, he did not encourage visitors in odd hours. Even though we were aware of this, we requested that the security person went inside to wake him up. Half-heartedly, a person emerged from inside. When he spoke to us, he learned that we were disciples of Swami Rama. "I, too, am a follower of Swami Rama," he said, welcoming us inside and making arrangements for our stay for the night. The next morning, he arranged breakfast for us and later bade goodbye to us. We finally reached Chopta. Now for the steep trek onward to Tungnath!

Pattabhiramji was not in a position for the strenuous trek. Hence, he opted for the pony. Narayan walked along with him. Doctorji, Nirmala, and I followed them on foot.

This Himalayan experience was new to me. I stood there admiring the beauty of the majestic mountain ranges. Slowly, I continued on my way. All of us were on our own, walking at our own pace but within hearing distance of each other. Since the weather was very unpredictable and it could rain any time in the mountains, we all wore our raincoats, which we had bought locally. We also carried water bottles, clothes, and accessories for one night's stay. As we started climbing, I reached for my bottle to drink some water when I heard a voice.

"Picnic ke liye aaye ho kya?"

"Have you come here for a picnic?" is what it meant, and I quickly looked around to see the source of the voice. No one was around. The people whom I was with were scattered around. No one seemed close enough to have heard the voice. Just as I was wondering who it could be, I heard the question again. "You should take the purpose of your visit more seriously," was additional advice given to me by the voice.

"What is the purpose of my visit here?" I wondered and was puzzled. I was not sure of any particular purpose of this visit to Tungnath!

However, I did become solemn from that moment onwards. I followed the voice that commanded me, "Come with me." I could clearly see two slim legs, from the knee downwards, clad in white pyjama, walking in front of me. Above the legs, I could not see the person, but I just began to follow those legs!

There is no fear of losing the way enroute to Tungnath. There are steps that take us there. Yet, I followed the legs that called me to follow them. After walking for some distance, those legs disappeared. By then, I had made a solemn conviction - whatever happens; I will not sit down anywhere till I reach Tungnath!

All along the ascent, on either side, there are rough benches for people to rest. Tea stalls were there, too. But as per my conviction, I continued without any stop and reached Tungnath. I stopped only to touch the bell at the main entrance of the temple. Until then, I did not stop anywhere as intended and reached before anyone else in our group. I sat down on the stone bench near the temple and looked around to see where the others were. In the distance, I could see the pony coming up. One by one, everyone in our group reached the place where I was waiting.

When I sat and thought about all that happened, I understood all about them. At the ashram, the feet that danced saying, "I'm Yog, I'm Anand," were the same feet that said, "Come with me," and led me to Tungnath without even needing to rest! These were the same legs I had seen at the ashram. It was none other than Bengali Baba himself who asked me to be solemn in my journey and have a strong intention. He then showed me the way to reach here!

By the time I understood all this while sitting at Tungnath, Pattabhiji had also reached and rung the temple bell, as I had done. He was tired and wanted to rest for a while. During that time, he shared the experience he had on the way up. He had seen a thick black smoke emanating from his own body and rising into the sky. Bengali Baba had brought him here for that very purpose, he said. Pattabhiji had been suffering from myriad health issues in the recent past. The doctors also could not give a suitable treatment or solution for his problems. We felt that this was some kind of black magic done by people who did not like the growth and progress that Pattabhiji had made in his life. That day, he saw with his own eyes all that dissipating into the sky as black smoke and felt relieved. We now clearly understood why Bengali Baba had instructed us to come to Tungnath!

We stayed the night at Tungnath. It was extremely cold, and none of us had come prepared for it. After resting, we had roti and dal in our tent, and on a pitch-dark night, we watched the beauty of the mountains in the flash of lightning. As if to say that night was very special, the sky put up a grand show of thunder and lightning for about 15 to 20 minutes. The surrounding mountains were bathed in the brightness of this extraordinary light and sound show, which we had never seen before!

In the days that followed, as I carried on my Sādhana, the truth came to me in a flash. The extraordinary light show was sent to us as a gift with lots of love. With Bengali Baba's blessings, Chinnamastā, the deity he dedicated his life to, had taken the pleasure of bestowing this gift on us!

After that incident, many times, Bengali Baba made an appearance. However, that was the first time with him. I had a conversation with him without actually talking at all. The Guru's kindness is eternal! Within no time, he had effortlessly neutralised the effects of the mysterious witchcraft that was done to Pattabhiji. Such is Gurudēva Bengali Baba's benevolence!

***

38

A CAGED, ENLIGHTENED SOUL

Coming out of my meditation, I instructed them all to collect their mobile phones. I turned around and noticed the same sanyasi seated among them. Clad in saffron, he stood out among all those present. I was stunned. Looking at him, I wondered how he suddenly appeared when he was nowhere to be seen!? Just as my eyes fell on him, he immediately got up and started to leave. Even as he left, he uttered loudly, "Atmajnani Pinjde mein hain" (The Enlightened soul is in a cage) not once or twice but thrice.

***

It was almost a year and a half since Pattabhiji had passed away, and I was in intense grief. While on the one hand, my daughter Sadhana's education was not yet complete, on the other hand, the responsibilities of the 'Swami Rama Sādhana Dhama Ashram', all of these were affecting me. Under these circumstances, it was decided to go to Tadkeshwar in Uttarakhand; altogether, about 20 to 22 disciples from Hyderabad, Delhi and Bengaluru joined. Tadkeshwar is the spiritual abode of Bengali Baba and Swami Rama, the holy place where they undertook penance. Swami Rama's ashram is located next to the Tadkeshwar Mahadev Temple, where we stayed for a retreat. A Sanyasi had also come to stay there, who, despite not having both hands, would go about doing his work energetically. I clearly remember him saying that he wanted to visit Jyotirmath. Was he referring to me? I wondered!

As the retreat was coming to a close, arrangements were made for me to conduct a meditation session in the meditation hall under a canopy en route to the Temple the day before we were to leave. Everyone turned up that evening, and since it was a guided session, they kept their mobile phones near me to record it. Just as all of them closed their eyes and settled into meditation mode, I noticed the Sanyasi seated amongst them! I looked at him surprised, wondering when he had come. I had not even noticed his arrival. He, in turn, kept looking at me; his gaze made me intuitively feel, "While the master of meditation is sitting here, how can I teach meditation to them all?" I started to think, what is the worst that could happen?; unmindful of the fact that I was not saying anything to guide them, everyone would continue to meditate; maybe a few might open their eyes slightly to check why I was not talking, and some might even get confused, not knowing what to do. That's about it, I thought to myself. Once I closed and opened my eyes, he was gone! I thought, "He was sitting right here." The sanyasi had left the moment I closed my eyes, so he could not have gone far; even if he had walked off, I should have been able to spot him. But the very next second, though disappointed, I began to meditate as if I had forgotten about all this, and conducted the session as usual.

It was a wonderful session; everyone had their own unique experience. Without much effort, they were able to attain a meditative state yet were able to experience the power. Post the Meditation, I instructed everyone to collect the mobile phones and turned around when I noticed the same sanyasi was seated among them. Clad in saffron, he stood out among all those present. I looked at him, stunned, unable to recollect when he returned. I had walked around during the session, correcting the postures of some of the participants and observing them, he was not to be seen all the while. Now, where did he appear from? Just as my eyes fell on him, he immediately got up and started to leave. Even as he left, he uttered loudly, "Atmajnani Pinjde mein hain," meaning The Enlightened soul is in a cage, not once or twice but thrice in a loud booming voice. Everyone present could hear him clearly, but when he said it for the third and final time, to me, it felt like an unearthly voice. My whole body went numb because I could experience the words coming from the sky that were specific to me! The interesting part of this incident was that just before he spoke, all the participants had taken their mobile back. So, it could not be recorded. Everyone had heard what he said, but no one understood the meaning of it!

We were supposed to leave for Rishikesh the next day, return to Swami Rama Ashram, and catch a flight to Bangalore the following day. Some of the people in the group wanted to see Rishikesh and left. I had been there several times in the past, so I was not interested in visiting again. Post lunch, some of the participants began to discuss the meaning of what the Sanyasi had said; though I understand Hindi very well, I could not then decipher the esoteric meaning of what he said. I concluded that if Guru desires, then I will understand. Yet those words kept repeating in my mind. I was alone in the room at night, trying to get some sleep, but his words kept coming back. In order to avoid missing the flight in the morning, having slept late, I set the alarm for 4 A.M. and went to sleep around 2 A.M., hoping the alarm would wake me up. Even in my sleep and dreams, the incident kept repeating. At one point in time, I turned to my right in my sleep, and my consciousness came forth out of my sleep. In a flash, I understood the entire message of the Sanyasi!

The Atmajnani he was referring to was Pattabhiji. We cry a lot when our loved ones depart from us, and we become very sad; though they have left us, we are not prepared to let go of them emotionally. You may have heard elders advising us not to cry when someone dies as it will prevent the departed from moving on. Though Pattabhiji was an Atmajnani, my love for him had locked him in an emotional cage. This was the essence of "Atmajnani Pinjde mein hain," which I finally understood.

In the one and half years that had passed since the Death of Pattabhiji, I had gone into a state of hopelessness; his loss was hurting me, and I was unable to continue my spiritual practices. Those were days of immense sadness. "You need to free the Atmajnani from the cages of your emotions. It is only by your Grace that he shall be at peace and continue his journey further." was the message he conveyed to me. He was responsible for bringing about a profound change in my heart. He was none other than Bengali Baba himself!! I realised the true purpose of Bengali Baba appearing in the form of a Sanyasi and staying with us in the ashram.

I came back and narrated everything to Rā Sā Gurugalu and asked him if my interpretation was correct. Looking at me intently, he replied, "Hmm," and I was convinced of its esoteric meaning. It paved the way for me to erase the emotional tower I had built; as I continued on my journey, Gurugalu cleared the path of any and all remainders.

This experience serves as a guiding light in the path of all those enlightened souls. Does it not?

***

39

WHEN GURU VISITS AS A FRIEND!

When ever Pattabhiji spoke about leaving his body, I jokingly used to remark, "Both of us are going together, right? Gurudeva has given that blessing to us. There is no chance that it will turn out wrong. So why do you talk about leaving this body?" However, when Pattabhiji's departure became a reality, it gave a big jolt to me. In this aspect, I got annoyed with Guru Paramparā and Baba. Baba did not keep up his words, and I felt annoyed by that," I said. Just as I finished saying this, I could see anger on both their faces. They looked at each other. Rahul had a questionable look on his face!

***

We were busy with the preparations for the retreat that had been planned at Swami Rama Ashram in Tadakeshwar in Uttarakhand. We had conducted many Srividya and Tantra retreats before this. This was probably the third year since we started Srividya retreats. Each time, Swami Rama and Bengali Baba came at some point during the retreat and gave us darshan and guided us. As a result, the number of people showing interest in joining the retreats and doing the Sādhana consistently increased. However, since the ashram was quite small, only 22 people could be accommodated. So, each time, it was a challenge to limit the number to 22.

The day of the retreat was fast approaching. One day, when I was talking with my daughter, Sadhana, I said, "For the last 2 to 3 years, Bengali Baba has been visiting. This time, I wonder how he would grant us darshan! It would be very nice if Bengali Baba and Swami Rama came together." Sadhana jokingly said, "If they come in the form of Sanyasis or some other form, we may not be able to converse much with them. This time, Sanketh and I are also coming. If they were to come in the form of youngsters like us, how nice it would be, isn't it Amma? We could go around with them, chat with them, probably go on a trek with them, and spend a lot of time together. How nice that would be!"

Since it was jokingly expressed, I also added by saying, "Good idea, Sadhana. You pray to Baba for this, and I will do so too." We just dropped the matter there and got busy with other work. We did not take this conversation very seriously and completely forgot about it, since it was just humorous banter.

The retreat commenced. Sadhana and her husband, Sanketh, were also present. A team of 22 of us had come together for this Tadakeshwar retreat. The environment also was very conducive to doing Sādhana. It had rained and just then stopped. The place was drenched in warm sunlight. Fresh air and a cool breeze added to the charm. Amidst tall deodar trees that almost kissed the sky, with Lord Tadakeshwar's temple and Swami Rama's ashram, the atmosphere would bring a divine experience to every heart. In this serene environment, everyone was happy. Meditation, lectures, debates, Satsang, and question-and-answer sessions were all progressing one after the other as per schedule.

That day, we scheduled a guided meditation session in the Tadakeshwar Mahadev temple premises. The way to that temple is very beautiful. Every day, walking through this hilly jungle path for meditation at the temple hall was in itself a very exhilarating experience. On that day, we had scheduled a trek in the afternoon. A person from the ashram was supposed to come along with us as a guide.

As usual, on that day, I finished the guided meditation and returned on the same path back to the ashram. There is a small kitchen in the ashram and a dining area nearby. I went inside and sat down to have breakfast. Sadhana had already started eating. One of the camp members got me a plate of breakfast. As I started to eat, I noticed two young men sitting outside, waiting to see me. A camp member told me about them. I said, "Ask them to come here. Please serve snacks for them, too."

The two young men came and sat in front of me. They introduced themselves as Rahul and Dhanush. Rahul was a bank employee. As we enjoyed our snacks, we continued our conversation. Suddenly, Rahul came near me and said, "We feel very sad about the demise of your husband, Pattabhiji. It is very bad news. Please accept our condolences." I was a little taken aback by his words and did not know how to respond. As soon as he mentioned Pattabhiji's name; my eyes filled with tears because the pain was still very raw inside me. Despite my efforts, I was still going through the pain of grieving, but at the same time, "Who are these young men? Why are they saying this?" was the question in my mind.

Among these 2 friends, Rahul was the talkative type. Dhanush was quieter. While I was still dealing with the shock of the moment, Sadhana had finished eating and approached us. "Pattabhiji's daughter, Sadhana, a Ayurveda Doctor" I introduced her to the 2 men. Rahul immediately responded, "Oh, is it? Ayurveda Doctor? We heard about your father's demise. It was shocking," he said.

"We both travelled all through the night on our bikes to reach here. I have a cold because of the chilly air. I have tiredness too. Can you suggest some remedy to bring down my cold?" asked Rahul, addressing Sadhana. I took this opportunity to compliment her abilities. "She is a very capable doctor. She also has the blessings of Swami Rama. She will ensure you recover very soon," I said. "Oh, is that true? I will take this as a challenge," teased Rahul. Sadhana laughed and said, "I will get you the medicine right away," and went inside.

When Guru visits as a friend!

As soon as Sadhana left, they started talking about Pattabhiramji again. "Pattabhiji was a very nice person. He was a great yogi; we have a lot of love and respect for him," they went on. "Why are they speaking so much as if they know everything about us? Who are these people?" were the thoughts going on in my mind. Even though these conversations upset me, I continued.

"At quite a young age, he passed away. He was just 59, wasn't he?" they went on. I was further feeling disturbed.

"It was not an age to die. He had Gurudēva Swami Rama's blessings too. But his behaviour seemed like he was stubbornly willing for it to happen. He would often say "I should go. I am done with this body. I want to be relieved from it soon. What is the use of keeping this disease-ridden body and there is no need for me to be alive.". At least 10 times a day, he used to say, "I want to go." He suffered pain in both body and mind. I used to calm him down saying "In life, we are bound to have many challenges. We should not buckle under them.". But he had made up his mind firmly to go. I do feel a deep sense of pain because of this." Saying this, I concluded the conversation as tears flowed down my cheeks.

"Please calm down. He had to go. His time had come, and that's why he left," said Rahul. Not just that, he turned towards Dhanush, who was quietly sitting next to him and asked, "Isn't it Dhanush? What do you say about this?" asked Rahul.

"Yes, yes. The time had come for him to leave. He had to leave." Dhanush reiterated Rahul's words.

I responded, "I'm not sure why you are saying all this. But when I first had mantra diksha by my Guru Swami Rama in 1992, he had said, 'Bete, I love you a lot. On this auspicious moment of mantra diksha, I wish to give you a gift.' He continued, 'I do not want you both to be separated for any reason. Therefore, I am giving you this gift. Both of you are going to leave your body on the same day at the same time together,' he had said. Therefore, whenever Pattabhiji used to talk about leaving, I would jokingly say, 'Both of us are going together, right? Gurudēva has blessed us that way. It cannot go wrong under any circumstances. So why do you talk about leaving this body?' I used to chide him. However, I feel quite angry about Baba and the Guru lineage. I feel frustrated that Baba did not keep up his word," I concluded.

Just as I finished saying all this, I could see both their faces becoming grim with anger. They both looked at each other. Rahul's face seemed like he was questioning, "What is this lady saying?" He turned to look at Dhanush. Dhanush responded, seemingly understanding Rahul's predicament, "No, it was not like that. But he had to leave, that's all," he said. They both again looked at each other and slipped into silence. Seeing them become quiet, I also realised I had probably spoken a little too much about Baba and decided to maintain silence.

In a few minutes, Rahul again started his banter. His face seemed calm again. He got up with a smile and said, "We are feeling tired after the long journey. We will rest for some time." They both went outside to cover their bike, which was kept in open parking. Their passion for their bike was evident. I felt strange seeing all this. I invited them to join the next lecture session if possible. Having said this, I went inside to rest for a while.

Two of the camp members had come to my room to accompany me to the lecture hall. Since the route was hilly and uneven terrain, they had come to extend support in case I needed it. As I came out with them, I saw Rahul sleeping on the bench outside. He seemed fast asleep. My disciples said, "Oh! Rahul is sleeping. Probably, he will not attend the lecture."

"Let him sleep. He must be tired after the long journey. But why is he sleeping here, I wonder. He could have rested inside the room. Anyway, let us not wake him up now," I said, proceeding further.

It felt very special that day, though I wasn't sure why. I felt like calling this retreat "Messages from the Sages." Accordingly, I wrote the same words on the board. It wasn't something I had thought through earlier and decided. It was something that had just occurred to my mind, and I went ahead with it. Everyone liked the name very much.

For about 10 minutes all of us meditated together. During the meditation, I sensed that it was not just the people in the room, but there was the presence of other beings. Probably there could be some sages in their subtle bodies, I thought. My idea of naming the retreat in such a way could have also been because of this. It was not just me; everyone in that room felt that meditation was wonderful and special.

Subsequently, there was a lecture for about an hour, after which we all returned for lunch. At that time, I felt Rahul and Dhanush should have attended the lecture. But when we returned, Rahul was not there. Maybe he got up or left the ashram; I was not sure. Without much thought, we all had lunch and went to get some rest, as we had to prepare to go on a trek shortly after.

Due to the rain the whole previous day, the atmosphere was very pleasant. The soothing sunshine was just apt for the trek. After resting for a while, I got ready to go on the trek and stepped out. I felt it would be ideal to carry a stick for support during the trek and proceeded to ask the people of the ashram. By then, one of the retreat members had already arranged for it. At the same time, Rahul and Dhanush appeared from inside, dressed up and prepared for the trek!!

The retreat member who had arranged for the stick had also tied a piece of saffron cloth to it. In the lineage of Shankaracharya, this system of tying a saffron cloth to the stick is a norm. I turned towards her and asked, "Who made this?" By then, Rahul came and handed the stick to me with a smile. "There is no surprise you might have been Shankaracharya in some lifetime of yours!" he said and laughed. I was confused and slightly irritated.

By then Rahul looked at Dhanush and asked, "You didn't bring the cap and cooling glasses?" "Would we need it?" asked Dhanush. "For sure, we need," said Rahul. Dhanush ran into the room to get them and joined us just as we set forth for the trek.

Rahul had a good camera. He was very interested in photography. He took a lot of pictures all through our journey. Due to the rain of the previous day, the pathway was full of fallen branches and posed small challenges. We all moved forward supporting each other on the way.

Some interesting things happened during the journey. The cap and cooling glasses that Rahul insisted that Dhanush carried were actually meant for me. They put them on me and said, "These look very beautiful on you." Sadhana and Sanketh were walking close by. Rahul looked towards them and said, "Sadhana, you must be missing your father very much, isn't it?" She didn't respond, but her eyes were filled with tears. "Don't worry, Sadhana, your father is in a good place now. Wherever he is, he is very happy too," he said, looking towards me. Again, he tried to console Sadhana by saying, "Don't worry, Sadhana, I'm sure of what I'm saying. Your father has reached a very safe place. He is very happy there," reiterated with conviction.

I was very surprised by his statement and the conviction in it! As we moved forward on our way, there was a big tree that had fallen, blocking our way. It was easier to crawl under the tree and go over to the other side, which everyone did. Rahul stood there instructing everyone to move without disturbing the spider's web on it. He said the same thing to me when my turn came to cross over. I carefully moved over to the other side. "Guruma is the only one who crossed over successfully without disturbing the spider's web," declared Rahul. I did not know whether to take this seriously or as a joke.

Talking, joking, and laughing together, we moved forward and did not realise that it was already an hour since we had started walking. "This is the cave where Swami Rama had done penance. We will sit here and meditate for a while," I said to both of them. "Is that so?" said Rahul, and he looked at Dhanush. "Isn't it interesting that we are going to the same cave again?" he said. I was very surprised to hear his words. I could not fathom why he was saying this!

When Guru visits as a friend!

"We had come here the previous year too. Due to rain and wind, this cave is dilapidated. It seems difficult to accommodate all 25 of us in this cave," I said.

"Oh, you think so? Is it not possible for all of us to fit in? Let's go there and check it out," said Rahul, looking at Dhanush and laughing.

We reached the cave. "One by one go into the cave and sit down," I instructed. There was a rock in the centre of the cave. One by one the team members entered the cave and sat down in an orderly manner. Surprisingly, there was place for everyone. At first glance, it seemed impossible to accommodate 25 people, but I wondered how everyone was able to be seated inside. Rahul and Dhanush sat on the rock in the middle.

"Does anyone have hot water to drink?" enquired Rahul. Since he had a cold, he wanted hot water to drink. Sadhana's medicines had given him considerable relief, and Rahul appreciated her by saying, "You are an amazing doctor. You have chased away my cold in just a few hours." One of the members had brought hot water in a flask. He poured it into a cup and passed it towards Rahul. The cup was passed through many hands before it was handed over to Dhanush, who was sitting next to Rahul. Just as Dhanush received the cup, a bit of hot water spilt on him. He was wearing shorts, and the hot water scaled his thigh, and Dhanush cried out in pain. Someone wiped the water with a cloth, but Rahul was laughing!

He got down from the rock and said, "Jyothiji, come, you sit here on this rock." "I'm quite comfortable here," I protested. However, he insisted, and I gave in and sat on the rock. The cap and cooling glasses that they had put on me were now with Sadhana. They took them from her, and Dhanush put the cap on me while Rahul had me wear the glasses. They laughed happily together.

Suddenly, Rahul became serious. "Ok, let's stop joking now. Time has come to reveal a secret," said he. "I will now tell you a story. It is a very nice story and I'm sure all of you will like it," he continued.

"Before you start the story, Sadhana will say a prayer in praise of Guru. After that, all of us will listen to your story," I said. Sadhana recited Shankaracharya's Guru Ashtakam while everyone joined in the chorus singing, "Tatah kim, tatah kim," and it converted into a bhajan session. After 2 stanzas were done and when the third one was being recited, I could not control my sadness. I started crying inconsolably. Memories of my Guru flooded my mind. After the recitation was done, Rahul came close to me and wiped my tears, "Calm down, don't cry. Why do you cry?" he asked. "I have still not been able to get over the loss of my Guru Swami Rama. Whenever we think or say prayers to the Guru, these tears always well up in my eyes." By saying this, I wiped my tears. They both looked at each other. Rahul started narrating the story.

***

Once upon a time, there was a king. He did not have much devotion to God. But God's Grace was always on him. He was very fond of hunting. Whenever he went hunting, he would take his favourite minister along with him. This minister was a very devoted person. "Everything happens for good" was what he believed in, and he always used to quote this to the king. The king always used to set his words aside and put forth his arguments.

One day, the king went hunting in the forest. The minister went with him. They spotted a cheetah and shot it. The king went near to check if the cheetah was dead. But the cheetah pounced on the king. The minister fought to save the king, and in the process, the king lost one of his fingers. Although his life was saved, the king was furious that he lost a finger and ordered the minister to be imprisoned.

"Now, do you think this also happened for good?" taunted the king.

"Yes, Maharaja, this is also for my good, and I strongly believe in it. God knows exactly what to give us. He is all-powerful. I have immense faith in him. He can never go wrong," said the minister, and went to prison as per the king's order.

Many months rolled by. The king again went to the forest to hunt. He lost his way in the forest and was caught by a wizard. The wizard was looking for a person to perform a human sacrifice ritual. The king was his prized catch for the purpose. As he was about to sacrifice the king, he noticed the missing finger. Since a person with any kind of handicap is not fit to be sacrificed, the wizard released the king! He returned to his kingdom and ordered the release of his minister, who was in prison. "Now I understand the mistake in my thinking. God is truly very merciful. He first took away my finger and now saved my life," said the king, narrating his experience in the forest. He also put forth another question to the minister. "I am still curious to know this. If God was that merciful, why did he make me put you in prison?"

The minister responded, "Maharaja if you had not imprisoned me, I would have accompanied you to the forest when you went hunting. Because of a missing finger, the wizard would have released you, but because I do not have any such flaws, he would have used me for human sacrifice. To save my life, God kept me in prison." The king nodded in agreement, "Everything happens for good. There is a reason for everything."

It is quite normal to have ups and downs in life. "Jo hota hai, acche ke liye hi hota hai! Which means, "Whatever happens, happens for good." If something bad or unpleasant happens in life, we indeed feel sad. But if we always live with the understanding that whatever happens, happens for good, we will be free from our sadness. Rahul narrated this life lesson through this in a very amazing way! I also realised that this story was about my present state of mind!

***

After narrating the story Rahul said, "We have now come to the last segment of the retreat. Everyone, please introduce yourself and along with it, state one of your desires."

All of them introduced themselves and shared information about their profession and their desires. The desire of one member was unusual. She expressed her wish to become like Guruma in the guru lineage and build an ashram. Both Rahul and Dhanush looked at each other. "This is a good idea," they laughed.

When it was the turn of Dr Ashok Bhat couple, his wife Nirmala said, "We wish for the Guru lineage protection and blessings to always be on us. That is all we want. Pattabhiramji had told us that Swami Rama had done penance in this cave for a long time and had also done a comparative study of Srividya and Patanjali's Yogadarshana. Our visit to this cave reminds us of that," she added.

Rahul looked surprised. He turned to Dhanush and said, "Is it? Did you do Omkara sadhana here? I had completely forgotten this! How could I forget it?" Then they spoke something to each other which I did not understand.

Why do their conversations seem like riddles? The more I contemplate, the more it seems complicated. This question started bothering me. Who are these people? They became friendly in such a short time, and now seem like people who are very close to us. They seem like very important people in our lives whom we need. At the same time, the mind sometimes seems clouded when understanding any of this. It sometimes seems like a dream and sometimes real, like the play of light and shadow. It seemed like our minds were not in our control, and someone else was directing it!

We finished the trek and returned to the ashram. We had tea and biscuits and in the meanwhile Rahul and Dhanush got ready and came. "We're leaving now, it's getting late for us," they said and happily left. After going away for a distance, they turned around and waved at us.

There was satsang that night. Since we were all tired, we finished the satsang early and went to bed. I had a good sleep. The next morning, as I was washing my face, a light suddenly shone inside of me. "Oh! The whole of yesterday, the wonderful time we had all had was with none other than Bengali Baba and Swami Rama! They had been with us the whole of yesterday!" This thought dawned on me!

Once again, the faces of Rahul and Dhanush came in front of my eyes. Among the two, Dhanush was very fair. He had a handsome face. His smile was also similar to that of Swami Rama. Rahul had a darker complexion. He was lean built, with a thick moustache and a small beard. They both came across as two close friends. But Dhanush was always submissive to Rahul's words. He came across as an obedient disciple who followed his Guru's words diligently. Indirectly, Dhanush demonstrated Swami Rama's obedience to his Guru!

I called Sadhana and asked, "Didn't you feel that this Rahul and Dhanush were Bengali Baba and Swami Rama?" "Yes, Amma, I too felt so. I forgot to tell you something. This morning, I got up quite early. When I sat to do my Japa, I heard a voice, "Whenever it rains accompanied by thunder and lightning, know that we have come. When I come, I will bring rain, along with thunder and lightning. Not only that, after the rain, I will bring bright sunshine." This was the message I received. I felt this message came to me from Bengali Baba's side. I completely forgot to tell you," she said!

There was no room for doubt! Whatever we had discussed for fun turned into reality! Bengali Baba and Swami Rama had come as friends. They had spent the entire day yesterday with us happily, talking, chatting, and joking. They had left after giving us the memory of a wonderful day together, exactly as we had desired and discussed!

If the disciple calls out with love and affection, will the Guru not come?! This is the glory of Guru!

***

Section 7

- Mother Renuka
- Can't the Mother inside not come out?!

40

MOTHER RENUKA

Conversing with mother Renuka!!

Anyone who has heard stories from the ancient scriptures would know about Renuka Devi as the spouse of Sage Jamadagni and as the mother of Sage Parashurama - an incarnation of Lord Vishnu. But her existence is not limited to only these aspects. She is also popularly known as the incarnation of Mother Parvathi herself, and her birth was to help elevate mankind from its miseries. As such, she is considered the Goddess of the universe; and referred to as Lokmata.

Appeased by the devout Yajna performed by King Renu, Mother Parvathi manifested from the fire as his daughter. As directed by Sage Agasthya, he gets his daughter married to Sage Jamadagni, who is also known as the incarnation of Shiva. Jamadagni is known for his fiery anger. Out of rage, once he commands his sons to behead his devout wife, Sage Parashurama follows the orders of his father and beheads his own mother. These are some of the snippets of stories many people would be familiar with.

Mother Renuka is prayed to across south India as Yellamma Devi and also prayed to across northern India as well. She is also the family deity for many sects in India. In the states of Uttarakhand and Himachal Pradesh, around the banks of the Yamuna River, many villages have exceptional respect and devotion for Mother Renuka. There are many temples dedicated to Mother Renuka in these places. I had an opportunity to visit such a temple once. Having summoned me to her, she graced me with an engaging and long conversation. I am presenting to you the gist of that direct experience and the conversation that ensued.

***

41

CAN'T THE MOTHER INSIDE NOT COME OUT?!

"We have travelled a long distance to see Renuka Mātā. Do you have the keys to the temple?" saying that I tried to take a peek inside to get a glimpse of the deity through the closed door. It was dark inside. I couldn't see the deity clearly. "I can't see Bhagawathi properly from here; if only you had the key with you, we could have opened the door and had darshan of the Goddess," I said, turning towards her. Staring at my face- "Can't the Mother who sits inside not come out?" she said as she laughed.

***

That was Uttarkashi. A mesmerising place surrounded by lush green fields, and tall, majestic mountain ranges. Pleasant air filled the environment with peace, though it was a valley, the ground was flat. There was no one there except us, standing in front of that little Renuka Mata temple that was painted red and white.

"*Koi hai?*" I called out.

No answer! I repeated myself, this time a little louder, "Koi hai?" and yet, there was no response. The presence of divine silence was so strong that we could hear our own breath. Turning towards Gaurav, who accompanied me, I said, "You call out; maybe someone might hear your voice since it's louder."

As if he wasn't inclined to disturb the solemn silence of the place, he went around the temple in the hope of finding someone there. But there was no one. With the hope that the temple bell would reverberate to a farther distance than our voices, he rang the temple bell.

At the strike of the bell, I spotted a lone older woman coming from the right side of the temple. She had a sickle in her hand, which she placed near the havan kund on the right side and walked towards us. As she approached us with curiosity to know who we were, our car, which was parked about 700 metres away from the temple, suddenly sounded the alarm. This was the car's safety feature in case someone tried to open the door of the car. Since the car's alarm kept ringing on and on, Gaurav felt the need to go and check what happened. Or maybe he had to leave so that my special occasion could unfold, with her.

***

There was a strong reason for us both to come to the Renuka Mātā temple. On the occasion of Gangotri's visit, Gaurav felt a strong pull to go to the special temple in a village called Devidhar, which is about 18 kilometres before Uttarkashi. The reason for that is a book- "At the Eleventh Hour," written by Pandit Rajamani. He is Swami Rama's senior disciple and the present director of the Himalayan International Institute of Yogic Sciences and Philosophy, USA. Rajamani writes that Swami Rama himself instructed him to visit this temple along with his American disciples' entourage. Abiding by his instructions, while on his way to Gangotri, Rajamani describes his visit to this temple and his unique experience of meeting Renuka Mātā herself there.

A special thing to note here is, without even knowing the name of the village, we went in search of the temple. Our search continued for a long while and we finally stayed near the same village, which we discovered the next morning before visiting the temple. After some enquiry, we discovered that the temple we were looking for was not too far from our accommodation, which came as a surprise to us both. We reached the temple around 11 o'clock in the morning.

Back in the past, one had to trek to this temple. However, we can now access the temple by vehicle. One would have to park a little before the temple and walk a couple of metres through the agricultural fields. We parked the car under a tree at a distance and came to the temple. Although the temple was small, it was maintained neat and clean. Since it was *pithrupaksha*, the priest had locked up and left quickly after finishing his worship rituals.

When Gaurav went to check on his car, the workers sitting under the tree said, "We don't know what happened. Your car began sounding the alarm on its own. We didn't do anything." After cross-checking the car's status, Gaurav enquired why the temple was closed and came to know- that the temple doors would open only by evening. He got the phone number of the temple priest from the men under the tree and returned to where I was. Looks like all of this would've taken about half an hour or more. A very special conversation took place between Mother Renuka and myself during this half-hour window.

***

"Where do you hail from?" "Is that your son who went to check on the car?" A conversation that began with basic pleasantries took a turn in a completely different direction. "We've come from a long distance to see Renuka Mātā. Do you have the temple keys?" I responded, trying to get a glimpse of the deity through the gaps of the shut gated door, but it was dark, and I could barely see the Goddess through the dimly lit oil lamp inside the temple. "I am unable to see Bhagavathi clearly from here. If only you had the keys, we could have opened the doors, and we could have had darshan of the Goddess," I said, turning to her. Staring at me with a straight face, she replied, "*Andar baitee huee Ma, bāhar nahi ā sakthi hai kyā?*" (Can the mother sitting inside, not come out?) and laughed.

Not only that, but she also approached the stairs not too far from her, "*Idhar āvo beti, baitho baitho*" She insisted strongly by slapping the floor with her hand, as she kept calling me to sit next to her very affectionately.

I obeyed her insistence and did as she said, side by side we sat, hanging our feet down from the temple steps. "I have heard many stories of Renuka Mātā, but I feel like I need to hear it from your mouth. Would you please share?" I re-engaged her in a conversation. "I remember Renuka Mātā's stories well since I grew up listening to them." she enthused.

The old lady had a very special style of storytelling. Her narration was so unique that one may not find it even on the World Wide Web. The story of Parashurama beheading his mother Renuka at the behest of his father Jamadagni is well-known. However, her overall story including that story was not only different but also very special. And thus she began narrating the story in an engaging and intriguing style in Pahadi Hindi.

"There are two Renuka Mātā Mandirs," she stated.

"Oh really? I wasn't aware of that. Have we come to the right one, then? Or should we have gone to the other temple? Besides, where is the other Renuka Mātā temple?" I asked her.

"It's not like that. There is no need to go there. I'll tell you a story. Look over there, at the mountain peak; that's where she is. The one who is here is considered Choti Bahen Renuka; the one out there is considered the Badi Bahen Renuka," she said, pointing out to the mountains at a distance.

"Oh! In that case, what is the difference between the one here and the one there?" I enquired.

"The *Badi* Renuka Mātā, who resides up top of that mountain, mostly has businessmen as her devotees. The rich and fortunate believe in the Goddess who is up there. The goddess here is a *choti* Renuka. She's always thinking and pondering about the big one out there." she said very matter-of-factly.

"Why does she think that way?" I retorted. The old woman continued her story and got me drawn and engaged in her conversational narrative.

"The one there, she's a King's wife. She hails from a great family. Affluent and great people visit her. This *choti* Renuka here, always wonders how to become like the one out there. She's also saddened by the thought sometimes." with this, she begins to narrate the story of Renuka Mahatmya - The Great.

Once upon a time, a group of traders loaded with their goods trekked up the mountain to do their trade. An old man, like everyone else, a trader desired to go up there. However, he couldn't climb the height of the summit. He sought help, asking for someone to carry him along as they carried their trade goods. 'We have enough baggage of our own; we can't take on your load, too,' they responded as they left him. Finally, a merchant happens to chance upon this old man and feels sorry for him. He said, 'I can help you up the mountain; I have less load to carry.' and picked him up along with his luggage. Since he was carrying an old man, he trekked the climb very slowly and cautiously.

All the merchants who had refused to carry the old man had already reached the top, set up their stalls and wound up quite a bit of trade and sales by the time this merchant reached. They teased and laughed at the merchant who came late since he was carrying the old man. "We warned you not to engage with the old man, but you did not pay heed to us. You will face the consequences now. We have all made excellent trade and profits. How are you going to compensate for your loss now?" they said as they laughed at him.

"What else can I do now? I will sell whatever goods I have on me," he said as he laid his luggage down. The moment he opened his luggage, to his shock, all that he had carried had turned to gold. Everyone was puzzled about where this gold came from. "I am clueless. I only carried a sack of salt," said the merchant. And just like that, the news of a sack of salt turning to gold articles spread like wildfire. Thus, everyone became acquainted with the glory of

Renuka Mātā. That day is marked as a very special day to celebrate in the calendar, and even today, on the marked day, they host Renuka Mātā's fair.

"In that case, I should visit that temple too, don't I?" I shot a question to Renuka, who sat beside me.

"*Nahi bete*, No. There is no need for that. What's out there? The one out there is '*duniyaadari*.' She resides there for the people of the material-mundane world. But you have found yourself here, right? Do you know who resides here? All the rishis and sages are here! Ask here; everything is here. Stay right here. Do you understand?" she said.

That's it! My eyes flooded with rivers of tears!

"*Bete*, why do you cry? Unburden all your worries and sorrows at the lap of the mother. Everything will be taken care of." she wiped my tears with affection.

I replied, "These are not tears of sadness. I am very happy to spend this time with you and listen to you."

"If these are tears of joy, then good. There is no worry, my child," she emphasised. She seemed relieved.

Gaurav had returned after checking in on the car at the exact moment my eyes welled with tears. Until then, the only witnesses to the unique conversation that unfolded were Renuka Mātā Mandir, she and I. That's it!!!

Sitting beside each other, both our eyes moist with joy. I bowed down and touched her feet which were beside my own, she reciprocated immediately by bowing down and touching my feet. I didn't know how to respond to this sudden move of hers.

"*Tumne mere paironko chuā, meine tumhare paironko chuā, Hum barābar ho gaye!*" (You touched my feet, and I touched yours. We are, therefore, equal now) she declared as she left me stunned with her words.

***

Later, Gaurav and I gave her Dakshina and bowed in reverence. "Why do you hold my feet again?" she said, "The mother is inside; give her also your offering," she said, pointing towards the goddess. She noticed me trying to deposit some money offerings through the gated door of the temple and said, "You don't need to deposit that big money." Not knowing what else to do next, as I turned towards the old lady, she simply replied, "No worries. Mother will take it."

On the way out, next to the Havan kund, was a small Shivaling. A roofless Shivaling that was completely open to the sky. Crossing the Shivaling, she began looking at me, then the Shivaling and then back at me! Attracted by the Shivaling due to her back-and-forth gazing, I approached the Shivaling and very unconsciously bowed and touched the Shivaling, not once, not twice, but three times! The sensory experience of that touch was awe-inspiring. Although I am usually not one who would do something like that, on that day, she made me do it!

The uniqueness of this experience could not be explained in mere words; although it had come to my field of awareness, it took about 2-3 days for me to process and understand it. A few months before, when we had gone to Kashi, a special experience similar to this had happened. "*Bholenath ko touch karna hai kya?*" some lady with a mobile phone had asked me in the crowd. These words resonated in my mind again. Even amidst all the push and pull, I managed to get a feel for and touch Lord Kashi Vishwanath. The fact that my mind was not fully satisfied then had now been fulfilled by this touch here facilitated by Renuka Mata herself came to my realisation.

She came to the temple gate to see us off. Before leaving, she told Gaurav, "Serve Amma well; come back again sometime."

***

Meanwhile, she had a long conversation with Gaurav about his life, his next moves and so on. His mind was flooded with questions and conflicts. We got into the car and turned it towards Gangotri as we had the Darshan of Renuka Mātā, to our heart's content. But it was far from over. The awareness that there is more for us to experience came when we locked eyes with him!

Looking at the man who stood in front of the car, I said, "He seems like the priest, just enquire." He also stared back at us. Gaurav pulled down the window and asked, "Are you the *pandit* here?" "Yes, Indeed!" he responded, "where are you coming from sir?" he followed up with a question.

As soon as we asked him about the temple visit, he said, "Since it is *pithrupaksha*, the temple will open only at 4:00 pm." and invited us to his house. He did not give an opportunity to even consider another option. "Okay, let's go and see," I said as I got out of the car. Gaurav parked the car, and we were about to head towards the house; again, without any reason, the car began sounding the alarm. The alarm went on and on for a couple of moments and went silent on its own. A car that had no issues, no battery draining problems, no electrical problems had sounded the alarm twice that day without reason!

The pandit made tea for us. Gaurav hinted to me that he had to share something. When Gaurav asked this, we did not know that the man was not only a temple priest but also an astrologer. As he engaged us in a conversation, he brought out a diary from inside the room. On it was written- *'Himalayan Institute, Jolly Grant'* "You were also talking about Swami Rama; this dairy is also from there." he said as he showed it to us. He stated some life events and situations that had unfolded in Gaurav's life.

***

The next day, we visited a Sādhu, well-known as Pāndava Guhfa Baba. While in conversation, he stated, "You are the Goddess herself" out of the blue. These words, coming from a Sadhu who was very stern, spoke only when the need was dire and mostly maintained noble silence was a great validation to the words of Mā Renuka - "You paid your obeisances at my feet, and I paid my obeisances at your feet. Now we are equals!"

***

If Swami Rama prayed to Mā Bhagavathi for his disciples, why would she not come to give darshan? Tell me.

A month after this incident, Gaurav went alone in the same car to the Jolly Grant Himalayan Institute Hospital campus. He had parked the car and was about to walk away to meditate in Swami Rama Memorial Hall, the car again had sounded the alarm three times and stopped on its own. It was a definite message from Baba 'It was my blessings and will, that you could have Mā Renuka's darshan.'

The car never showed this kind of behaviour any time after that day!

***

Section 8

- Bhole Baba's instructions and Bholenath's presence
- Kalabhairava on a Varanasi twilight
- Darshan of Lord Kashi Vishwanath
- Saptharshi Pooja – A Divine Experience

42

BHOLE BABA'S INSTRUCTIONS AND BHOLENATH'S PRESENCE

Pouring rain; the wipers of the car were busy wiping off the raindrops, being clear at one moment and full of raindrops the other!

In a similar moment of clarity and haziness on our part, the old man had appeared. His kind grace was what took us to Varanasi! What is special about this esoteric pilgrimage centre is that while the original triangle (Moola Trikona) of Sri Chakra Yantra of Srividya practice is manifested as the land of Bharata (India), the three corners of the triangle are taken as Kashmir, Kanyakumari, and Nepal, as the tantric equivalents. The Bindu (●) in the Sri Chakra Yantra and the triangle are accepted as Varanasi by the tantric adepts in practice. Hence, it is regarded as the point and place of liberation.

To be more specific, it was as per the instructions of Bhole Baba that we reached the sanctum sanctorum of Bholenath!

How did that happen? Who was the old man? What is the connection between him and Swami Rama? You may be puzzled by all these questions coming up in your mind. Answers to all your questions will be answered in the forthcoming chapters of this book.

```
K                                    N
 \                                  /
  \                                /
   \                              /
    \                            /
     \                          /
      \                        /
       \          ●           /
        \                    /
         \                  /
          \                /
           \              /
            \            /
             \          /
              \        /
               \      /
                \    /
                 \  /
                  \/
                  K
```

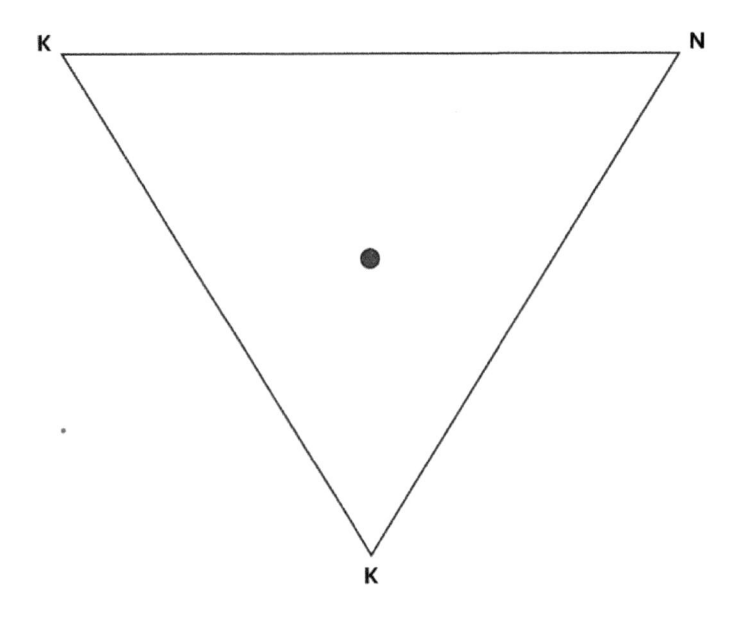

For now, let us bow down to the feet of Goddess Renuka Devi at Gangotri and proceed on our journey towards Kashi. Varanasi is a power centre of spirituality. Lord Vishwanath's power is unveiled only to the sincere seekers and sadhakas. The Ida, Pingala and Sushumna nadis are represented by the rivers Ganga, Yamuna, and Saraswati. Along with Yamuna and Saraswati, the Ganga River flows, and on her banks, the town of Varanasi is the holiest abode of God. Gurudēva Swami Rama was not someone who would send us here without a reason. So, what was his purpose? How did he reveal that?

Dusk was setting in. As I bowed down to the holy Ganga, a tall, dark, and handsome person appeared before me. Who is he? What is the background to this? Come, let's find out!

***

43

KALABHAIRAVA ON A VARANASI TWILIGHT

"A terrifying face. Pitch black form. Sunken cheeks. Protruding cheekbones. Bountiful crown hair and heavily bearded with moustache. His lean, bony stature made one feel he might crumble at the slightest touch. In a grim voice, he said, "Your mission of arriving here is to go to Satyaloka."

We were dumbfounded."

***

It was the time when the bright noon sky mellowed into the warm red of the evening. Heavy public crowding was common in Kashi. It was even more so on weekends and during vacations. But without the slightest hunch of this fact, I landed at Varanasi one blistering noon. I was anxious at the very first sight of the swarm of people gathered. The little energy I held onto just evaporated away in the simmering heat of Varanasi. Gurudēva Swami Rama's mandate - I landed at Kashi. We just had two days' time. Baba had only intimated us about visiting Kashi, but we had no inkling of what we had to do or where we had to go. I stood there along with Gaurav, completely mortified, and staring at the sea of people like two lost children at a fair, not knowing where to go next. We decided to just loiter around the place until we received further instructions from Baba and do as per his guidance once we received it.

There was no end to the ocean of people in our sight at one side, and on the other side was the calm, graceful, meandering waters of Ganga Mai, even in that bustling din of a crowd. Generally, the boatmen cater to visitors when paid and help visit all the ghats of the vicinity. There was an opportunity to witness the Ganga arathi at the banks of Ganga Mai as dusk approached. I decided to visit all the ghats, threw caution to the wind, and asked Gaurav to engage a boatsman. By luck or ill fate, we didn't get any. A few diesel boats were available. But I did not want to engage any diesel boats that heavily polluted the air and disturbed the tranquil serenity with their cacophonous noise. My maverick heart did not agree to engage the boat.

I said, "Gaurav if Baba asked us to come here, there must be some reason. Let's both walk down the shore of Ganga Mai for a bit. Let's sit down at a place that's less crowded. Let's watch Ganga mai for a while." The place had small lanes and choc-a-bloc with people brushing past, not minding personal boundaries of touch, claiming to directly witness the Lord, rickshaw drivers calling out for customers, there were coughers, spitters, and misers. Gaurav and I walked our way through this, not knowing where we were to go.

We just walked for a long time with no destiny or charter in mind. We got exhausted. We were looking forward for further instructions from Baba. As we walked, we finally arrived at a place with less crowd. I said to Gaurav "Let's go sit there." We sat at the stairs letting our feet dip into the waters. The soothing touch of the soft waves of Ganga Mai washed away the exhaustion from our tired feet.

It was the hour of dusk that harmonised day and night. The peaceful flow of Ganga Mai soothed our weary minds and bodies. A few people were swimming in front of us. Here and there, boatsman anchored their boats at the shore. A few boats that were just nearby where we sat bumped along by the effect of the winds and waves over Ganga Mai. This place was indeed serene. Abruptly, the people seated there got up and scooted away one by one as if they had just remembered an urgent work. We two were the only ones left there, barring an aged person who was swimming in front of us.

Suddenly, a white dog appeared in front of us, trying to get off the middle boat anchored near us. We wondered how this dog appeared out-of-nowhere. There was quite a bit of space between the boat and the shoreline. It was not feasible to reach it without getting into the waters. As we were watching, the dog jumped to the boat on the right. It looked for a way off that boat, too. There was no way out. It jumped back to the boat at the centre and then hopped to the boat on the left. It kept hopping between the three boats. I said to Gaurav, "Maybe the dog is looking for a way off the boat and wants to come ashore. See if you can find a way to get the dog ashore."

He loved canines, but on that day, he said, "Amma, this is unfamiliar territory; that dog is not acquainted with us. It would be difficult if I trigger an attack by trying to do something. It won't come even if I pull it this side. It might bite me if I force it to come aside" and he left it at that. My mind was a bit restless, thinking that the dog might be stuck there if nobody tried to get it ashore. I felt sorry, wondering what might happen to it; the dog kept hopping around the three boats without making a clear attempt to come ashore. My mind lingered on the dog.

The twilight set in as time passed by. There was a mild light from the streetlamps. A man came by the lane. He had steel buckets in both his hands. We kept chatting with each other, observing the swimmers in front of us, assuming that the man was just passing by. Just as I was preparing to start my chanting practice, that man came to us. He kept those buckets right beside us. This was unexpected for both of us. He, just like that, came near us. It was evident from his confident gait that he was a person belonging to the locality. I thought we must ask this man what and all we could see in Kashi.

By then, about 30 dogs came near where we were, howling loudly all along. Many of the dogs were black. Some were a mix of black and white. They surrounded that man. The man unflinchingly started disciplining the dogs as he kept muttering "sushh sushh." There were some plates in the steel buckets he had got. It had food. We couldn't see much clearly since it was getting dark. We could only see with the dim light from the streetlamp. He served equal portions of rice on the plates for all the dogs there. Being dogs, they were constantly eyeing each other's plates and jumping here and there. He disciplined the dogs with the sway of a stick and a cautioning voice, not allowing the dogs to eat off each other's plates and keeping them to their respective plates. The dogs ate their food and were as noisy as a class of naughty children. He looked at us occasionally. He turned to Gaurav and spoke to him in English, asking, "Where are you coming from"? They both started talking to each other. Despite all these, the white dog remained in the boat. I felt pity since that dog was stuck there while all the dogs were eating there. I was telling Gaurav to request the man to get that dog here.

I wondered, "Why is that one dog stuck there? Doesn't it want to eat? It might not get food if it doesn't eat now?" Gaurav enquired with the man. The man saw the white dog. But his attention was towards the other dogs. He said, "That dog is like that only. It does not come anywhere here when these dogs are here. It is shy. It's been like this since it was a puppy. I am the one fostering it." It felt weird. I did not feel comfortable thinking that the dog might not get anything to eat since all the other dogs would finish the food. By then, the men swimming there pushed the boat with a stick and encouraged the dog to jump off the boat and go eat. It did not budge a bit. It would just jump away from them into another adjacent boat.

Almost 20-25 minutes passed this way. The dogs ashore had their fill. Some started loitering around there itself. We prepared to leave as we realised the passage of time and the man too was about to leave. Just then, the man looked at the white dog and called out "Ajao" asking it to come.

The dog immediately jumped into the water and came ashore in a jiffy. I was so disturbed looking at the state of the dog in the past 20-25 minutes and it came by so swiftly like a good child. When it came near, the man placed its plate of food for it. It started eating very calmly. "Does it always behave like this?" asked Gaurav. "Yes, it always does this and is very dear to me" replied the man.

After it ate, the man picked up his steel buckets and must have placed just 2 steps before turning to Gaurav. That is when I looked at him properly. It was a face that triggered fear! Pitch black form. Sunken cheeks. Protruding cheekbones. Bountiful crown hair and beard with moustache. His lean, bony stature made one feel he might crumble at the slightest touch.

In a grim voice, he said, "Your mission of arriving here is to go to Satyaloka," pointing his finger upward to the sky. We wondered how he knew all of this and were dumbfounded. He then asked, "Have you come with your mother?" Gaurav replied, " She is my Guru."

He enquired, "What are you learning?" Gaurav replied, "I am learning Srividya. Ours is the tradition of the Himalayan Yogis as taught to us by Swami Rama." He said, "Take Mother along with you." Gaurav must have been nervous then, and he kept quiet, looking at the man. He said, "Have you heard of Lahiri Mahashaya?" Gaurav nodded to say yes. The man continued, "His samadhi is here only. I stay right near Lahiri Mahashaya's samadhi. It is called Satyaloka. You can go there tomorrow. You must take Mother along," this time showing his hand to the left of where he was standing.

We both stood dumbfounded. Why did lift his finger upward towards the sky mentioning Satyaloka? And who is he? I felt he was not an ordinary person, as we had assumed.

As we passed the ghats, there was a horde of people going for Saptarishi ārathi and returning from the temple after darshan. I was very tired. There was no space for any vehicular movement in that narrow lane, but cycle rikshaws were allowed. I do not engage in a cycle rikshaw where another fellow human has to pedal to make the journey. It felt inhuman to me. I had conveyed the same to Gaurav when he suggested that I take the cycle rickshaw. Gaurav replied, "Amma, please do not be adamant. Understand the situation. You are very fatigued. You cannot walk that far. For the time being, there are only cycle rickshaws here. The rickshaw driver also can earn his livelihood. You can pay him more if you wish to. I will walk down." I could see no option but to agree. Gaurav called the cycle rickshaw and engaged him in pushing it instead of pedalling. He then walked down together with us.

I boarded the cycle rickshaw, and it was a flood of people wherever I saw. Amidst all this, he was pulling the cycle rikshaw and coming.

I felt the cycle seat to be very high since all the people around seemed to be at a much lower height. It was a weird feeling. My seat was like a throne or pedestal, and I felt like I was seated like Devi on her throne. The place was lighted by streetlamps. There was a man by the flight of stairs near a building who was calling for people to come to visit Lord Kalabhairava. Later, we realised that the building wasn't just any building but a consecrated temple.

The moment I heard the name of Kalabhairav, it flashed to me that the man we met at the banks of Ganga Mai was no ordinary man but Kalabhairava himself.

The dog is the vehicle of Kalabhairava. It is said he is the protector of this Kshethra or the zone. As per the Āgama Shāstra of the tantric tradition, one must first visit and offer obeisance to Kalabhairava and then visit Kashi Vishwanath and Visalakshi temples. I was aware of this. But I was not familiar with the city of Kashi. We had less time on our hands. Looking for Kalabhairava's temple and then visiting Vishwanath's temple was a luxury we couldn't afford since it took much more time. As we left the ghats, we decided to stand in queue by 5 am the next morning to seek the darshan of Kashi Vishwanath and Visalakshi. Lo and behold, we received Kalabhairava's darshana. I conveyed the same to Gaurav.

Readers might find it weird to understand that the man we met was indeed Kalabhairava; in fact, you might even feel him to be a normal human. You might want to understand by what logic I recognised that man to be Kalabhairava himself. One can understand this if one understands the invisible mysterious energy behind Varanasi. Only the sādhakas may perceive this. Particularly, Sri Vidya Sadhakas enjoy even the respect of the devathas or heavenly beings. It is not surprising that Devathas would come to visit such Sādhaka. This has been elucidated in our scriptures. But they stun us enough in their presence so that we do not realise who they really are because our behaviour would then change in the face of their stark reality, and the situation may change, too. This is a spiritual truth. But this cannot be proved in a laboratory. This is an internal realisation. In retrospect, we realised this is Baba's first intended experiential blessing for us in this journey to Kashi. As per Āgama Shāstra, he can be inferred to be Kalabhairava as well. In Sanskrit, death is one of the interpretations of the word Kāla. Before true absolution at the Feet of the Divinity, the trivial self must face death. This death begets no rebirth. Witnessing Kalabhairava means accepting this death wholeheartedly. Without Kalabhairav's consent, one may enter the temple but not attain the divine spiritual purpose of the visit to Kashi. But Baba wanted us to have this experience.

Suddenly, Gaurav had a thought, and he asked, "Amma, what do you think of the white dog?"

"That is you only, dear. Kalabhairava created a replica of you out there." Said I.

"I, too, felt the same," replied Gaurav. "Why did you feel like that?" I prodded.

"Kalabhairava said one thing. The white dog did not like to compete with the other street dogs. Even I am like that. I like to enjoy my Sādhana. If somebody does better than me, I am never interested in doing better than them. I don't see anything beyond your love. But I do not know where to go with all this. My mind just keeps jumping here and there. Perhaps that's why the middle boat of the three over there was a bit wide and spacious. The other two were smaller. I felt the flanking smaller boats represented the Ida and Pingala, and the middle boat represented the Sushumna. I felt I was jumping between these three, not knowing what to do." replied Gaurav.

"This is Varanasi!" I exclaimed.

Shivapurana explains thus about Varanasi. Ganga, Yamuna, and Saraswathi, these three rivers represent the ida, pingala, and Sushumna nadis of our body. The pristinely auspicious Ganga flows along with Yamuna and Saraswathi in Varanasi. Lord Vishwanath dwells in such an auspicious place. This is a place of complete absolution at the feet of the Supreme Divine.

Moreover, Kalabhairava indicates the concept of death. Going to Kashi is to overcome death. When man overpowers all his boundaries and limiting definitions of the self, he overcomes death. To be defined by one's cultural times and nationality is one's limitation. To overcome this definition, one must overcome kāla/death. Shiva exists beyond this oscillation of the duality of life and death. Shiva manifested is Shakthi. Kalabhairava helps Jeevas along the path by guiding them in overcoming limitations. To realise the Vishwanath - the lord of the universe within, one must overcome these limitations or the death that shadows us. Kalabhairava aids us in this. Only with His guidance can we realise the Vishwanath or Shiva dwelling within us.

I realised that Baba has shown these truths to me. For the seekers, on a subtle note, this perceptive understanding is feasible. For the rest, this becomes a tell-tale string of coincidental events. That's all. In fact, everybody has spiritual experiences daily, but does not comprehend them for the lack of right perception.

***

Lahiri Mahashaya:

Yogi Shyama Charan Lahiri was well-known as Mahashaya (greatly respected). He lived between 1828 and 1895. He initiated the Gurukula of Kriya yoga, teaching Kriya yoga. He was the disciple of the great Guru of the Himalayas, Mahavathar Babaji. Paramahamsa Yoaganandaji has explained about Lahiri Mahashaya in his book "Autobiography of a yogi." His final resting place is in Varanasi. A meditation hall is also present.

Messages from the Himalayan Sages: Timely & Timeless

44

DARSHAN OF LORD KASHI VISHWANATH

I saw a monk on the roadside, in the highway underpass, and with the attitude of an Emperor! At that moment I only understood "Both of you have to go", by his hand signals. After a long time, I realised that it was Baba himself, directing us to go to Kashi. As per the instructions, when we went to Kashi, the divine experience that we had cannot be explained in words!

***

"Vishwanath ko touch karna hai kya"? (Do you want to touch Lord Vishwanath?) asked a voice in Hindi from very close by. I turned around in surprise and saw a lady talking on her phone. In between her conversation, she turned towards me and asked again, "Vishwanath ko touch karna hai kya?" We were standing near the main entrance of the Kashi Vishwanath temple. The queue was probably a kilometre. As we went to join the queue at the far end after depositing our footwear in the designated area, I heard this voice. I had never seen her before and did not know who she was. She was around 35 years of age and had surprised me by casually asking this. The first couple of times when she asked this question, I assumed it was meant for the person on the phone and just looked at her without responding. The third time when she repeated, I understood. I nodded in affirmation.

Then she continued her conversation as if nothing ever happened. Her question was still ringing in my ears.

"Vishwanath ko touch karna hai kya?" were not her words. She could not have realised that she had uttered these words. This question was directed to me through her. That was very clear. I asked Gaurav, who was standing next to me. "Did you hear that? We are now going to enter the temple and touch Lord Vishwanath." He looked at the serpentine queue in front of us and said, "Amma, look at the queue! Forget touching Lord Vishwanath; I doubt whether we will be able to enter the temple itself." I just repeated in a kind of trance, "We are going to touch Lord Vishwanath." He just stood puzzled. The queue moved slowly forward. Just then, a boy wearing ochre robes stood before us and asked us in Hindi, "Would you like to take darshan of the Lord? Shall I escort you inside?" Many people like him are seen all over Kashi. For a few rupees, they escort people into the temple for darshan. Gaurav thought this person was probably also one among them and asked, "How much will you charge for it?" After a brief pause, "I don't want any money," said he. "They all say this, but once inside, they demand a lot of money. Please tell us how much you will charge," asked Gaurav vehemently. The boy looked towards me and repeated, "I do not want any money. I will take you inside for darshan." With an affirmative glance, I beckoned to Gaurav to say that we would go with the boy. Gaurav agreed.

What a surprise! The youth treated us like VIPs and escorted us towards the sanctum sanctorum for darshan. He signalled to the security personnel who stood near the barricades, and he also made way for us to go in. After we walked a few steps, the youth shouted out to another person who was standing there, "Take these people for darshan," and he disappeared into the crowd. The second person took us forward into the temple. We finally entered the sanctum in a way we had never imagined it would happen!

My mind alternately meditated upon my Gurudēva Swamy Rama and Lord Kashi Vishwanath. Swami Rama, whom we affectionately called "Baba," was also called "Bhole Baba." Everywhere around us, we could hear chants of "Har Har Mahadev" and "Bhole Baba" reverberating in the temple. "Bhole Baba" means someone who is filled with innocence, which indicates Lord Shiva's nature. Momentarily, I felt that my Gurudēva and the Lord were not two entities but one! When I was given the highest diksha of our lineage, called "Shambhavi Diksha," my Gurudēva had mentioned that he was doing so in the presence of Lord Shiva himself! At that time, I did not understand his words. Now, I was slowly able to comprehend what he meant by that.

The name of the place we were in, Varanasi, can be split into two parts: Varana and Asi. Varana indicates the Ida Nādi, and Asi indicates the Pingala Nādi. These naadis traverse on either side of our backbone. The rivers Ganga and Yamuna are seen in comparison with these energy channels. The river Saraswati, which is said to flow under the surface of the Earth and is understood as a secret path of spiritual seeking, is compared to the central channel called Sushumna Nādi in our body, which is also believed to lead a person attain Moksha or salvation. The Kashi Vishwanath temple, has special significance because it is in between these two holy rivers, the Ganga and Yamuna. The important significance of the Shivaling in Kashi is that it is said to be the Sahasraara of the Universe. I had received an indication earlier that we would be able to touch Lord Vishwanath, and now we also have the blessings of Gurudēva. It somehow felt that Gurudēva Swami Rama himself had given us the indication to visit Kashi!

***

One afternoon, I went to the house of my disciple, Srilakshmi, for the Guruvandana programme. Gaurav had accompanied me. As I alighted from the car at the destination, Gaurav felt that, for a fleeting moment, my face appeared like that of Swami Rama! All through the Guruvandana programme, as I was accepting the offerings, I felt the presence of my Gurudēva. It felt like I was not the one accepting the offerings, but it was my Gurudēva doing so through me! I felt Baba was within me and getting all this done. Few of the people present there also experienced a divine presence!

It was softly drizzling as we proceeded from there towards the ashram in Ramanagara. "Let's go to Channapatna. We must purchase ghee for homa," said Gaurav. We continued without taking the turn to the ashram. Just then, Gaurav looked at me and said, "Amma! Someone seems to be sitting below this flyover. I feel like meeting him!" I felt a bit strange when I heard his words. Anyway, there were lots of fruits in the car, which people had offered during the Guruvandana programme. If we see any beggars there, we could give them these fruits. I thought about it and suggested it to Gaurav. He reversed the car and proceeded to drive under the flyover.

As we drove off the Mysuru Expressway towards the underpass of the flyover, the drizzle became heavier. The windscreen wiper was busy in action. A little ahead under the flyover, sometimes clear and sometimes blurry, I could see a monk with the attitude of an Emperor! He had dark sunglasses on and was wearing an ochre shirt. On that was a red blazer and an orange scarf. He looked around 70 years or so. He was lean and seated on the sand by the road, but he had the attitude of sitting on a royal throne with his head held high like an Emperor, with both his hands crossed behind his head and cross-legged!

Gaurav fetched some fruits from the boot of the car and handed them to me. He reached into the dashboard to get some money to offer along with the fruits. He laid his hands on a 500 rupee note. He took that, and both of us moved forward toward the monk. Without changing his royal pose, the man looked towards us. His sunglasses added to the attitude on his face. I handed over the fruits and the money to him. Without bothering to see the currency note, he just kept it aside. I wondered if he realised it was a 500 rupee note and would lose it by just carelessly keeping it aside. I pointed towards the note and said, "That is a 500 rupee note. Keep it carefully, don't forget"! He looked towards the note and nodded.

He did not seem to be a Kannadiga. Yet I spoke in Kannada and asked, "Where are you from?" He murmured something under his breath. I could just see his lips move. I repeated my question. Just as he answered, a noisy truck came by. I saw a truck driver who had parked close by with the engine on, and I could not hear what the beggar had responded. By then, Gaurav came closer and asked him loudly, "Where do you stay?" The old man gestured towards a place afar. We could see only fields in that direction. We felt he pointed in that direction to indicate our Swami Rama Sādhana Dhama ashram. We also felt that we were unable to communicate with him as he could not understand whatever we were saying, so we turned to leave. Just then, he said something that we couldn't comprehend. He gestured that we both should go to where? We did not understand.

He showed his index and middle fingers as if to say, "the 2 of you" and gestured far away and said we should go there. We could not comprehend where we had to go, but both of us had to go was what was said. This much we understood. Dumbfounded, we did not know what else to say, and we took leave.

After driving away for a distance, it suddenly occurred to me! This person was none other than our Baba! As long as we were in his company, he had used his mystical powers to cloud our intellect, so we didn't recognise him! I turned towards Gaurav and said, "That was Baba!" Gaurav looked into my eyes and said, "Amma, I too felt the same. I was just waiting for you to say it!" My mind was in turmoil. On the one hand, I felt delighted that Baba had given darshan to us. On the other hand, I felt he could have accompanied us to the ashram; we all could have sat down together and had a chat. All these fancy ideas crossed my mind. It settled down after some time, and I realised that Baba was telling us to visit Varanasi!

This was not the only indication we had received from Baba asking us to visit Varanasi. Around a year and a half ago, Baba had visited Gaurav in his dream, wherein Gaurav was on a call with Baba sitting in the bus. But this experience was very vivid and unlike a dream. It seemed more like a vision because when he woke up, Gaurav recalled and narrated every little detail. If it was a dream, generally, we tend to forget many things when we wake up. Even if we remember some portions, it would not be with complete details. But Gaurav could remember every little detail of what he dreamt. Baba was on the phone with Gaurav while Gaurav was travelling in a bus.

Gaurav said, "I love you, Baba," and Baba replied, "I love you, beta"! Suddenly the phone went dead. Gaurav called the number again, but someone else received the call. Gaurav requested to speak with Baba, saying he had a call from that number, and it had been disconnected. The person on the line responded, "Baba is in Varanasi," and cut the call.

After this incident, he asked me, "Amma, is Baba asking me to go to Varanasi, or is this an indication that he is asking me to do internal Sādhana? As per references seen in Shiva Samhita, as I have explained earlier, "Varana" represents the "Ida" naadi, and "Asi" represents the "Pingala" naadi. Kashi stands for the "Sushumna" nādi in the middle. "Could this be about internal Sādhana or the geographical city called Varanasi?" he asked. "For now, you continue your Sādhana. If it is meant that you must visit Varanasi, you will get another indication again, then you can visit," I had told. Gaurav had responded, "Amma, how can I go alone? If I get any experiences there, I will not be able to comprehend them. Let us both go together."

***

In another instance, as we were all returning to Bangalore after a trip, near Attibele we spotted a board that said, "Varanasi 1,742 kms"! At that time Gaurav's mother also was with us. All 3 of us had seen the board. We had never spotted that board earlier whenever we had travelled on that road. All of us were puzzled – where is Varanasi and where is Bangalore, to show the distance in kilometres?!

Many experiences like this were indications from Baba that we should visit Varanasi. But the time had come only now.

***

While we were waiting in the queue at Lord Vishwanath's temple, I recalled all these instances, and my mind went into a meditative state. Meanwhile, the jostling crowd in the temple pushed us around from one place to another. People were screaming at each other. But my mind was as calm as a ship in the middle of the ocean. Moving ahead slowly, we finally stood in front of Lord Vishwanath. We were within touching distance of the Lord. But because of people crowding, I could not bend down and touch the Lord despite having come so close to Him. Gaurav was standing at a distance with flowers in his hand. "Amma, were you able to touch the Shivaling? he asked loudly from there. "No, Gaurav, I couldn't bend down," I responded. Somehow, he came to me, held me by the hand, and pulled me even closer to Lord Vishwanath. With his other hand, he tried to keep the teeming crowd away. "Now bend down and touch Him," he signalled. I bent down and touched the Shivaling. A deep feeling of gratitude overwhelmed me.

We had stood in the queue for darshan at 5 a.m. and it had taken around 4 and a half hours for us inside the temple. It was now around 9.30 a.m. I said to Gaurav "We were asked so many times Vishwanath ko touch karna hai kya, and now we have finally done it." He had a smile on his face. I could see immense gratitude in that.

***

45

SAPTHARSHI POOJA – A DIVINE EXPERIENCE

Light!

Golden light!

Those seven Rishis with a divine glow on their faces!

Athri, Bharadwaja, Gautama, Jamadagni, Kashyapa, Vasishta and Vishwamithra!

These were the Saptharshis. They have descended from their Loka and invoked in these 7 priests who are now performing pooja to Lord Vishwanatha.

The boundary between the earthly and heavenly planes has slowly diminished and everything at that moment seemed like just Lord Shiva!

Even though I wanted to keep my gaze constantly on, my eyelids closed by themselves in pure devotion. Tears of joy flowed!

***

Gurudēva, who had asked through that lady, "Vishwanath ko touch karna hai kya?" had now given the next indication, "Saptharshi Pooja."

The ticket for this pooja was exhausted the previous day itself. Amidst this, we overheard a conversation between two priests.

"Someone from the Commissioner's side has come, he is supposed to be permitted inside."

"Does he have a ticket?"

"No."

"In that case send him back. No one without a ticket can be allowed inside."

"Okay, Swami."

Gaurav looked at me. "Don't get influenced by what you just heard. Go and enquire with them," I said. He went directly to that person. He was a rotund man, very fair and immaculate looking. But his eyes were big, harsh, and authoritative. A large tilak of vibhuthi with vermilion in the centre adorned his forehead. His beautiful, divine face had a shadow of sternness.

"We want to witness the Saptharshi Pooja," Gaurav enquired, sceptically. "Do you have tickets," he asked. "No, this is my Guruma. She would like to witness the Saptharshi Pooja," answered Gaurav.

"Without tickets, there is no entry inside. Do one thing: buy tickets for tomorrow's pooja at the counter," he carelessly responded.

"No, we have to leave tomorrow."

"So, what can I do? How can you be allowed inside without tickets? You must just stand here and watch; that's it!"

"Here? But from here, we cannot see the Pooja happening inside?"

I intervened. "Namaskara, we are Srividya Bhagavathi upasakas. Both of us have come here under the indication of our Gurudēva," I said.

"Ok, but Mataji, you don't have the ticket required for the darshan," he insisted firmly.

"I'm a Srividya upasaki. The Saptharshis who descend here come in my meditation, too! They guide me! My Gurudēva has instructed me to witness this pooja. Based on his instructions, we are here. We are unaware of the rules and regulations here." after saying all this, I was still not confident that he would accommodate us. Such stories may be given by each of the lakhs of devotees who visit every day.

But a miracle happened at this point. Up until that time he, who was talking with authority and firmness, turned towards me. His stern facial expression slowly softened.

"Mataji, now there will be darshan facilitated for the public. It will go on till 6.30. Then, the people who have tickets for special ārathi will have darshan. That will conclude at 7. After that, the sanctum sanctorum will be cleaned up, after which the Saptharshi Pooja will commence. Please stay here till I tell you," he said respectfully. Further, he arranged a bench for me to be seated.

I sat there till I got an indication from him. After some time, the barricades were moved, and he took both of us inside. No one else could cross the barricades. Once again, we got another chance to touch the Shivaling and pour milk over it! Then, he found a place for us to sit and instructed us not to move from there and disappeared into the crowd.

The man standing in front of us moved slightly to the side. What a surprise! Lord Vishwanath was just in front of us! We were very close to the Lord. We realised that he had made us sit right in front of the Lord. After some time, the cleaning process commenced. It was a question of cleaning up all the flowers, milk, and plastic covers left behind by thousands of devotees. It was a big challenge to clean up all this. But they did it very quickly and in a matter of just ten minutes the place was sparkling clean! Even a small petal of a flower was not left behind; they had cleaned it thoroughly. Darshan of just the Shivaling without any decorations and with just a strip of silver around it! It was an unexpected moment of pure bliss!

After the cleaning process was completed, those seven priests arrived. The priest whom we had met outside made us both sit right behind these Saptharshis I had never thought we would get an opportunity to sit so close by. Pooja commenced grandly. Every ritual was happening right in front of my eyes. The entire atmosphere was filled with divinity. The mind and heart were held in magnetic focus. As we watched, the facial expressions and emotions of the priests performing the pooja underwent a subtle change. Due to many years of practice of meditation, I was able to comprehend these things. It seemed like celestial beings were invited and present in these priests! Such was their body language. It was not just a belief that the great Saptharshis themselves descended to perform pooja to Lord Vishwanath; it was the truth unfolding right before my eyes! Loud chanting of mantras in a divine rhythm – the place was reverberating and overflowing with vibrations. The facial expressions, the music of drums, and the Damaru .... witnessing all this was Gaurav and me. It was a moment of complete dumbfoundedness. The language of communication with God at that moment was just silence.

At this point, I want to remind you that Swami Rama had given me the Srividya "Shāmbhavi Diksha" in 1992. After he left his body in 1996, Baba sent Pattabhiji and me to Mysuru Srividya guru Mahamahopadhyaya Padmashri Dr. R. Sathyanarayana (initiation name Shri Sathyanandanatha) to continue our learning in the south Indian tradition of Srividya. I had once asked him, "What is the purpose of the remaining part of my life?" "It will be revealed to you tomorrow in your meditation," he had said. The next day, during meditation, I saw "Āgama Shāstra" written in golden letters!

The pooja system that I witnessed here in Kashi was the essence of Āgama Shāstra! It was because of Baba's grace that I could witness it!

In between all this Gaurav was repeatedly prostrating to the Lord and wiping his eyes. "Amma, it feels like I'm in a different world," he said.

A few years ago, Baba said, referring to my spiritual experiences, "Whatever you write will become a historical document." My Mysuru Gurugalu had said, "Whatever you write should be the closest expression of the truth." He also added that it "should be welcoming" to the reader. Those words came to mind at this moment. I must record all these experiences in that book, I thought to myself. But I felt the need to record this moment in some form. Phones were strictly not allowed in that place, and hence, we could not even take pictures. We had left our phones outside. I was wondering what to do. I just kept quiet, thinking Gurudēva would show some way. In a few minutes, a professional photographer arrived there and was clicking pictures of the pooja that was underway. I turned towards Gaurav and said, "Tell him to click a picture of us, too." Gaurav signaled to him, requesting a photograph of us. But the photographer appointed by the temple trust just gave us a cold stare and got engrossed in his job. "Tell him that I have requested for the photograph," I said to Gaurav. He signaled and communicated the same to the photographer again.

The last segment of the pooja was going on. My hands were in Yoni Mudra. I had lost myself in the rituals that were unfolding. At that moment, without my knowledge, the photographer had captured a shot of us. So it seemed like Baba had fulfilled that desire of mine, too!

***

Āgama Shāstra

The literal meaning of "Āgama" is "to have come." This word is also used as a synonym for heritage. In a deeper sense, "gama" also means knowledge or awareness. It is also seen as an alternative to Vedas or Shāstras. This is a text which is related to the worship of the Gods. To see the formless Shakti in a deity form, certain procedures are needed. Ritualistic poojas are needed for this. Āgama Shāstra gives details of all these aspects. There are three prominent sections in Āgama Shāstra - Shakta, Shaiva, and Vaishnava. They are further divided into many sub-sections. As a whole, Tantra, Yoga, and other aspects are included.

Section 9

- Divine experience in the city of Palaces
  – Dr. Rā. Sathyanarayana
- The grace of Samadhi by a mere gaze
- A plane that does not fly, and Satyavan Savitri's story
- Guru's Dentures in my hands!
- Srividya – Universe in a Capsule
- Tantric practice system and Srividya
- Guru lineage is there!
- The Journey from Savithri to Sakalamaa
- Guru lineage continues!

46

DIVINE EXPERIENCE IN THE CITY OF PALACES – DR. RĀ. SATHYANARAYANA

I was in denial when we received the direction from Swami Rama, 'I am sending you to a Shastri in Mysuru. I want you to learn Srividya from the South Indian tradition.' When the great Himalayan Yogi Swami Rama is my Guru, why should I go to any other guru? Baba is irreplaceable, and he is my only guru; I won't accept anyone else as my guru - such were my thoughts and the deterrents for me to accept the command. But Baba, being himself, knew this very well as someone who knew the past and future and as someone who had tuned thousands of disciples all over the world; preparing disciples like me was a minuscule task for Baba.

I eventually gave in when I realised Baba would not relent on his command. My Srividya learning commenced again at the lotus feet of my Mysuru Gurugalu. I once had complained to Baba when he was in the body, 'You do not give me enough time' In response to this, Mysuru Gurugalu gave me ample time. In the southern tradition of Srividya, starting with the Ganapathi Mantra, he showered me with his grace all the way to the Maha Shodashi Mantra, which is considered to be the pinnacle of all initiations in the path. By being both compassionate and disciplinarian, he engaged with me to demonstrate how a disciple's personality could be nurtured to shine like an ornament. I am mesmerised when I remember how he graced me with the direct experience of instant Samadhi, just by a mere gaze, in our very first meeting.

Bowing to his lotus feet, I am sharing with you my association with him and the greatness of the mantras he bestowed upon me.

***

47

THE GRACE OF SAMADHI BY A MERE GAZE

He was all set to start Lalitha Sahasranāma, a pinch of vermillion in his right hand, a piercing gaze, and a single-minded focus. But for some unknown reason, Gurugalu smiled and said, 'I am about to begin!' I simply looked at his face. For what felt like hours, I was outside my body!!

***

For many years, I knew Ra. Sathyanarayana is a world-renowned musicologist and danceologist. I have met him numerous times to seek his guidance regarding dance and music. Of all the meetings, I would like to recall an episode in 1999. This incident occurred primarily during the Navaratri Festival. During those nine days, Gurugalu spent his entire day immersed in Devi pooja; imagine 8-9 hours were dedicated to various rituals and ceremonies and an equal amount of time for homas. He was at the peak of his sadhana.

Gowri Amma, Rā Sā Gurugalu's wife, was a Hindi teacher in School. In one of our conversations, she mentioned Gurugalu's routine during Navratri. Since she was working, she had to leave home by 9:30, so during these nine days, Gowri Amma said, 'I used to prepare and keep all the things required for his pooja and homa before I stepped out for work, Jyothi. The following 8-9 hours were dedicated to his pooja; by the time he finished, it used to be evening and only then would we have lunch.'

Coming back to 1999. That year, the Department of Kannada and Culture invited our dance troupe to perform at the famous Mysuru Dasara. Along with Sadhana, my daughter, who was hardly a few years old, we were all set to perform a dance ballad called 'Navarasa Devi.' Our performance was scheduled for the evening, and we had reached Mysore by morning. I vividly remember that around 11:30 a.m. I felt this intense urge to visit Rā Sā Gurugalu; mind you, I wasn't his disciple then. It just took over me since I had already visited him a couple of times for guidance and discussion on music & dance and was familiar with his residence; without much thought, I boarded an auto, and the next thing I knew, I was standing in front of his house. What happened next is surreal and beyond logical explanation.

He was sitting on a sofa, wearing a "Red" panache and angavastra, mostly worn by Srividya adepts, during religious ceremonies in south India. I noticed that there was no power. I realised that he must have taken a break from his pooja since his pooja room wasn't well-lit, and he was awaiting the power to return and resume his pooja. But for a brief moment, it all looked welcoming; I felt he was awaiting my arrival. I would have missed meeting him if he hadn't taken that break due to a power failure. Guru's resolution was more potent and graceful to me on that day. As soon as I entered the house, Ra. Sa. Gurugalu said, 'Hmmm, I am happy you made it. I am about to resume my pooja; join me. I am sure you don't mind witnessing the rituals, is it not?' He showed me a place from where I could observe all the proceedings. Interestingly, power came back. He said, 'OK then, shall we proceed with the pooja?'

He went in and sat in the pooja room, and I sat near the door. He was all set to start Laitha Sahasranāmarchane; a pinch of vermillion in his right hand, a piercing gaze, single-minded focus. But for some unknown reason, Gurugalu smiled and said, 'I am about to begin.' I simply looked at his face. I remember watching with eyes open until the third name of Devi. Clearly, I was there from Śrī mātā.., Śrī mahārājñī..., Śrīmatsinhāsaneśvarī and then. I am clueless about what happened to me; I am seated but motionless, and Sahasranāma is audible but unclear as though from a far-off place, and then I am not there. I wasn't in my body. I don't have the slightest clue how many hours I was in that state. Through his gaze, Gurugalu had bestowed me with a state of trance, i.e. I experienced Samadhi on that blessed day of Navarathri.

Guru's grace is boundless, and I am eternally grateful to have him in this life.

***

Losing Pattabhiji was one of the most harrowing experiences in my life. Grief engulfed me for the next two years. The void that his loss created consumed me. I felt an indescribable ache, and I fell into depression. During those despairing times, I could only connect to Gurugalu, and the rest of the world ceased to exist for me.

The situation in which I lost Pattabhiji was such that Sadhana, my daughter, was still in the process of completing her Master's Degree in Medicine, her education was incomplete, the ashram that Pattabhiji built was a huge responsibility to take on, and I had no clue how to run it as I had never looked into its functioning until that point in time. There were plenty of difficulties on the family front as well. There were a lot of hard decisions to be made and questions to be answered. Will I ever be able to manage such a vast responsibility? Since I was already on a spiritual path, do I need to take up such worldly obligations if I don't want to? How do I let go of them? Until then, we used to share all the responsibilities, and his sudden passing had created such a vacuum, and I was struggling to make peace with it. I felt helpless without that Love.

During these testing times, I met Gurugalu at his residence. He had finished his pooja and was in meditation; he could be in Samadhi stithi as long as he desired. I must have waited about half an hour before he opened his eyes and walked out of his meditation room. He looked luminous. Gurugalu radiated with rudrakshi around his neck, a red vermilion, and a holy ash-smeared forehead. He walked towards me, asking, 'Hmmm, How are you?' My sadness overtook me, and I could hardly answer this question. He sat down, met my eyes, and angrily enquired, 'When are you gonna be fine?' Failing to face his anger, I put down my face and didn't move. He persisted and said, 'Look at me.' I looked into his eyes, and he said, 'I am releasing you from all familial and worldly ties. From today onwards, you are free from all bondages.' That was it. Gurugalu, in a fraction of a second, had severed all my worldly ties.

Believe me when I say, since that day, all forms of attachments, need for belongingness, and grief distanced themselves from me. I no longer felt dejected. You might wonder what form of grace this is. All forms of relationships come into existence because of Karma. If Gurugalu hadn't showered me with Grace and discarded all my Karmas, I would have continued struggling with worldly relationships for aeons to come. The Guru will not hesitate to undertake the cleansing work upon himself to smoothen the forthcoming spiritual path of his disciple.

***

48

A PLANE THAT DOES NOT FLY, AND SATYAVAN SAVITRI'S STORY

"Savitri!

This is my birth name, Gurugale! There's a story behind it," I said and laughed loudly. "She defeated Yama and got her husband, Satyavan, back to life. What a brilliant personality she had!" Gurugalu said mystically.

I wondered what connection was there between a plane that wouldn't fly from Delhi to Munich, the story of Satyavan and Savitri, and me. Thinking about this, I got ready to leave for the airport.

***

"My dear, do you really want to go to America?"

I heard the unexpected question from Gurugalu and was confused. My heart sank. I was anxious, too. "Not that I surely have to go. But Pattabhiji has made all the arrangements. Tickets have also been booked. I just have to prepare to leave. We waited all these days to finish the Guru Purnima pooja and then leave," I said.

"Ok. So if you feel you should go, then carry on." Saying this, Gurugalu blessed us. With a worried expression, I looked towards Pattabhiji, who was having a conversation with someone at a little distance.

It was Guru Purnima Day. Mysuru Gurugalu's house was teeming with disciples. All around, there was a celebration – the chanting of mantras, the perfume of agarbatti in the air, Guru Mandala pooja happening with the guidance of Shri Gurugalu and many more such activities. All of us disciples participated enthusiastically in all these celebrations.

The programme was very divine and to perfection. Meals were served thereafter.

I finished my meal and approached Gurugalu. I prostrated before him and said, "Gurugale, Pattabhiji and I are shortly proceeding on a trip to America in two weeks' time. As usual, we are planning to finish a series of lectures and spiritual programmes and return." He looked at me and said, "Do you really have to go, dear?" asked Gurugalu. I was worried when I heard his words.

As per our plan, we went from Bengaluru to Delhi by air. Generally, when we fly to America, we take an international flight from Delhi. At midnight that day, there was a flight from Delhi to Munich. There was a stopover at Munich. Security checks at Delhi airport were uneventful and clear. We got on the plane at the appointed time. We then informed our family members and our hosts in America.

All the seats in the plane started filling up as passengers boarded. We expected the flight to take off in a few minutes. But even after 10 to 15 minutes beyond the departure time, there was no indication of the plane taking off. The pilots and cabin crew were all standing outside. Even after a long time, they did not come inside the plane. We were wondering what the reason for this delay was. We did not know what was happening and whom to ask. Time was slipping by, and the passengers' patience was wearing thin. The air conditioners were also not switched on. There was no fresh air inside the cabin, and it was sweltering inside. Our mouths were becoming dry, and we started feeling very thirsty. Unable to bear it, passengers started demanding water. The cabin crew quickly came inside and provided water to the passengers.

As soon as they came in, people crowded around them. "What is happening? Why are we not taking off?" there was a barrage of questions. The cabin crew struggled to calm down the impatient passengers. "In a short while, we will be on our way. Please cooperate," they appealed.

Another hour went by like this, and the passengers were agitated and irritated.

At last, at around 2.30 am, an officer came. The passengers, who were sleepy and irritated, sat up in anger and took him to task. He calmly explained the reason why the delay had happened. "We have been trying for an hour and a half. There has been an engine breakdown. Our technical staff has been working on it to solve the problem. However, they have not succeeded. We have called for senior experts from Germany. We expect them to arrive by the afternoon. Soon after the repair work is done, we will be ready to take off. We regret the inconvenience caused to you all. We have made arrangements for your stay at Hotel Leela Palace. Those of you who want to leave urgently may board another plane, which will leave shortly," he said.

Soon after hearing this, passengers started murmuring among themselves and got up from their seats. We were not in a hurry and decided to stay in the hotel that was arranged for us. We reached the hotel and rested. Since the experts from Germany were expected only by afternoon, there was no need for us to get up early. We got up leisurely and had our breakfast there. We still had some time on our hands, and Pattabhiji started a phone conversation with the organisers in America.

I felt a strange restlessness and anxiety. A feeling that somewhere something has gone wrong. I remembered Gurugalu and felt like talking to him. The time was around 11 am. This is the time that he would generally be free. I thought I would feel better if I spoke to him. I made a call. Gurugalu answered. I told him about the instances of the previous day. "We are staying at the hotel, Gurugale. We will be proceeding to the airport shortly," I said.

"Oh! You might have faced so much hardship, my dear," he asked with lots of concern.

Immediately, as if something flashed to his mind, he said, "I will tell you a story. Do you have the time to listen?"

"Most certainly, Gurugale. We still have some time before we have to leave for the airport," I responded.

"Do you know the story of Savitri and Satyavan?" he asked.

"Yes, I know it well, Gurugale. In my childhood, my mother narrated this story to all of us. Another interesting fact is that my birth name is Savitri," I said.

"Is it?" Gurugalu asked.

I laughed and went on to narrate the story of my birth. "My parents had a total of 10 children. Two of them had died, and 8 of us survived. But my mother wasn't in favour of my birth. She was tired of giving birth repeatedly. Poverty was also another reason why she did not want another child. As it was in vogue those days, she consumed papayas and pineapples to abort the pregnancy. But I remained strong and came into this world!"

Since my mother did not want another baby yet I was born, she decided to name me "Saak Savitri." This was a well-known phrase in those days. She brought me up, however, with a lot of love and affection. Although she gave me the name "Savitri" as my birth name, Amma liked the name "Jyotsna" very much. So, when it was time to put me in a school, she decided to give me the name "Jyotsna." But this name was a little difficult to use often, so gradually, I was called "Jyothi." I said this and started laughing.

Gurugalu did not laugh. He patiently listened to everything I said with a lot of seriousness. Then, "This is all correct. Shall we proceed with the story?" he asked. "Most certainly, Gurugale," I said. Although I knew the story of Satyavan Savitri, it was a joy to hear it again from Gurugalu.

He narrated the story nicely, and I listened attentively as if I was hearing it for the first time.

"This story appears in the Vana Parva of Mahabharata. While answering a question from Yudhishthira, Rishi Markandeya narrates the story of Satyavan Savitri. Ashwapati was the king of Madra Desha. For many years, he had no children. He prayed to Goddess Savitri and did penance for a long time. By her Grace he had a girl child. He named the baby after the Goddess who had granted him the child. Baby Savitri was brought up with a lot of love and affection and became a fine young woman.

When Savitri comes to a marriageable age, the King starts thinking of getting her married. "My daughter, please select a suitable match for yourself," he says and leaves the choice of a suitable husband to his intelligent and sensible daughter. Savitri agrees to her father's words, goes in search of a suitor, and visits several ashrams in the forests. She receives the blessings of many Rishis and Munis. She does a lot of charity work. She travels to many kingdoms. Finally, when she passes through a thick forest, she meets Satyavan and falls in love with him at first sight. Satyavan, too, is love-smitten by her. Satyavan is the exiled son of a blind King called Dyumathsena.

With a lot of excitement, Savitri shares the news of having selected a suitor with her father. Brahmarishi Nārada being present at that time, hears about Savitri's choice, and his face shows worry and concern. The king notices this and asks Brahmarishi why. "The young man that your daughter is in love with is intelligent, just, generous, and handsome, but his life is short-lived. He just has another year to live," Rishi Nārada informs. On hearing this, King Ashwapathi repeatedly pleads with his daughter to select another eligible bachelor. But Savitri has a firm resolve. If she has to marry, it would only be with Satyavan, is her strong conviction. Rishi Nārada himself is taken aback by her firm decision.

Then, Savitri addresses Sage Narada, "Revered One! Even if Satyavan has only a year to live, I will pray to God and extend his lifetime. Please bless me that my efforts bear the fruits I seek. The sage is appreciative of her mental strength and conviction. "May all the challenges that come in your life be resolved very quickly, and may happiness multiply," he blesses Savitri. Satyavan and Savitri get married. After the wedding, Savitri proceeds to the forest along with her husband. They both spend many happy times together. When challenges come, time seems to hang heavy and not move. However, when one is happy, time seems to fly. In this manner, it was almost going to be a year since their wedding. The countdown to the end of Satyavan's life begins.

Savitri is aware of this and is constantly watching over him. One day, while cutting wood in the forest, Satyavan complains of chest pain and loses consciousness. Savitri is anxious and makes him lie on her lap. A short while later, Satyavan opens his eyes and realises that his life is coming to an end. He looks at his young wife and feels very sad. "Savitri, even after knowing that I would not live long, you remained firm and married me. I feel a lot of pain to see your plight. See, my life will end in a very short time," laments Satyavan. Soon, Satyavan passes away.

Savitri feels disoriented. She could see Lord Yama approaching on his buffalo with a lasso in his hand. Immediately, she calls out to him, "Lord Yama!" Yama is surprised because mere mortals can neither see nor speak to him. Since this young woman can see him and addresses him by name, he realises she is no ordinary woman. "Young lady, because you are a staunch devotee of God, you can see me. But I must take away people whose lifetimes have come to an end. That is my duty." Saying this, Lord Yama continues.

"Lord Yama, stop! I know that only mortals of virtue will be able to see entities from Devaloka. I demand the fruits of my virtue from you," Savitri declares stubbornly. "Whatever happens, it is impossible for me to return your husband's life." Saying this, Lord Yama proceeds on his way. Savitri persistently follows him.

"Oh Lady! You are a mortal. You can't follow me. There is no way you can save the life of your husband anymore. Go and prepare for his last rites," says Lord Yama, trying to send her away. But the determined Savitri continues, "Lord Yama if I am truly a virtuous wife, you have to grant me the boon I wish," he firmly says. With no option, Lord Yama relents, "Okay. Except for your husband's life, you may wish for anything, and I will grant it for you," he says and offers her three boons.

Savitri wishes, "My father-in-law should be able to see again."

"So be it," says Lord Yama and grants her boon. "We should get our lost kingdom back," wishes Savitri. "That's all! The one who usurped your kingdom will himself return it to you," declares Lord Yama and proceeds further.

The determined Savitri does not stop there. "You have been so benevolent and granted me these two boons, Lord Yama. You are so gracious. Can you please grant me one more wish?" Savitri pleads. "I do not have time. Ask quickly," says Lord Yama. "I want the boon of becoming a mother and giving birth to a child," asks Savitri. "So be it. I will grant this boon, too. Now leave," insists Lord Yama, in his hurry to go on his way. "Oh, Lord Yama! You are such a generous one! You have granted all the wishes I asked of you. Now, you must keep your promise and give me the pleasure of motherhood. But without my husband, how can I birth a child?" Savitri binds Lord Yama with her clever words.

Lord Yama is very surprised to hear the young woman's words. "Daughter, you have defeated me with your clever use of words. Till now, I have not granted anyone a boon like this. To save Markandeya's life, Lord Shiva Himself had to come down and challenge me. But a mere mortal that you are, you have trapped me with your clever play of words. I agree to return the life of your husband. Both of you shall live happily for many more long years." By saying this, Lord Yama blesses Savitri and returns the life of Satyavan.

Satyavan gets up as if from a long, deep slumber. Her in-law's vision returns. They get back their lost kingdom and live happily ever after.

Gurugalu concluded the story thus. I had a small doubt after listening to the entire story with rapt attention. I went ahead and asked him, "How is it that you wanted to narrate this story to me now, Gurugale, that too on the phone? I am surprised."

He laughed. "Nothing in particular. You are also aware of the most important part of this story. But since you have asked, I'm saying this. This Savitri was a very virtuous wife. She had immense respect and love for her husband, to the extent that she went ahead to challenge Lord Yama, the God of Death Himself. She challenged Him and won back the life of her husband, Satyavan. What a personality she had! It is a very exciting story, and that's why I felt like narrating it to you," said Gurugalu.

At that point, I did not think too much. Maybe what Gurugalu was saying was right, I concluded.

"Gurugale, it is time for us to leave. May I take leave of you?" I asked.

"Yes, dear. Do you know another thing? Many years ago, I was in Russia to speak about aesthetics at a literary conference.

"Oh yes, Gurugale. You are a world-renowned musicologist. You are a scholar in dance as well. Who else can speak on these subjects other than you?" I said proudly.

"That's a different thing, my dear. But this is different. I was returning after the conference. When alighting from the aircraft, I overheard a conversation with a lady walking ahead of me, talking to another woman. "Oh my! I never thought we would land safely. How many problems have we had? Probably a great person must have been travelling with us. Because of his holy presence, we have safely landed." I overheard this talk. I thought of mentioning this to you," he concluded and disconnected the call.

I took some time to snap out of the inertia of Gurugalu's call.

I started thinking. What is the connection between a plane that did not take off from Delhi and the story of Satyavan Savitri? Why did Gurugalu choose to tell me about it at this point? Why did he become stoic when I mentioned my birth name as Savitri? And finally, what is the experience he had indicated? Although on the surface all of these seems like different incidents, there seems to be a connection between all.

In my hometown in coastal Karnataka, during rainy seasons at night times, many fireflies fly around, shining brightly and soon disappearing into the darkness. Gurugalu's words also sometimes seemed clear but the next minute the mind became empty. Unable to comprehend, I got ready to leave for the airport.

***

49

GURU'S DENTURES IN MY HANDS!

I puzzlingly looked at those dentures held out by my Gurugalu. I thought, 'What should I do with these dentures? What might be Gurugalu's intention?' and looked at his face. He was carefully watching me. I asked him, 'Should I clean this Gurugale?' He responded with a thoughtful 'hmmmm.' I took those dentures, which were dirty with food particles and filled with saliva.

***

Srividya tradition is a journey that a disciple undertakes with his Sri Guru. Knowledge and wisdom are revealed in phases, but they are not limited to just the technical details about Srividya. We are more familiar with learning the technicality of a subject; modern education is time- and syllabus-driven. Year after year, a student is taught theories of a subject, which may be an outcome of the Westernisation of education.

It is not the same when a Guru is from an authentic Rishi Paramparā. Knowledge is not limited to the Guru's physical plane; instead, the Guru is well aware that he doesn't own this flow of knowledge but is a conveyor or medium for it. Guru Paramparā selected him and trained him for this role. The required knowledge is disseminated to him in Silence. He is like a trustee of the knowledge gained through silence. He acts as a link between the practitioner and Guru Paramparā but never establishes his ownership of this flow of knowledge because this supernatural, perpetual, and eternal knowledge existed before and will continue to exist after him. The flow is not limited to Guru's physical plane. So, Guru Paramparā is an infinite flow of knowledge through the medium called Guru. The Guru is the energy centre which leads the practitioners from darkness to light and from ignorance to knowledge.

Unlike modern education, learning is a very subtle process in Guru Paramparā. The technical aspect of knowledge is imparted to the discipline without his awareness. It's akin to the gentle diffusion of musk's fragrance, an exquisite beauty that permeates and enriches the disciple's understanding. In our tradition, learning isn't confined to spirituality; it encompasses our rich cultural heritage and wisdom. We share every detail in an easily understandable way. Playfulness is at the heart of our approach; students aren't stressed or anxious about their progress. There's no exam-like pressure; instead, learning is driven by curiosity. Daily tests are part of the journey, but they're not written or spoken; they unfold silently. Students aren't aware of when or how they're being tested. That's the essence of learning in our ancient tradition—it happens in the serenity of silence.

Like tests, disciples are clueless about results. At times, we are least expecting, but when the time is right, the results are revealed. That is when the practitioner surprisingly realises, 'Oh! I was tested and had answered these questions. Today, what I received was the result of that test!' One crucial aspect is the absence of preparation; even if a practitioner insists on preparing for his unknown test, the Guru will change the topic of the test itself. This means the Guru will conduct a different lesson altogether, and all the preparation turns out to be meaningless.

Therefore, Srividya is a journey that a disciple undertakes with an authentic Guru, which makes it all the more joyful and equally challenging. It won't end until it touches the essence of one's being and transforms it from the inside out. The Guru's effort is much more prominent in this transformative journey than the disciple.

Getting to spend a few hours with a Srividya Guru is decreed by destiny that I had the privilege of spending days with Rā Sā Gurugalu, to my heart's content, immersed in learning, it is a boon bestowed by Himalaya Bhārathi Paramparā, the grace of the entire rishi gana. They have been very benevolent with me. I feel incredibly blessed for the time I spent with Rā Sā Gurugalu. This sentiment is rooted in an encounter with Swami Rama in Mysuru, where Pattabhiji requested, 'Swamiji, we would like to talk to you. Could you spare 10 minutes for us?' Swami Rama, extending his hands towards the universe, replied, "Why 10 minutes? I will give you ample time." spreading his wide large arms.

However, in later days, meeting Baba became challenging as he became deeply involved in the Jolly Grant hospital project which was his way of offering Guru Dakshina to Bengali Baba. While understandable, the inability to spend time with him was equally frustrating. On one occasion, I expressed my disappointment to Baba, saying, 'It is challenging to secure an appointment with you through your secretaries. Even if, by chance or luck, I manage to bypass all your secretaries and meet you, I hardly get a few minutes to discuss with you, Baba, and I feel disappointed.'

Due to his commitment to the Jolly Grant project, Baba couldn't fulfil his initial promise of giving us ample time."

Baba is one to remember his promises. It was precisely for this reason that he directed us to Rā Sā Gurugalu, where we received time and guidance and effortlessly immersed ourselves in learning. While Gurus may appear physically distinct from one another, this distinction is merely a creation of the mind's assumption. The mind tends to assume that one Guru is vastly different from another. Swami Rama and Rā Sā Gurugalu may differ physically, coming from different locations and experiencing different life circumstances. However, claiming they are fundamentally different based solely on their physical dissimilarities would be foolish.

Our minds struggle to grasp the non-dualistic reality of the universe because the very nature of the mind is rooted in dualism.

Whenever we perceive something, the mind interferes and creates confusion, fostering a sense of duality. If the mind doesn't create division, it transcends into intuition or inner consciousness. Intuition represents the highest form of our mind—it serves as the bridge between our current existence and divinity. Without intuition, our minds cannot ascend to the highest realms of spirituality.

Returning to my Gurugalu, he has consistently offered me abundant time and boundless knowledge. I never experienced him holding back or sensed any shortage of time or wisdom on his part. He wasn't just a Guru; he guided me through life's journey as a mother, father, and relative combined. Since my initiation into the Srividya path, I've never felt lacking in any aspect of life, whether wealth or wisdom. Gurugalu blessed me with affluence in every sense.

Even when my bank balance was nominal, I would receive money when the need arose from some source. Most of the time, when I planned visits to the Himalayas in North India, money was never a concern because it manifested from unknown sources. Abundance is possible when we practise Sri Vidya. Abundance is one of the signs that our practice is moving in the right direction.

Life possibilities unfold effortlessly when we faithfully practise the mantra every day. Surrendering completely to the path allows it to guide us hand in hand.. Srividya encompasses Goddess Bhagavathi and Guru Paramparā. There is no difference between the Guru in the physical form, the divinity, the mantra, and Guru Paramparā. As mentioned in Bhāvanopaniṣath, a pivotal text in Sri Vidya tradition, Śrī Guruhu sarvakārana bhūta śaktihi, which translates as Guru is the energy behind all manifestations.

When I completed practising the Mahāṣōḍasi mantra, Gurugalu told me, 'I have given you everything meant to be given, done what is expected of me. Henceforth, life will move as it is supposed to be. It will be a delightful journey for you.' While in this phase, one day, I met Gurugalu, and we discussed Sri Vidya. The conversation was moving in a good flow. Gurugalu was in a festive mood and sharing his spiritual experiences; this went on for 30-45 minutes when he suddenly opened his mouth and, using his tongue, dislodged his dentures; until then, I hadn't realised that Gurugalu had artificial teeth. With wonder, I looked at those sets of artificial teeth. He removed and held those dentures in his hand and stretched towards me. I puzzlingly looked at those dentures held out by him. I was not sure what he wanted to convey through this—a few minutes passed in this manner. I stared at his face and those dentures in his hand. He was observing my thoughts and my reactions closely. He was examining my inner dialogue; our response to any given circumstance is our samskaras, isn't it? Polishing those thoughts and then expressing those thoughts is not our true personality.

It looked like Gurugalu was deeply sifting through my inner consciousness. But at that point, I was thinking, 'What should I do with these dentures? What might be Gurugalu's intention? My actions are supposed to please my Guru and should not be a reason for his displeasure. So what should my action be?' I looked at his face. He was carefully watching me. I asked him, 'Should I clean this Gurugale?' He responded with a thoughtful 'hmmmm.' I took those dentures, which were dirty with food particles and filled with saliva.

The dentures appeared unclean, with food particles from breakfast still stuck on them and saliva making them even dirtier. At first glance, anyone would have thought, 'How dirty!' I might have felt the same initially, though I'm not certain now. That's the nature of the mind; it reacts immediately. We can't prevent the mind from thinking, but I chose to move beyond the initial response and considered what needed to be done next.

I went to the backyard of the house and cleaned the dentures with fresh water. Afterwards, I searched for a clean cloth to wipe them, considering that his wife wasn't home, and his son was busy with Japa, which I didn't want to interrupt. After a few minutes of searching, I noticed my dupatta which I was wearing on my shoulders, which was clean. I used it to wipe the dentures, leaving no trace of water. I then returned them to Gurugalu, who smiled warmly and placed them back in his mouth. We didn't have any further discussion about it.

As I discussed, this is one way a Guru may test his disciple; at the outset, this is such normal behaviour. He handed over his dentures, which I cleaned and returned to my Guru. It was a simple process, nothing complicated. Did my Guru test me on that day? Did I pass the test?

I must have passed many such tests, few with distinction, and a few I might have also failed. We will only know if our Guru explicitly discusses them. Sometimes, they indirectly point out that you should not have behaved that way. That is when we realise what we must have scored in that situation. As I mentioned earlier, in Srividya Guru Paramparā, there's no predefined process for gaining knowledge or a model question paper to answer. It doesn't adhere to the timelines of our everyday lives.

Sri Vidya is indeed an incredible journey, where the time it takes to reach a particular stage can vary greatly—some may achieve it in two years, while others may need three to four years. I received a mantra, dheekshe, from Swami Rama in 1992, and my learning journey continued until 2016. However, after my husband Pattabhiji passed away in 2016, the next three years were particularly challenging, and my Gurugalu supported me in every possible way. Later, Mysuru Gurugalu also renounced his physical form in 2020, yet my learning journey under their guidance continues. The process of leaving the body has not been a challenge for either of my Gurus.

Interestingly, even after their physical departure, my Sri Vidya learning continues silently, and the connection and communication remain unbroken.

***

50

SRIVIDYA – UNIVERSE IN A CAPSULE

I will grant you 'Double promotion' - instead of śōḍaśī, I will initiate you to Mahāśōḍaśī Mantra, said Gurugalu.

My eyes welled up with exhilaration.

By the grace of Sri Guru and Mā Bhagavathi, the day I received Mahāśōḍaśī Mantra intuitively - considered to be the most crucial mantra in Srividya practice, was one of the most blessed moments of my life.

***

Guru works in mysterious ways. It is like an onion, mysteriously layered and nuanced. Similarly, truth is layered and nuanced; it unveils itself in unlimited possibilities and meanings. Likewise, every word of Guru is a ray of light; they are not ordinary at all. The meaning and relevance of the Guru's words transform with the intensity of our practice and the situations we face in life. Guru might have shared some words of advice, or at times, Guru might have spoken good words to you, which may not have been significant at that moment. At times, the Guru's words might have been sharp, piercing the disciple's core belief. Those words, though harsh, often transform into guiding lights during different phases of the disciple's life. It will often become a source of courage and vigour to navigate the storms of life. When the time is right, these words will reveal themselves. Mind you, they reveal that they are not just meant to be understood but also to open up a world of new experiences.

Likewise, some of the Sri Vidya mantras are meant to 'appear' in one's meditation, and a few mantras have the power to bestow countless siddhis. It all gets revealed in stages according to our eligibility, Sādhana, and desires.

"What is Srividya, Gurugale? Is it a sequential method like Asana, Prāṇāyāma, Dhyāna, and Dhāraṇa, mentioned in Yogasutra? Are these part of Sri Vidya's practice? Or is it something beyond it? Why is it you never explain?" I asked Gurugalu. Those were my initial days as a Sri Vidya practitioner under his tutelage.

He listened patiently to my questions and smilingly responded, 'Your question is akin to you savouring palm sugar and asking what is this?!!'

What he meant was, as a practitioner of this path, you don't have to practise Astanga yoga or individually perform Chakra Upasana, or for that matter, perform any other rituals. This does not mean one should not gain knowledge of these practices; seeking this information would help Sadhakas to make sense of their experiences during Sādhana. However, there is a path to attaining siddhis even without these practices, which is merely chanting the mantra. That path is Srividya. The Srividya mantra encapsulates the entire Viśva prajñe, i.e. Universal Consciousness!

The very term Universal Consciousness encompasses everything, be it nadis, chakras, or Pranayama; nothing is exempt. The tiniest of particles is part of it. Sri Vidya is the subtlest of all Paths; a sadhaka may not even sense how and when he gained all that knowledge. There are instances where a practitioner hasn't realised that he is liberated... so subtle. That's why this is considered the supreme path to liberation. In Tantra, Sri Vidya is referred to as Kundalini Path. This path offers a Jīvanmukta (liberation while still alive) state; those who tread this path would attain immense strength to move the world around them without raising a finger.

Sri Vidya practitioners don't have to fret and worry if someone asks them about Pranayama or Chakra Upasane. For a moment, you might feel confused. Why hasn't my Guru taught me these? Not knowing these words might lead to self-doubt, like, am I on the right path? Is my practice deep enough? What am I even practising? Don't get into this loop of thoughts; because other Paths progress in a segmented order, they divide and observe each process. On the other hand, Sri Vidya is all-inclusive, i.e. observing the process as an undivided whole. So when someone asks a Sri Vidya Guru what a sweet taste is like, he simply gives a piece of palm sugar without a word. It is all experiential science, in silence.

The Mantra is this universe in a seed form, the more you nurture it with Japa, the deeper and broader it grows, just like a Banyan tree. Yoga Sādhana feels never-ending if our practices don't deepen or reach a state. For instance, after starting Asana practice, one realises it is just the beginning and that there is a long way ahead. These are good practices, no doubt, but they may or may not lead to a resting point. However, there should come a resting point (Vishrantha state) for your spiritual Sādhana. Otherwise, what is the use of these practices in this world? Most of us start these practices so that the activities of this mind cease, and all paths focus on the mind. Ways of reaching this goal differ; for example, Ashtanga Yoga believes in progressively attaining mastery over parts, starting with the body, breath, mind, and intellect, which are sequential. However, it is possible to give all this knowledge in a single consolidated capsule form, that is, the Sri Vidya Path.

It is a marvellous journey in itself, which is why I say Sri Vidya is the Universe - Brahmanda.

Early in my practice under Rā. Sā. Gurugalu, I became aware that the Guru who shows us and leads us on this path is as important as the mantra and Mā Bhagavathi. Guru always thinks about his disciple's well-being and progress, and to enable it, he might jolt them in unimaginable ways. Gurugalu convinced me about these realities at a very early phase of our association.

Our practice continued sequentially for the next few years as per Dakshinachara tradition under Ra. Sa, Gurugalu's guidance. In the sequence, the last and ultimate mantra is the 16-lettered

Sōḍaśī mantra. As per tradition, a Guru gives his disciple up to the 15-lettered Panchadasi mantra, but the 16th one is supposed to appear to Sadhaka in their meditation!! So, this mantra isn't given by the Guru, but he will systematise it after it appears to the disciples.

By the Grace of Bhagavathi and my Gurugalu, the Sōḍaśī mantra appeared to me, and my happiness was limitless that day. However, what came next left me in awe!!

After the Sōḍaśī mantra appeared to me, I immediately rushed to Gurugalu to update him about this magical moment, at which point he asked me to recollect the mantra, which I did. He said something that came like grace in abundance. It felt as though the entire Universe had showered Grace on me.

He said, 'I am giving you a double promotion so you will get the Mahāsōḍaśī mantra instead of the Sōḍaśī mantra.'

My eyes welled up with exhilaration. I still remember when I heard these words: There were no bounds to my happiness or inexplicable joy, and my feet were not on the ground. On that day, I bowed down to him and surrendered my body, mind, and consciousness at his lotus feet.

He initiated me to the Mahāsōḍaśī mantra and asked me to recall it, which I did. Then, he corrected the sequence of the mantra, wrote it down on a piece of paper, and handed it to me so that I could refer to it later. Which I carefully placed inside my handbag.

In Srividya, after Panchadasi = Mantra of 15 letters, it is Sōḍaśī = mantra of 16 letters. There are 2 more highly acclaimed Mantras, which are described at length in a very well-known Srividya text, "Soundarya Lahari" by Sri Bhagavan Adi Shankaracharya. One is Astadashakshari – a mantra of 18 letters and Mahāsōḍaśī – a mantra of 28 letters. Now you may wonder, does it mean that the more letters, the greater the power or shakti? The answer to that is both yes and no! The Mystery of Srividya is packed up in the encapsulated Mother Divine's Matrka Chakra science. This information may be gleaned by referring to the related texts. However, if it is not revealed internally through one's Sādhana of Mantra Japa, it can never become your knowledge. This inner revelation comes only through the Divine Mother's Grace and the Guru's blessings. In this context, the revelation of 28 lettered Mahāṣōḍaśī mantra is one of the most divine moments in my life.

After the initiation, I left the same evening for the Swami Rama Sādhana Dhama Ashram. On my way back, while in the bus, I recollected the chit Gurugalu gave me. Since it was a 28-lettered mantra and appeared only once, I wondered whether I remembered it. I closed my eyes, recollected the mantra, repeated it twice or thrice, and then opened the chit given by Gurugalu. Surprise!!! It was exactly as I recalled.

The following day in the ashram, I thought of offering my profound gratitude to Swami Rama, as I believe this miracle was purely his blessing. With this thought, I started my mediation; I chanted Mahāṣōḍaśī 21 times and ended by saying, 'Dhanyōsmi Gurudēva' As soon as I uttered it, Swami Rama appeared in my meditation. I had not envisaged it!! Baba said, 'A long time ago, when I initiated you to Srividya, I had done the Sādhana of all the Sri Vidya mantras, and for the convenience of my disciples, I encapsulated all the mantras into one and bestowed that one mantra to you. But you didn't practice it intensely, so I had to send you to the Shastri in Mysuru.'

Puzzled by this, I recalled the moment Baba had given me this mantra. Swami Rama was right because then I wondered how such a small mantra would help me realise a topic as vast as Sri Vidya. Though I continued practising that mantra, it was not to my Guru's satisfaction; I lacked in my Sādhana. Baba must have caught my drift and thought, 'She feels the need to learn in a prolonged way, like starting from LKG and completing post-graduation. She hasn't understood that I have granted her a direct PhD, so her mind isn't ready to accept it yet.' This revelation by Swami Rama jolted me to the core; suddenly, the big mystery was revealed to me as if I had woken up from slumber.

***

Messages from the Himalayan Sages: Timely & Timeless

TANTRIC PRACTICE SYSTEM AND SRIVIDYA

Srividya has a pivotal role to play in the Tantric practice system. Among many systems of Tantric practices, Shakta tradition is female deity-centred; Shakti Bhagvati grants both Bhoga (enjoyment) and Moksha (liberation) to the seeker. Let us briefly understand about Trantra before we glance at "what is Srividya"-

Tantra? What does it mean?

The definition of the word tantra in scripture is: 'Tan means "to expand;" Trai is "to protect" – Tanoti iti trayate iti tantraha.' In totality, tantra is "Protection by way of expansion." It is a practice system (Prayoga Shāstra) to protect the spiritual seeker by expanding his or her soul or self-knowledge. Tantra is a process of expansion of one's consciousness.

There are 6 systems in Tantra Shāstra, based on different deities.
1) Ganpathi – Gānapatya Tantra
2) Kumara or Subrahmanya – Kaumāra Tantra
3) Vishnu – Vaishnava Tantra
4) Shiva – Shaiva Tantra
5) Surya – Soura Tantra
6) Shakti – Shākta Tantra

A notable point in these Tantra systems is that the main male deities are worshipped along with 'Shakti' as their associated wives as Sankalpa, resolution of "Along with Shakti" – Shakti – Sahita, for example, Lord Ganesha along with "Siddhi – Buddhi," female deities, Lord Vishnu with Mahalakshmi, Lord Shiva with Parvati devi and so on.

The Status of Sri Vidya in Tantra

Among these 6 tantra paths, the Shakta tradition is called by the name Srividya. Devi, or the female deity, is worshipped, and her names are "Sri" and "Vidya." The yantra in Srividya is Sri Yantra; 'Sri' Akshara, or alphabet, is her supreme mantra. This 'Sri' deity is the one who grants the 4 types of boons, namely Dharma – Righteous path, Artha – wealth and abundance, Kāma is desire and wish fulfilment; and lastly, Moksha – liberation; Hence, Srividya is granting Bhoga and Moksha – enjoyment and liberation.

The popular modes of practice in Srividya are Lalita Sahasranama, Durga Saptashati, Soundarya Lahari, and so on. Chandi Homa (sacred fire offerings), Sri Nitya Devi Homa, Sri Chakra Homa, and Sri Chakra worship rituals – like this are all meant to fulfil one's desires in life. Hence, they are very personal practice.

Primarily, Srividya is Kundalini yoga of awakening the Kundalini. The only way to obtain this vidya is through Sri Guru, a preceptor, or a Sri Vidya adept.

The dimension of Srividya worship is oceanic. The major practices are termed "Dasha Mahavidyas" – The 10 great wisdom goddesses – Kali, Tara, Lalitha Tripurasundari, Bhuvaneshwari, Bhairavi, Chinnamastā, Dhumavati, Bagalamukhi, Matangi and Kamalatmika. These 10 deities are further classified as terrible and benevolent; Sundari, Bhuvaneshwari, Matangi, and Kamala are benevolent deities or Mahavidyas. Kali, Bhairavi, Chinnamastā, Bagalamukhi, and Dhumavati are terrible forms of Mahavidyas. Tara is terrible in blue and benevolent in white. The most popular among them is Lalitha Tripurasundari in Samayacharya Srividya Tantra.

Another aspect of Srividya is the worship of Durga Deity in 9 forms – Shailaputri, Brahmacharini, Chandraghanta, Kushmanda, Skandamata, Katyayini, Kalaratri, Maha Gowri and Siddhidhatri. Also as Mahasaraswati, Mahalakshmi and Mahakali. Srividya Bhagavati is worshipped in several ways in the 51 Shaktipeethas in India.

Srividya is 'Upasana' – which means practice oriented wisdom. It means that through spiritual practice, this wisdom is brought into the state of experience and not the wisdom concerned with the Buddhi or intellect. Our Spiritual adepts have ascertained this wisdom to be experiential alone.

Srividya Shōdashika – Chitkala – 3 by Mahamahopadyaya Dr R Satya Narayana, Padmashri Awardee, Deekshanama – Sri Satyanandanatha.

Srividya is Brahmavidya, the wisdom of self-realisation, the wisdom of the Self. It is the method of contemplation, Meditation, Japa (sacred chanting), worship, and Adoration (Sthuthi) of the Self in relation to the Deity Srvdiya. Shakti tantra base is our ancient Vedas (revealed knowledge system) as a philosophy. Srividya, thus, is Advaita path of the Non-Dual state of the Absolute – one without the second.

Srividya – Swami Rama perspective

"There are three schools of Shakti Sādhana: Kaula, Mishra, and Samayāchārā. These schools correspond to the mental state and preparedness of the aspirant. All are concerned with awakening Kundalini energy from its dormant state at the base of the spine and leading it to the crown chakra."

Shakti Sādhana – Steps to Samadhi by Pandit Rajamani Tigunait, PhD – Introduction by Swami Rama.

The Kaula path is a systematic and highly disciplined system. It uses external objects such as Yantra and Mandala. It is more of an external worship called Bahiryaga. This practice helps the seeker open up the spiritual centres and finally awaken the kundalini energy at the Muladhara Chakra.

The Mishra path is a combination of external and internal contemplation and meditation that transforms consciousness from an outer orientation to an internal state of meditation. In this path, the Kundalini awakening happens at the Anhata Chakra (heart centre).

The third one is the Samayāchārā path. Scriptures claim this system to be the supreme and highest, and it is practised by the yogis and the adepts. Samayāchārā has the existence of 10,000 years in vogue, perfectly protected by the Himalayan Sages. This wisdom is the manifestation of the radiant sages, the Manasa putras (born out of the mind) of Brahma, the creator – Sage Sanaka, Sanandana, Sanat Kumara, Sanat Sujata. In the words of Swami Rama, 'Samaya' means "I am with you," – which is a Brahmee state – the state of supreme enlightenment, which is an inner awareness in Yoga.

To a fully prepared Sadhaka, if there are any subtle obstacles, the Spiritual Master clears the path by either touch or gaze.

Last words from Swami Rama to you:

"Tantra offers the highest protection, which is the highest state of attainment."

***

52

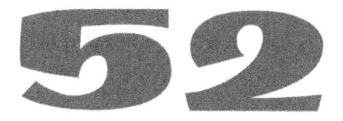

GURU LINEAGE IS THERE!

He pointed towards me and said, "There is the Guru lineage!"

It was a time when Gurugalu had been very unwell, subsequently recovered, and had just returned home from hospital. I had told Dr Ashok Bhat from Delhi to come to Mysuru to take the Darshan of Gurugalu. Dr Ashok Bhat was one of Pattabhiramji's favourite disciples. He, too, had received a mantra from Rā Sā Gurugalu just recently. It is always good to have Darshan of Gurugalu at any given opportunity, and hence, I asked him to come. He also came to see Mysuru Gurugalu with a lot of devotion and respect. I used to say that whenever we went to meet our Guru, we should never go empty-handed. Whether they accept or not, we should carry something for them as per our capability and offer it to Gurugalu. The nature of Dr. Ashok Bhat was that he would never offer anything small or insignificant as Gurudakshina. Even during Pattabhiram's time, he was like that. Accordingly, he had brought an envelope with a big amount of money in it to offer to our Gurugalu. We all went to Gurugalu's house. In between the conversations, Dr. Ashok Bhat put the envelope in front of him in all humility and prostrated before him. "What is this?" asked Gurugalu. "Nothing much, Gurugalu, just a small offering," said Doctor. "No, no, you should tell me what is in this right now," said Gurugalu.

I had earlier told Doctorji that sometimes Gurugalu does not accept any offerings. Why he does so is not known to anyone. I also told him not to feel bad about it and to just keep it near the Shri Chakra in his puja room and offer it to Lalitha. In any case, Lalitha and Gurugalu are one and the same.

As far as I had observed, Gurugalu would generally not accept any Gurudakshina from anyone. He used to be very firm on this. Surprisingly, he would always accept my offer whenever I gave it to him. In one instance, I had set out to go to his home. It was already quite late when I left. I could not reach Mysuru at the time I had anticipated. So, as soon as I got down from the bus, I hired an auto and rushed to Gurugalu's house. "You just came without bringing anything for me?" he questioned, to my surprise. How much love and affection he had for me that he made this remark! I, too, gave him an equally humorous reply, "Please forgive me, Gurugale. The next time I come, I will make up for not bringing anything for you this time."

"That's ok, I was just joking," he said. It was clear that he was very observant of even the minutest actions.

Similarly, when Dr Ashok Bhat offered Gurudakshina to Gurugalu, "Money? For me? Why?" he asked. Doctorji didn't know what to say and looked at me. "Gurugalu, this is not for you. It is for our lineage of Gurus; it is for the tradition," he said. Immediately, Gurugalu smiled and said, "Ah... ok! What you say is right!" He then said, "Guru is here," pointing to himself and then pointing towards me, "Lineage is there," he said. "Tradition is sitting there," he added. Doctorji was quite sensitive to these things. He turned to me and said, "Amma, Gurugalu, and you are the same for me." With that, he put the envelope in front of me and prostrated. Gurugalu did not give up until that envelop of money was handed over to me.

Gurugalu had never once mentioned to me that I should or would work for the tradition, or that I would manage an organisation or give mantra diksha to other disciples. But he had perfectly communicated all this silently in this manner!

***

53

THE JOURNEY FROM SAVITHRI TO SAKALAMAA

It was a quiet dawn. As usual, I was in meditation. Suddenly, a name appeared in front of my closed eyes. I studied the name closely with my inner vision. "Everything is Bhagavathi" was the essence that came up.

***

"My birth name is Savithri, Gurugale," I said and laughed.

It was an incident that happened years ago. We were on the way to America for a spiritual programme. Gurugalu had subtly indicated his disagreement for our intended journey while blessing us. Past midnight on the scheduled date, we boarded the flight to Munich. However, due to technical issues, the plane did not take off. The next day, when I called Gurugalu to inform him about our situation, "Do you know Satyavan Savitri's story?" he had asked. "Savithri is my birth name, Gurugale," I told him and laughed loudly.

There was a reason for that, too. After the birth of 10 children, my mother was tired of having babies and did not want any more. At that time, I was born. Since my mother did not want another baby yet I was born, she decided to name me "Saak Savitri." I narrated this incident humorously to Gurugalu, but he was not amused. "It is right," he said as if he had a moment of realisation!

He then went on to narrate the story of Satyavan Savitri very nicely. At that moment, I did not realise the purpose of that story. But because of Gurugalu, I happened to recall my birth name, which I had almost forgotten. In early childhood, I was Savitri, and later, when I went to school, I was called Jyotsna, which later became "Jyothi" for ease of usage. That name has stuck with me ever since. I then went on to step into the world of spirituality. At one point, the name, too, had to change!

It was the period of COVID-19 (coronavirus), a microscopic virus that shook up the world. There was a need to bring strength, courage, hope and divinity into the lives of people who were in great anxiety and stress. But no one could venture outside. Since I was used to having my students in front of me during my spirituality classes, the online format of remote teaching did not appeal to me. But my Guru lineage instructed, "Change your core values," and urged me to walk along with changing times and accept the new norm.

The stage was set for new responsibilities. Until then, I was known to the world as "Jyothi Pattabhiram," the dance Guru. Now, there was a need to don the role of a spiritual Guru and spread the message of my Guru lineage to the world. This required a change of name too. There was a dilemma of which name to use, as keeping the one I already had would not work.

The work I was embarking on was in line with my Guru lineage. I would feel blessed if my divine spiritual masters themselves would give me a new name. It was a quiet dawn. As usual, I was in meditation. Suddenly, a name appeared in front of my closed eyes. It was "Sakalaa." I studied the name closely with my inner vision. "Everything is Bhagavathi" was the essence that came up. My heart was filled with gratitude. Much after meditation, my mind continued to remain in a meditative state of bliss. The name suggested by my lineage, "Sakalamaa," became my identity for the path I was embarking on. While this was the name I was blessed with, the initiate name given to me by my Gurugalu of Vidyaranya tradition was "Poorna Shaktyāmbā."

In this way, from the name "Savithri," given to me by my biological mother, to the name "Sakalaa," given by the Divine Mother herself, the journey of my lifetime has come a long way. My heart overflows with gratitude for this Divine Grace.

***

54

GURU LINEAGE CONTINUES!

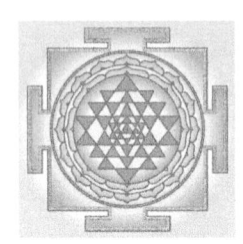

If I look back at my journey through the Srividya lineage, I'm both surprised and elated. During my childhood and youth, I had absolutely no awareness about Srividya.

Later in 1992 when I met Swami Rama also, I had no clue that my journey through this lineage was about to begin. But once this journey began, what transpired was beyond ordinary human comprehension.

At one point, when Swami Rama indicated, "You should go to Mysuru to meet Gurugalu and learn Srividya in Dakshin Bharat tradition," I opposed it because changing the Guru was not my way. Later, to adhere to Baba's words, I met Gurugalu in Mysuru. There, too, I had the experience of abundant knowledge, love, and grace of the Guru!

At one point in this journey, a desire to become part of the Guru lineage and take these teachings forward, did occur to me. However, I was not ready to accept this idea. The Guru's Grace guided me forward in this as well.

I had once taken a group of spiritual enthusiasts to Gurugalu. When one of them wanted to offer him a big sum of money as a donation, Gurugalu pointed towards me and said, "There is the

Guru lineage." As I was rooted in shock and surprise, he made me understand the purpose without saying a single word.

This is the elegance and essence of Srividya!

Here, no choice is completely ours. As the Gurus in the lineage choose their eligible disciples, the lineage also chooses suitable adepts to become Gurus and take the lineage forward. We are just the torchbearers of knowledge and tradition. Through us, this knowledge reaches itself to the deserving and most eligible. Here, the knowledge is not limited to the Guru's physical presence. Neither does he own the knowledge. He just remains the channel or a tool that shares this knowledge with the deserving people. In this manner, the lineage continues by choosing the eligible people to carry on the tradition.

Even after Gurugalu had communicated to me, the thought of taking the tradition forward as a Guru brought a vague denial and confusion to my mind. But the choice of the lineage could not be turned down! I had to bow down and give in to the instructions given. To take the Guru lineage forward, I donned the role of Guru and accepted the responsibilities that came with it. I began to be addressed as "Guruma" and became a guide to people who were curious about this knowledge and encouraged them to experience Srividya.

As times change, making subtle changes and spreading the knowledge to people is a challenge for the Guru. The Vedas and Upanishads were not easy to comprehend. When it came to Bhagavad Gita, it became easier. Later, it came down to Puranas. Making changes according to changing times, identifying people's level of understanding, and sharing knowledge in a way they understand are always challenges for the Guru. The Guru lineage, in all its kindness and grace, looks for people who are suited to the current period. The lineage aims to carry forward the teachings that have been coming down for ages and impart this knowledge to the world. Too much importance is not given to the methodology of how it is taught.

For example, during COVID times, when social interactions were largely restricted or avoided, the question of online mantra initiation came up. At the outset, I rejected the idea. "The disciple should be physically present in front of the Guru for the initiation to happen. That was the right way," was my point of view. But Guru's orders arrived! "Moving according to times and yet imparting this timeless knowledge is the only way," was the message! He shouted, "Change your core values!"

Without further arguments, I started doing Satsangs and mantra initiations online.

Many people think that this position of being a Guru is a luxurious one. Far from it! It is like a throne of thorns - in reality, and only a person who is Guru would know this. In a world that is entangled in the clutches of Maaya, attachment, and desires, the Guru must be skillful enough to bring people out of these illusions while himself/herself remaining unaffected. The price the Guru pays when performing this herculean task is through spiritual energy. He/she must exercise a lot of dexterity in this.

Along with the Guru's own strength and capability, the abundant Grace of the lineage also joins hands in leading the world from darkness of ignorance to light!

In this manner, as a representative of both Himalayan Bhārathi and Shri Vidyaranya traditions, I have been guiding my disciples, who are like my children, addressing me as "Guruma" as well as Sakalamaa. In this manner, I am in service of the tradition, with all honesty and responsibility. By choosing me, a middle-class, ordinary woman, to don the role of Guru, it is proved that Srividya is not something beyond reach. Even people from ordinary backgrounds can rise to the level of becoming a teacher, which is what this shows. The possibility of lighting the lamp of knowledge within oneself while also leading others out of the darkness towards that light has been proved to the world by the Guru lineage by choosing me to be on this journey. Before I conclude, I bow down in utmost reverence to such an enlightened lineage of Gurus and Masters.

Guru lineage continues!

Om, Sarve bhavantu sukhinaḥ
Sarve santu nirāmayāḥ
Sarve bhadrāṇi paśyantu
Mā kashchit duḥkha bhāgbhavet
Oṁ Shāntiḥ, Shāntiḥ, Shāntiḥ

***

Messages from the Himalayan Sages: Timely & Timeless

Parameshti Guru
MUKTHI BABA

Parama Guru
BENGALI BABA

Swaguru
SWAMI RAMA

Guru Sakalamaa's Himalayan Guru Lineage

Sri.CHANDRASHEKARABHARATI SWAMY

Sri.BRAHMAVIDYANANDANATHA

Sri.PUNDARIKAKSHANANDANATHA

Sri.SATHYANANDANATHA

Guru Sakalamaa's Dakshinachara Guru Lineage

Guru lineage continues!

Natyashree award ceremony

Guru Sakalamaa, and her 25 dance disciples who did their Ranga Pravesh

Guru Sakalamaa with her daughter Sadhana

Awards

Guru lineage continues!

Gaurav, after his meditation in the Ramanagara hillocks

Pooja mantra initiation at Roma and Pradeep's home

Parampara photos at Guru Nivas

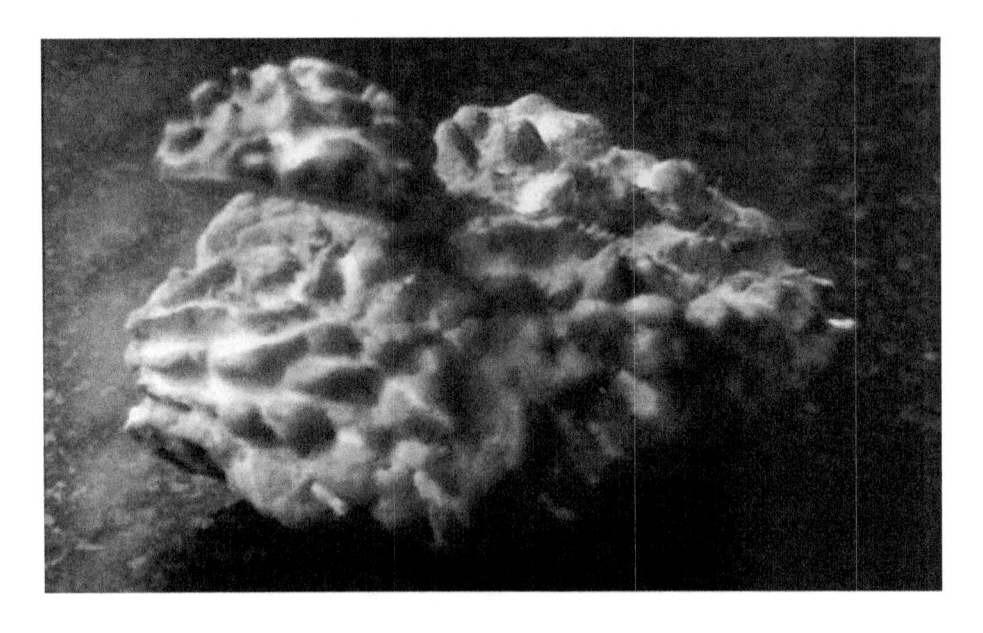

*Eka mukha rudhraksha brought by Kulkarni ji,
at the behest of Bhole Baba Swami Rama.*

Guru lineage continues!

Guru Sakalamaa and Gaurav getting to witness Saptarshi Pooja in Varanasi

After one of the retreats at Swami Rama Ashram at the Tadakeshwar dham

As the dance teacher and performer

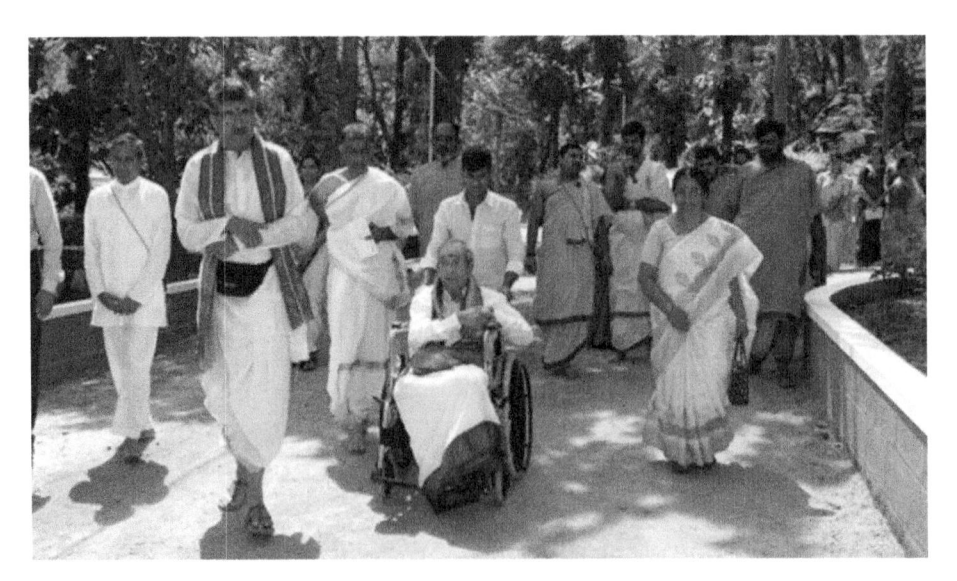

Rā Sā Gurugalu inaugurating Rasarishi block at the Swami Rama Sadhana Dhama Ashram

Guru lineage continues!

Rā Sā Gurugalu inaugurating Rasarishi block at the Swami Rama Sadhana Dhama Ashram

Bhole Baba Swami Rama

Swami Rama's compassionate glance towards his desciples

Swami Rama giving mantra deeksha

Guru lineage continues!

Rā Sā Gurugalu gracing the Swami Rama Sadhana Dhama Ashram

Guru Sakalamaa's recent family portrait

Messages from the Himalayan Sages: Timely & Timeless

Team Sakalamaa

Dr. Ashok ji and his wife Nirmala ji

Printed in Great Britain
by Amazon